THE MEN OF TH

THE MEN
OF THE NORTH

The Britons of Southern Scotland

TIM CLARKSON

First published in Great Britain in 2010 by
John Donald, an imprint of Birlinn Ltd
Reprinted 2014, 2016, 2017, 2018, 2021, 2022

West Newington House
10 Newington Road
Edinburgh
EH9 1QS

www.birlinn.co.uk

ISBN: 978 1 906566 18 0

British Library Cataloguing-in-Publication Data
A catalogue record for this book is available on request from the British Library

Typeset by Hewer Text UK Ltd, Edinburgh
Printed and bound in Britain by Bell and Bain Ltd, Glasgow

CONTENTS

ACKNOWLEDGEMENTS

In writing this book I have benefited from advice and assistance given generously by a number of people. To them I express my gratitude for helpful comments and suggestions on specific points, or for providing me with useful information. I wish to particularly thank Hugh Andrew, Stephen Driscoll, Kevin Halloran, Alex Woolf and Michelle Ziegler. Any errors and idiosyncracies in the book are, of course, entirely of my own devising. On the editorial side I am grateful to Mairi Sutherland for her unwavering patience and attentiveness, and to Jackie Henrie for ironing out the crinkles in the narrative. Mark Brennand at Cumbria Historic Environment Service kindly gave permission to reproduce the aerial photographs of Liddel Strength. Other photography is the work of my wife Barbara who took on the additional role of *chauffeuse* along the highways and byways of Scotland.

TC

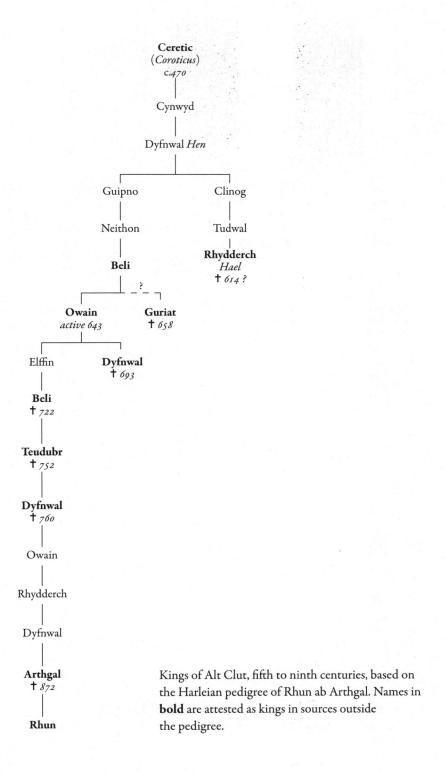

Ceretic
(*Coroticus*)
c.*470*

Cynwyd

Dyfnwal *Hen*

Guipno

Neithon

Beli

Clinog

Tudwal

Rhydderch
Hael
† *614 ?*

?

Owain
active 643

Guriat
† *658*

Elffin

Dyfnwal
† *693*

Beli
† *722*

Teudubr
† *752*

Dyfnwal
† *760*

Owain

Rhydderch

Dyfnwal

Arthgal
† *872*

Rhun

Kings of Alt Clut, fifth to ninth centuries, based on the Harleian pedigree of Rhun ab Arthgal. Names in **bold** are attested as kings in sources outside the pedigree.

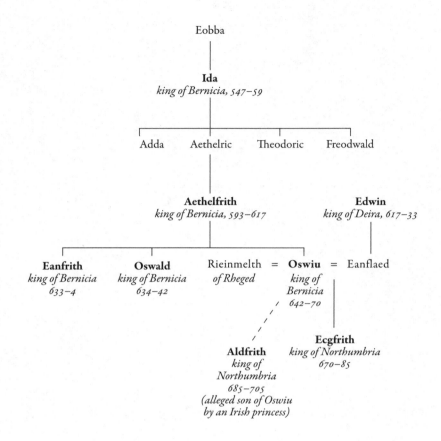

Eobba

Ida
king of Bernicia, 547–59

Adda   Aethelric   Theodoric   Freodwald

Aethelfrith
king of Bernicia, 593–617

Edwin
king of Deira, 617–33

Eanfrith
king of Bernicia
633–4

Oswald
king of Bernicia
634–42

Rieinmelth
of Rheged = **Oswiu** = Eanflaed
king of
Bernicia
642–70

Aldfrith
king of
Northumbria
685–705
(alleged son of Oswiu
by an Irish princess)

Ecgfrith
king of Northumbria
670–85

Bernician kings of the sixth and seventh centuries (dates derived from Bede).
Some siblings omitted in each generation.

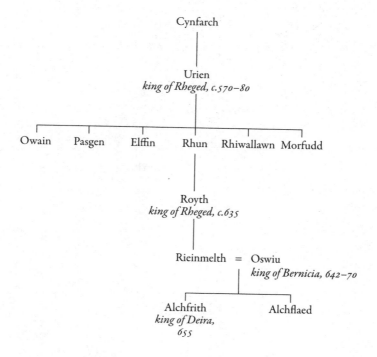

Cynfarch
|
Urien
king of Rheged, c.570–80

Owain   Pasgen   Elffin   Rhun   Rhiwallawn   Morfudd
|
Royth
king of Rheged, c.635
|
Rieinmelth = Oswiu
king of Bernicia, 642–70

Alchfrith   Alchflaed
king of Deira,
655

The family of Urien Rheged

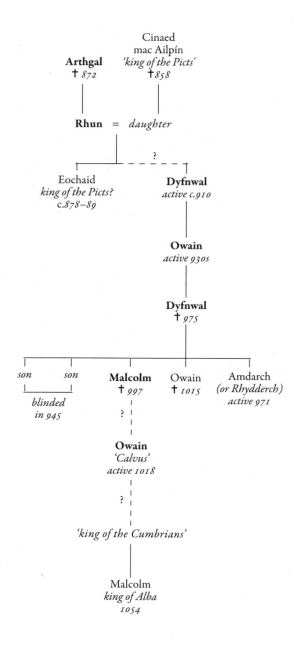

Kings of Strathclyde, c.870 to c.1060, shown in **bold**. Based on a table produced by Dauvit Broun (Broun 2004, 135).

INTRODUCTION

Gwŷr y Gogledd

The medieval kingdom of Scotland began as a fusion of different peoples, each with their own language and culture, who were brought together during a period of change spanning the ninth to twelfth centuries. Two groups in particular – the Scots and the Picts – are generally viewed as the most important players in the process, their 'unification' in the mid-ninth century being seen as the beginning of a recognisable Scottish identity. The other main groups were the Scandinavians, the English and the Britons, the latter two inhabiting what are now the Lowlands south of the River Forth. By c.1100 most people living north of the Forth spoke Gaelic, the language of the Scots, even if the speech of their forebears had been Pictish. Their neighbours to the south-east, in Lothian, had become subjects of the Scottish kingdom but many were English-speakers whose ancestors had been ruled by English kings. From the speech of these Lowlanders came the tongue we now call *Scots* or *Scottis*, essentially a northern English dialect. The lands west of Lothian were inhabited by a people who spoke neither Gaelic nor English. These were the last remnant of the North Britons, a group whose role in the shaping of Scotland is frequently ignored, forgotten, or overshadowed by the roles played by their neighbours. To their English-speaking contemporaries they were known as *wealas*, 'Welsh', and in Latin documents of the time they appear as *Cumbrenses*, 'Cumbrians'. Their language no longer survives but it was descended from an indigenous tongue, commonly termed Brittonic or Brythonic, that had once been spoken in almost every part of Britain. Brittonic survives today in several evolved forms as the living languages of Wales, Cornwall and Brittany but it ceased to be heard in Scotland 800 or 900 years ago. Its disappearance became inevitable in an age when those who used it faced strong pressure to adopt alternative tongues such as Gaelic and English.

Few traces of the North Britons have survived, hence their often minor presence in our history books. In terms of a general picture of Scottish medieval history they are far less well-known than the Scots, Picts and Vikings. Much of what we know about them comes not from Scotland but from Wales, from a body of literature in which their kings were praised as mighty warlords in a remote heroic age. To a thirteenth-century Welshman these kings of old were his fellow countrymen, members of an ancient British nation to which he himself belonged. In his own language he knew them as *Gwŷr y Gogledd*, the Men of the North.

Sources

This book represents one attempt to construct a narrative history of the North Britons. The sources involved in such a construction (or reconstruction) are not especially suited to the task, nor do they sit comfortably under the kind of close academic scrutiny to which they have been justifiably exposed in recent years. In many cases this scrutiny was long overdue. Some sources have indeed failed the strict reliability tests demanded by today's scholarship, usually because they have turned out to be far removed in time and place from the historical events they claim to report. Others pass the tests with certain caveats which mean that they can be used only with caution or in circumstances where no alternative source exists. Casual acceptance of information provided by these texts is no longer an option. All of them invite scepticism and none can be accepted at face value. In the chapters that follow some of the most important sources are discussed individually or in genre-groups. Space considerations and the needs of the narrative mean that no individual source is examined in great detail, although references point to further reading on particular issues. In this introductory section a brief and selective survey is offered as a preliminary overview of the literature.

The main time-period covered by this book falls between c.400 and c.1150. The first half of this span corresponds roughly to an era now termed Early Historic, a time when an indigenous tradition of historical writing began to appear in the British Isles. The foremost ambassador of this tradition was Bede, an English monk who lived in the Northumbrian monastery of Wearmouth-Jarrow during the late seventh and early eighth centuries. Bede is usually regarded as a fairly reliable historian, and in certain respects this is probably true, but he was not really a historian by any modern definition. His vision of the world perceived human history as the gradual unfolding of God's Will with regard to mankind in general and to the English in particular. This perception runs through his best-known work, the *Ecclesiastical History of the English People*, in which he presented a view of events in his homeland from Roman times through the ensuing centuries to the twilight of his own life in 731. He has much to say of northern Britain, including the parts later to become Scotland, but in the Britons themselves he had little interest. In fact, he frequently regarded them with disdain.

A rather less partisan approach to the Britons appears in a group of texts known collectively as the Irish annals. Unlike Bede's *Ecclesiastical History*, of which two early copies survive in manuscripts written between 737 and 747, the Irish annals are preserved only in manuscripts of much later date. Current opinion nevertheless regards their core as a set of annals compiled at the monastery of Iona from the seventh century to the eighth, with material thereafter being added in Ireland. Many entries are not, however, contemporary with the events they describe and were added retrospectively by scribes of a later period. The two major collections – the annals of Ulster and of Tigernach – both incorporate the earlier Iona material, and it is to Iona that we owe much of our knowledge of the early history of Scotland. For information on later times we are obliged to turn to less reliable sources of Irish, Scottish and English origin. Among the Scottish material is a text sometimes known as the *Scottish Chronicle* or, in more recent usage, the *Chronicle of the Kings of Alba*, a text found in a fourteenth-century compilation of materials relating to Scotland. The *Chronicle* deals with events from the ninth to eleventh centuries and, although much of its data is of uncertain provenance, it is generally regarded as an important documentary source. It provides useful information for the period covered in the final three chapters of this book. Other sources of Scottish or Irish origin include the enigmatic *Berchan's Prophecy*, the *Fragmentary Annals of Ireland* and various king-lists.

From England in addition to Bede we have the *Anglo-Saxon Chronicle*, king-lists, a brief chronology known as the 'Continuation' of Bede and several twelfth-century chronicles, including the *History of the Kings* attributed to Symeon of Durham. Sources from Wales include poetry, genealogical tracts, the *Annales Cambriae*, 'Welsh Annals', and a narrative chronicle called *Historia Brittonum*, 'History of the Britons'. Some of these Welsh texts are discussed individually in the early chapters of this book where their uses and limitations are noted. Finally, the genre of hagiography – writings about the careers of saints – provides a wealth of fact, fiction and folklore assembled in the guise of authentic history. The usual hagiographical format is a *vita* or 'life' of an individual figure, often written many centuries after his or her death. Hagiographical works of Scottish, Irish, English and Continental origin have been consulted during the writing of this book and are cited in the narrative where appropriate. As a convenient shorthand these and other primary sources are often abbreviated in the bibliographical notes at the end of the book. The abbreviations cited most frequently are:

AC	*Annales Cambriae*
ASC	*Anglo-Saxon Chronicle*
AT	*Annals of Tigernach*
AU	*Annals of Ulster*
HB	*Historia Brittonum*
HE	Bede's *Ecclesiastical History*
HRA	*Historia Regum Anglorum* attributed to Symeon of Durham
Scot Chron	*Scottish Chronicle*
VSK	*Vita Sancti Kentigerni*, 'Life of Saint Kentigern', by Jocelin of Furness

For each of the above an edition and English translation appear in the first part of the Bibliography at the end of this book. Annal entries are cited in the endnotes by source and year, for example *AU 685*. Where the annals show an erroneous date, the correct one is shown thus: *AU 638 = 640*. In instances where two sources report the same event they are cited as, for example, *AU/ AT 716*.

Terminology

The term Early Historic is used here in relation to c.400 to c.800, an era loosely defined as 'between the Romans and the Vikings'. Events of the longer period spanned by the fifth to eleventh centuries are described in this book as 'early medieval', although in a wider European context this term encompasses an era stretching from c.300 to c.1100. The boundaries between these chronological blocks are in any case fairly loose. A rather tighter precision is applied here to terminology descriptive of places and peoples. Thus, the term 'Scotland' is not used in the sense of a political entity until the later chapters, although throughout the book it occasionally appears in contexts relating to landscape and geography. In political contexts the more neutral term 'northern Britain' is generally preferred, primarily because the book makes frequent reference not only to Scotland but also to territories in what is now northern England. 'Britain' means here the island of Britain with its associated isles, excluding Ireland, but 'Britons' and 'British' are used in a much narrower sense to denote the native population at the time of the Roman invasion. Other ethnic terms such as 'Picts' and 'Irish' need no explanation, but 'Scots' is another term used here without its modern connotations. In this book the Scots are not the people of the country we now call Scotland but a Gaelic-speaking group based originally in Argyll. Occasionally their territory is referred to here as Dalriada, although without any implication of cohesion or unity among their separate kin-groups. The English of the early medieval period, from their first appearance in Britain during Late Roman times to their conquest by the Normans in 1066, are commonly known as 'Anglo-Saxons', a term used also in this book.

A final point of explanation relates to the book's title, *The Men of the North*, a term interpreted by some historians as defining a group of sixth-century kings who appear in Welsh heroic poems and genealogical 'pedigrees'.[1] In this book the term is used less restrictively to include any North British king whose ancestry was recorded in the Welsh genealogical tracts or whose existence was noted in other records. Since the genealogies include the pedigree of a king called Rhun who ruled on the Clyde in the late ninth century, this individual is regarded here as one of the Men of the North. Rhun's immediate successor is absent from the pedigree, but the death of Owain, a later representative of the dynasty, is briefly noted in the Welsh Annals at 1015. One historian regarded the first North British entry in these annals at 573 as the beginning of a 'historical horizon' for Latin records of the Men of the North.[2] By projecting this same literary horizon forward in time we eventually come to Owain's *obit*, the last Latin entry made by the Welsh annalists in relation to a North British king. This book duly assigns the era of the *Gwŷr y Gogledd*, the Men of the North, to the four and a half centuries between the years 573 and 1015.

Patronyms appear in this book in a style appropriate to the cultural group concerned. Those of Gaelic (Scottish and Irish) origin are shown with *mac*, 'son of', while Welsh and British ones have the equivalent term *ap* (from an earlier form *map*). Respective examples are Cináed mac Ailpín and Owain ab Urien (*ap* becomes *ab* when it precedes a name starting with a vowel). Spellings of some personal names are here given in forms that might now be considered 'old-fashioned', such as *Constantine* rather than the Gaelic or Pictish equivalents *Causantin* or *Custantin*, *Malcolm* rather than *Máel Coluim* and *Olaf* rather than Gaelic *Amlaib* or Old Norse *Anlaf*. There currently seems to be no consensus on Welsh and British names so 'traditional' forms such as *Owain* are used in this book, despite a recent trend towards older variants as found in the sources (e.g. *Eugein* for Owain, *Urbgen* for Urien). To modern Anglophones (English-speakers) some Welsh and Gaelic names look difficult to pronounce, but a useful starting-point is the 'hard C' rule whereby C is always pronounced K and never has the sound of S. Space forbids a lengthy pronunciation guide, but the following names are shown here with their approximate 'sounds':

Dyfnwal = Duv-noo-wal
Rhydderch = Hrutherkh
Owain = Oh-wine
Taliesin = Tal-yessin
Gogledd = Gog-leth
Gododdin = Go-dothin
Ecgfrith = Edge-frith
Óengus = Oyn-yus
Cináed = Kin-ayth
Áed = Ayth
Cenél nGabráin = Kenel Navrain

A very useful 'quick reference' guide to pronunciation of Gaelic, Welsh and Old English names can be found in Alex Woolf's recent book *From Pictland to Alba*.

Structure and Format

The primary theme of this book is political history. In an early medieval context this normally means the deeds of kings and the relationships between kingdoms. Other topics, such as social history and archaeology, are also encountered where the narrative requires reference to them. Detailed analysis of the literary sources is absent, as mentioned above, although some texts receive a lengthier summary than others.

In the first chapter we meet the North Britons on the eve of their conquest by Rome. A synopsis of the Roman invasion and occupation of Britain then brings us to the troubled years around AD 400 and to the period of transition from the Late Roman to Early Historic periods. We examine what happened to the Britons living on either side of Hadrian's Wall during the collapse of Roman rule and discuss their differing experiences during the great upheavals of the fifth century. Chapter 2 looks at the North British kingdoms that began to emerge into the historical record after c.500, taking the form of a political survey of the region between Hadrian's Wall and the Forth–Clyde isthmus. It is followed by a chapter dealing with the arrival of Christianity in the same region. The narrative then returns to political history with a look at four North British kings who appear in a controversial passage in the *Historia Brittonum*. One of these kings is Urien Rheged, the most famous of the *Gwŷr y Gogledd*, and here the conventional view of his kingdom's location is challenged. A similar challenge forms the second part of the next chapter (Chapter 5) where, after a study of the Battle of Arfderydd, the traditional identification of the place known in Welsh sources as *Catraeth* is brought under scrutiny. Chapters 6, 7 and 8 take the narrative onward through the seventh, eighth and ninth centuries to c.900. At this point in the chronology only one North British kingdom still flourished, its fate in the following two centuries forming the main focus of Chapter 9. The final chapter examines the disappearance of the North Britons and looks at traces of their former presence in place-names and folklore.

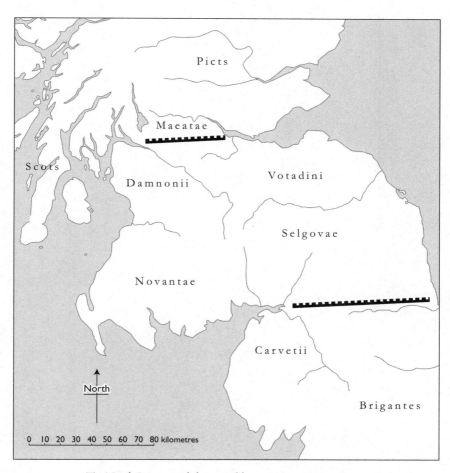

The North Britons and their neighbours in Late Roman times.

1

ORIGINS

Britain and Rome

The historical record first takes note of the peoples of northern Britain in the first century AD, when they encountered the military might of the Roman Empire. Rome's conquest of the island began with an invasion in the year 43 and many southern parts were rapidly subjugated. The region north of the Humber and Mersey remained unconquered for a time, largely due to a negotiated agreement with the Brigantes, a tribal confederacy holding power on both sides of the Pennines.[1] With the appearance of the Brigantes in Roman records we encounter an identifiable group of North British people, even if we are not told much about who they were or how they lived. What we do learn is that their confederacy of tribes or septs was ruled by a paramount monarch whose core domain lay in Yorkshire. In the years following the Roman invasion this was the formidable Queen Cartimandua, a shrewd politician who entered into a treaty with Rome. Brutal suppression of the southern British tribes by Roman forces eventually turned the Brigantes against their queen and she was deposed in a *coup d'état*. Rome responded by invading Brigantia in great force. The initial war lasted from 71 to 74, breaking the backbone of the native resistance. It was followed at the end of the same decade by a campaign of conquest led by Gnaeus Julius Agricola, a talented commander whose achievements in Britain were described by his son-in-law Cornelius Tacitus. Through the writings of Tacitus we meet not only the Brigantes but also other tribes further north, all of whom were subjugated in a series of campaigns lasting from 79 to 82. Roman forts were established in Brigantian territory east and west of the Pennines and in lands northward as far as the Forth–Clyde isthmus. Few native groups dared to risk a military confrontation and most surrendered to Agricola without a fight. Some, such as the Votadini of Lothian, may already have made treaties with Rome before Agricola's arrival on their borders. Others gave up their independence less willingly, preferring to risk defeat and death and the ravaging of their lands. The distribution of first-century Roman forts in the Tweed Valley and adjacent areas suggests that the Selgovae, the people of this central region, required putting down by force. Further west, in Dumfriesshire and Galloway, a confederacy of peoples called Novantae was brought to heel during the campaigning season of 82. The northern neighbours of the Novantae were the Damnonii of the Clyde whose territory encompassed Renfrewshire, Dunbartonshire and parts of Lanarkshire. Like the Votadini of Lothian the Damnonii may have voluntarily submitted to Rome, trading their independence for clientship and so avoiding the devastation threatened by Agricola's army.

In 83 the first Roman attempt to conquer the Highlands was launched by Agricola from military bases south of the Forth–Clyde isthmus.[2] A major northward push brought Roman troops across the River Tay and face-to-face with another tribal confederacy, the Caledonii of Perthshire, whose stubborn defiance was barely subdued by a crushing defeat at the battle of Mons Graupius. Not even this victory achieved sufficient gains to provide a springboard for permanent conquest and Agricola eventually withdrew. A frontier of watchtowers was established along the Gask Ridge on the southern fringe of Caledonian lands, but this was abandoned before the end of the century. By c.105 the north-west frontier of the Roman Empire had withdrawn to a line drawn between Tyne and Solway. Behind this boundary the Brigantes and other tribes remained in subjection to Rome, their freedom curtailed by a heavy military presence. North of the line, as far as the Forth and Clyde, the Agricolan forts were abandoned and the natives reasserted their independence.

The early second century saw the progressive Romanisation of Britain south of the Tyne–Solway frontier. This was part of Rome's standard package for newly conquered peoples and involved a restructuring of indigenous society. In Gaul and Spain the same process saw the total replacement of native languages by Latin and the dismantling of native cultures. In Britain these changes were never fully completed. Brittonic, the Celtic language of the Britons, maintained a strong presence among the subject population and continued to be the preferred medium of everyday discourse in many northern areas. In southern Britain below the estuaries of Humber and Mersey the natives were reorganised by Rome into tribal *civitates* administered from newly built towns and cities. In these centres of trade and administration an urban elite of wealthy, Latin-speaking Britons arose as an upper class whose members were probably descended – in many cases – from the old warrior-aristocracies of pre-Roman times. A few *civitates* were established further north, perhaps in an attempt to control the Brigantian heartlands. One of these was the *civitas Brigantiarum* centred on the eastern edge of the Pennines, while another was established for a people called Parisii who lived near the North Sea coastlands. Much of the former Brigantia lay under direct military rule. Forts garrisoned by units of auxiliaries from all parts of the Empire gave the Roman authorities tight control over the native population in this area, while a network of roads enabled troops to be deployed quickly to deal with outbreaks of unrest.

There appears to have been no significant attempt to Romanise the people of this military zone, but every effort was made to police them intensively and to deter any rebellious elements still lurking among them. Justification for such heavy-handed monitoring was demonstrated between 110 and 120 when a major revolt caused upheaval on the frontier. The insurgents were probably the Brigantes, possibly with aid or encouragement from fellow Britons dwelling north of the Tyne–Solway frontier. By c.119 the uprising had been suppressed and a measure of stability returned. To consolidate the frontier a massive stone rampart was erected on the orders of the emperor Hadrian who visited Britain in 122. Whether its primary purpose was to deter attacks from the north or disrupt communication between the Brigantes and their neighbours is unknown. It may have been built as an imposing display of Rome's prestige, or perhaps of Hadrian's. If it had any military or defensive purpose as a physical barrier, this was negated around the time of completion in c.140. In that year the new emperor Antoninus launched a second invasion northward, his campaign achieving a reconquest as far as the Forth–Clyde isthmus. Forts abandoned after the withdrawal at the beginning of the century were now re-garrisoned and the isthmus became the new imperial frontier. Antoninus fought and defeated one or more tribes – perhaps the Selgovae of Tweeddale – and compelled the rest to renew their submission to Rome. He then constructed a wall of his own, a rampart of turf rather than of stone, and placed a chain of forts along its length. The Antonine Wall ran from Kinneil in the east to Old Kilpatrick in the west and was evidently intended as a bulwark against raids from the Highlands. If defence rather than propaganda was indeed its primary purpose, the group it was most likely meant to deter were Agricola's old adversaries the Caledonii.

Another revolt in the 150s, probably by Britons living on either side of Hadrian's Wall, necessitated a major redeployment of troops and a withdrawal from the Antonine frontier. The isthmus was briefly re-garrisoned after the defeat of the rebels, but military requirements elsewhere in the Empire led to a second and permanent abandonment in c.160. Final withdrawal to the Tyne–Solway line did not happen immediately and, for a time, a handful of forts north of Hadrian's Wall were still manned. The political situation implied by these military outposts is that the Britons dwelling between the two walls – the Damnonii, Novantae, Selgovae and Votadini – remained tied to the Empire through treaties and therefore required monitoring. Similar relationships between Romans and natives existed on other frontiers, often taking the form of mutual promises of protection in the event of attack by a common foe. In the case of northern Britain in the late second century the chief menace lay beyond the abandoned Antonine Wall where two aggressive groups now posed an imminent threat. One was the Caledonian confederacy of Perthshire, the other a people known to the Romans as *Maeatae* who dwelt immediately north of the Antonine line. The Maeatae inhabited Stirlingshire and were independent of the Caledonii but apparently in league with them. Both groups attacked Roman Britain at the end of the second century, wreaking havoc as far south as Hadrian's Wall. They were eventually bought off with cash from the imperial treasury but could not be kept quiet for long and, as the third century dawned, they resumed their raids. In 208 the emperor Severus personally took charge of the situation, arriving in Britain with the intention of conquering the troublesome northerners. A brutal war against the Maeatae drove them to the brink of extinction and they were only saved by the death of Severus, whose son Caracalla negotiated a peace treaty. Caracalla promptly abandoned the campaign and returned to Rome, his departure signalling a final withdrawal from the Forth–Clyde isthmus and consolidation of the imperial frontier along the Hadrianic line. A reduced military presence was retained in the region between the walls: units still manned outpost forts at High Rochester and Risingham on the major road known today as Dere Street, and at Bewcastle and Netherby further west. The Britons of this area remained outside the Empire but benefited from guarantees of protection offered by Rome. In return they served as a buffer against raids from the North, their obligations as clients being periodically renewed at formal gatherings overseen by Roman officials. Throughout their lands imperial agents known as *arcani* undertook intelligence-gathering missions, seeking news of barbarian movements further north as well as keeping an eye on unruly elements closer to home. At Netherby a unit of *exploratores*, 'scouts' or 'rangers', undertook similar functions to the *arcani* or were perhaps identical with them. The new defensive system, based on a symbiotic relationship between the Roman garrison of Hadrian's Wall and autonomous Britons in the lands beyond, seems to have worked effectively for a number of years. Roman writers refer to no wars or incursions during much of the third century, although their perceptions of the population north of the Forth evidently changed. A new people, the *Picti* or Picts, emerge into the historical record in 297. The Picts included the Caledonii of former times together with other groups, all of whom were now collectively regarded as 'Pictish' by their neighbours further south. The new name may have originated as a pejorative label bestowed by external foes rather than as a reflection of social or political changes among the peoples of the far north. Whatever its origin or meaning the term passed into common usage along the imperial frontier and was soon adopted by contemporary chroniclers. By c.300 Pictish and Irish pirates were mounting seaborne raids on the exposed coasts of Roman Britain, a trend that steadily escalated as the new century progressed.

No more revolts by the Brigantes were recorded in the third century. By c.300 the native population south of Hadrian's Wall had seemingly accepted the presence of an occupying force. Nonetheless, a continuing threat from external foes compelled Rome to maintain a large garrison on both sides of the Pennines, and thus the entire region remained a militarised zone. In the third century Roman Britain consisted of two provinces which together constituted a diocese of the Empire. The old Brigantian lands north of the Humber and Mersey were part of a northern province, Britannia Inferior or 'Lower Britain', while the southern or 'Upper' province was designated Britannia Superior. In the fourth century the diocese was further subdivided to form a quartet of provinces, the most northerly being designated Britannia Secunda, 'Britain II', broadly coterminous with ancient Brigantia. Britannia Secunda lay under direct military rule, its administration operating from the fortress of the Sixth Legion at York. This province was a militarised zone in the sense of being tightly controlled by the Roman army. By contrast, the Britons of this area were a thoroughly demilitarised population. Even their elite class – the descendants of the Brigantian aristocracy – were weaponless and politically impotent. All civilians who lived under the army's jurisdiction were answerable to fort-commanders in their local area. All of them were part of an economy designed to serve the demands of the troops. There were few structures of local government and only a handful of urban settlements. Towns were established at York, Aldborough, Carlisle and Corbridge, but the urbanisation and Romanisation seen in the tribal *civitates* of the South were never more than a thin veneer in the North. Rome gave the southern Britons a measure of local self-government but there was little scope for such delegation in the northern military zone. A few 'local councils' were established here and there in Britannia Secunda, but their powers were limited to whatever scraps of authority the army saw fit to offload. Outside the walls of some northern forts civilian settlements sprang up to serve and exploit the needs of the soldiers. These settlements were called *vici* and their inhabitants were *vicani* or 'vicus dwellers'. Most *vicani* were Britons, often the wives and families of soldiers, or local entrepreneurs providing goods and services. The typical *vicus* was essentially a boom-town tolerated by the imperial authorities as an inevitable consequence of a prolonged military occupation. In economic terms all *vici* were utterly dependent on the forts and had no *raison d'être* without the army. The same comment applies to the entire native population of the military zone, for civilians and soldiers alike lived within an artificial economy generated by the presence of large numbers of troops. Every stakeholder in the system, from the peasant farmer producing barley for the local garrison to the fort-commander ordering wine for a banquet, knew that a major socio-economic catastrophe would befall the region if ever the army departed. The remainder of this chapter looks at the varied responses of the Britons, both north and south of Hadrian's Wall, when this fragile superstructure eventually collapsed.

The End of Roman Britain

Britannia Secunda, the northern province of the British diocese, was a region under military rule. Its centre of administration lay at York, the headquarters of the *Dux Britanniarum* or 'Duke of the Britains'. The rank of this senior officer implies command of imperial troops in all four provinces of the British diocese, but his primary responsibilities were Hadrian's Wall and the adjacent coasts. Further north, between the Wall and the Forth–Clyde isthmus, lay lands no longer formally governed by Rome but still important to the interests of the Empire. Since the abandonment of the Antonine frontier the people of this intervallate ('between the walls') region had regained a substantial measure of independence. They were Britons, like their neighbours in the Roman province to the south, but their society was more 'barbarian'. This term carries no implication of savagery and is merely used to indicate their separation from the Empire. It is possible that their fourth-century political divisions still corresponded to the four major groupings or tribal confederacies of earlier times, namely the Damnonii around the Clyde, the Votadini of Lothian, the Selgovae of Tweeddale and the Novantae of Galloway. In the case of the Damnonii and Votadini substantial continuity throughout the entire Roman period is implied by the evolution of their respective heartlands into later kingdoms. It seems likely that the relationship between the intervallate Britons and the Empire was based on treaty, imperial subsidy and reciprocal military obligations.

Beyond the Forth–Clyde isthmus lay vast tracts of territory that had never owed allegiance to Rome. This was a region where Agricola and Severus had tried and failed to subjugate the natives, an area whose harsh terrain would continue to challenge invaders for centuries to come. Here dwelt the Picts, a people whose language was closely related to that of the Britons but whose culture displayed sufficient differences to define them as a separate group. Their heartlands lay north of the Firth of Forth in what are now Perthshire, Fife and Aberdeenshire, but the Orkney and Shetland Isles were also Pictish and so were many parts of the central and western Highlands. South of the Picts, in an area broadly coterminous with what is now Stirlingshire, lurked the Maeatae, a people described by Roman writers as living immediately north of the Antonine Wall. Although the Maeatae were associated by Rome with the worst excesses of the Picts, they are nevertheless identifiable as Britons or, to put it another way, there is no evidence that their cultural affiliation was Pictish. Their status *vis-à-vis* the Roman authorities was, however, quite distinct from that of their fellow Britons south of the Forth–Clyde isthmus: they were regarded as enemies of the Empire and thus as a truly 'barbarian' people. West of the Maeatae and somewhat north and west of the Damnonii of Clydesdale lay the shorelands and islands of Argyll. This was the home of a people known to the Romans as *Scotti*, 'Scots'. Until fairly recently, a long-established conventional wisdom believed that the Scots of Argyll had come from northern Ireland as immigrants to Britain sometime around AD 500. This has now been challenged by an alternative view which sees them as an indigenous, Gaelic-speaking group whose ancestors simply adopted the language of the Irish as a result of social and economic contacts. More will be said of the Scots, Picts and Maeatae in subsequent chapters, but for the moment our focus switches back to the intervallate Britons and to their dealings with Rome in the fourth century.

The outpost forts in the region between the walls were gradually abandoned as the fourth century progressed. Since c.250 only four had been garrisoned and these were located not far north of Hadrian's Wall. With so few forward bases no intensive monitoring was possible, although the *arcani* and *exploratores* still patrolled this region. The *Dux Britanniarum* and his subordinates relied on accurate intelligence on what was happening in the lands beyond the frontier to enable them to anticipate raids across the Forth–Clyde isthmus. The main threat, as in previous centuries, came from the Picts. Other dangerous marauders were the Gaelic-speaking peoples of northern Ireland and Argyll – collectively the *Scotti* – and a mysterious group called *Attacotti* who perhaps came from the Hebrides. An additional threat came from Continental Europe, from barbarian nations living beyond the imperial frontier along the Rhine. Pirates from northern Germany were increasingly raiding the eastern and southern coasts of Roman Britain, from the mouth of the Tyne to the Thames estuary. In an effort to deal with these 'Saxons' a specific military command was created, headed by the *Comes Litoris Saxonici*, the Count of the Saxon Shore. His base lay in one of the massive fortresses that ran in a wide arc along the south-eastern coastlands facing the Continent. Neither he, nor the *Dux Britanniarum* at York, nor indeed any loyal commander in the Roman administration, was able to anticipate or prevent the catastrophe that suddenly engulfed them in 367. In that year, according to the historian and soldier Ammianus Marcellinus, the various raiders joined together to launch a combined onslaught, a 'barbarian conspiracy'.[3] Its objective was to paralyse the imperial forces by hurling them into disarray, thus allowing bands of pirates to penetrate far inland in search of plunder. The assault was successful: vast amounts of loot were taken, forts were destroyed, Hadrian's Wall was overwhelmed and the imperial infrastructure collapsed. Both the Duke of the Britains and the Count of the Saxon Shore were slain, together with countless soldiers and civilians. Barbarian warbands roamed freely, wreaking havoc across the countryside, while gangs of Roman deserters inflicted further misery on the defenceless population. Eventually a force of elite troops led by the renowned Count Theodosius arrived from Gaul to restore order. Theodosius duly repelled the raiders and regained control before undertaking a major overhaul of military and administrative structures. But the Roman world was changing and neither Britain nor any other diocese could turn back the clock. Manpower and resources were no longer available for a complete reconstruction. So it was that in the military zone behind Hadrian's Wall some forts were repaired or rebuilt while others were abandoned. Some troops were redeployed within Britain, but others were needed more urgently elsewhere and departed with Theodosius when he returned to Gaul. By the end of the century, after further troop withdrawals had depleted the garrison still further, the defences of Roman Britain were left perilously vulnerable. The role played by the intervallate Britons in these events is uncertain. They were perhaps overwhelmed by Pictish raids on their own lands while attempting to meet their obligations as clients or 'buffer states' of the Empire. We cannot even be sure that their relationship with Rome had not already broken down before 367, perhaps becoming an uneasy truce which left them less inclined to assist in her defence.

By 400, when the pirate raids were once again reaching critical levels, the imperial garrison in Britain could no longer cope. It was severely undermanned. Troops had been withdrawn to Gaul in 383 by the imperial usurper Magnus Maximus and were not replaced. More departed in 407 under the ambitious general Constantine III who, like Maximus, sought to make himself emperor of the West. With serious crises erupting even at the heart of Empire, the troubles of Britain became a lesser priority than those of Gaul or Italy. There was no real prospect of reinforcements, nor of any respite from barbarian assault. The soldiers still serving in Britain became increasingly demoralised, especially when their wages stopped arriving from the imperial treasury. These fifth-century troops were those of Hadrian's Wall and the Pennine forts, together with the surviving garrisons of the Saxon Shore fortresses in the South.[4] The northern frontier army, still nominally under the command of a *dux* or some other senior officer at York, was already so embedded in the landscape that it had become fossilised and immovable. Some units had continuously garrisoned their forts for 300 years, their personnel retiring to farm the local countryside while being replaced in the ranks by native-born sons. Intermarriage with British women had forged close bonds between fort-garrisons and local communities and had led to a system of hereditary recruitment from fathers to sons through many generations. Magnus Maximus and Constantine III left many of these garrisons *in situ*, withdrawing instead less-entrenched forces for their respective Continental expeditions. In some of the older forts in the Pennines and on the Wall the soldiers were barely distinguishable from the local Britons. When Rome at last relinquished her authority in the early fifth century, the frontier army had already begun to merge with the local civilian population.

Gildas

There is much debate and uncertainty about the end of Roman Britain. Most commentators focus on the year 410 when the Emperor Honorius sent a letter to the Britons in which he told them he could no longer protect them from the barbarians. He instructed them to defend themselves against raiders without further help from Rome. Historians have traditionally viewed this as heralding a new era of native independence. However, neither Honorius nor the recipients of his letter could have foreseen that no help would ever be sent, nor that the Western Roman Empire would collapse within the next 60 years. The Britons to whom Honorius wrote were the civilian authorities in the southern towns: the magistrates of the *civitates* and other key members of the urban aristocracy. A hundred years later an account by the Greek writer Zosimus described these elites seizing power in 409 after expelling officials appointed by Constantine III.

What happened next is unclear. According to Gildas, a British cleric of the sixth century whose writings provide a bleak retrospective commentary on the end of Roman rule, the newly independent Britons tried with varying success to fight off the Picts and Scots.[5] Gildas refers to the abandonment of towns and to the ineffectiveness of the northern frontier army before presenting a picture of social meltdown and economic collapse. This scenario is broadly consistent with the statements of Roman writers and with archaeological data showing large-scale desertion of urban centres and the end of a coin-based economy. Without Rome there was no centralised system of taxation and no bureaucratic structure. In the ensuing chaos taxes were paid as gifts or food-renders to local magnates who set themselves up in positions of authority. Gildas speaks of a 'council' of native leaders making decisions on a national scale but, if such a body even existed, its members may have held power only in southern Britain. Before the end of the fifth century their successors were ruling as kings of small kingdoms.[6]

In the North the garrison of Hadrian's Wall faded away. The end of the coin-based economy left no means of paying the soldiers and made their position untenable. There can be no doubt that the majority of regiments disbanded in the early 400s. Gildas speaks of troops manning the Wall forts at a time when Britain was independent, but his chronology is jumbled and his knowledge of both Roman walls extremely inaccurate. He believed, for instance, that the Antonine Wall was constructed before Hadrian's Wall and that the latter dated from c.400. His description of a military force, apparently composed of Britons, stepping forward to defend the post-Roman frontier owes more to sixth-century folklore than to fifth-century history. It is not supported by archaeological evidence for continuity of occupation or for later reoccupation. Slight evidence of fifth-century habitation has been unearthed at several Wall forts, but the data is too sparse to support the Gildasian picture. Only at Birdoswald, 16 miles east of Carlisle, is the evidence for continuity very strong, but this site appears to be exceptional and seems to have been the abode of a local warlord rather than part of a larger post-Roman defensive scheme. Gildas in fact sheds little light on what was happening in northern Britain after the end of Roman rule. He described the lands beyond the Hadrianic frontier being overwhelmed in the early fifth century by Picts and Scots who 'seized the whole of the extreme north of the island from its inhabitants, right up to the Wall'. This assault is probably fictional. We can infer that Gildas envisaged its victims as the intervallate Britons, a group to whom his narrative alludes so vaguely that he barely seems to acknowledge them as his compatriots.

Gildas envisaged the national council as still functioning as late as c.450, although it was now supposedly headed by a *superbus tyrannus*, a 'proud tyrant'.[7] Later tradition called this figure Vortigern, 'Overlord', and turned him into the fictional ancestor of a royal dynasty in Wales. Upon the *tyrannus* and his associates Gildas heaped much of the blame for the evils of the sixth century, blaming them especially for hiring 'Saxons' to defend Britain against the Picts. 'Nothing more destructive, nothing more bitter, has ever befallen the land', he complained, adding that the council had foolishly 'invited under the same roof a people whom they feared worse than death'. In the eighth century Bede understood these hirelings as springing from three peoples of northern Germany: the Angles, Saxons and Jutes. He used the writings of Gildas to construct his own version of what had happened, but both writers tell a broadly similar story: groups of German warriors arrived in Britain and settled with their families in areas vulnerable to Pictish attack. Eventually they began to arrive in greater numbers, settling mostly in eastern areas and demanding higher pay for their services. When their demands were refused, they rose in revolt, seizing the lands around their settlements. This was the beginning of the Anglo-Saxon conquest, a long process of conflict and assimilation through which a large part of Britain ultimately became England.

The North Britons after c.450

So much for the picture presented by Gildas. How much of it is history rather than folklore or guesswork is a matter of debate. Large parts of his account are obviously fictional. He clearly had major gaps in his knowledge and either lacked or ignored the additional information provided by Continental texts. We should remember that he did not call himself a historian, nor did his audience expect him to present authentic 'history'. His chief purpose was to remind his sixth-century contemporaries that they were in danger of repeating the mistakes of their ancestors. Lax morals and religious failings, he believed, were leading the Britons of his own time to disaster. In the final analysis his gloomy predictions bore fruit and much of his homeland fell permanently under Anglo-Saxon control.

His view of the fifth century divides the North Britons into two parts: those living between the Roman walls and their neighbours in the former province of Britannia Secunda. The latter he portrayed as a feckless rabble who made a half-hearted attempt to defend Hadrian's Wall after c.410. Archaeology, as we have already noted, does not support this notion of a post-Roman frontier army. A better interpretation of the evidence at places such as Birdoswald imagines widespread abandonment of the frontier before c.420 and the appearance of small political units centred on individual forts.[8] This kind of fragmentation, leading to a dispersal of authority and the rise of ambitious local elites, was an inevitable consequence of the end of Roman rule. The descendants of the Brigantes divided their allegiances among an unknown number of rulers. After being dominated for 300 years by an imperial commander at York they found themselves answering once again to a home-grown leadership. Whether or not this new elite had any hope of prosperity in a region where social and political disintegration was particularly acute is debatable. Some leaders may have managed to kickstart economic recovery in districts where agricultural production had been less dependent on the needs of the Roman army. Other communities undoubtedly failed, or remained impoverished and feeble. The *vicani*, for example, lost their reason for existence after the northern forts were abandoned. Urban living on a larger scale likewise ceased to be a viable option and the towns quickly fell into dereliction as their populations dwindled. The decline of large urban centres was chiefly a feature of the South where such settlements were common, but a small number of communities in the northern military zone were affected too. At York and Carlisle, for instance, the Romans had established sizable settlements, both of which were severely denuded of inhabitants by c.500.

The most successful post-Roman communities, those with well-organised elites and sustainable local economies, eventually evolved into the nuclei of viable kingdoms. In some cases 'royal' status may have been supported by claims of descent from the kings of old, a scenario which might explain how the Yorkshire-based kingdom of Elmet came into being in the ancient Brigantian heartlands. Once established and flourishing these embryonic realms in the former province of Britannia Secunda probably differed little from the older kingdoms of the Damnonii and Votadini north of the Wall. In the intervallate region the Britons had been ruled by their own kings for many generations, perhaps continuously since pre-Roman times. These lands probably experienced minimal economic disruption in the fifth century. They had never been permanently annexed to the Empire and therefore had strong, deep-rooted traditions of group identity and social stability. Such notions may have been more difficult to establish south of the Wall where the collapse of the Roman economy, coupled with total withdrawal of the imperial administration, had destroyed any real prospect of continuity between old and new. After languishing for so long under the heel of a Roman military boot the native upper class of Britannia Secunda faced the enormous challenge of transforming itself into a weapon-bearing aristocracy headed by kings. North of the Wall the kings and warbands had never disappeared, even if their activities had been periodically curtailed by imperial interference and intervention.

Coel Hen and the Illusion of Continuity

With the exception of Birdoswald, where occupation continued throughout the fifth century, the forts along Hadrian's Wall ceased to be inhabited in any significant sense in the early 400s. The archaeological evidence for abandonment is so persuasive that any hypothesis supporting the idea of continuity seems unsustainable. This has not, however, prevented such theories from being proposed, often on very flimsy foundations. Of these the only one with any real merit was Ken Dark's suggestion that the Britons may have re-garrisoned the Wall in the period after 410, an idea conforming to the picture painted by Gildas.[9] Dr Dark based his theory on evidence from Birdoswald and on a scatter of archaeological finds at other forts such as Vindolanda and Housesteads. His ideas were well-argued and thought-provoking but failed to achieve widespread support, chiefly because the evidence is simply too meagre. Of far less scholarly worth is an older theory proposing a similar scenario but based on little more than unfounded speculation. Its supporters envisaged large-scale continuity of the northern frontier army and of the Roman military bureaucracy. According to this hypothesis there was little or no abandonment of Hadrian's Wall and the Pennine forts. Instead, the last *Dux Britanniarum* at York proclaimed himself king of Britannia Secunda and established a hereditary monarchy. His name, we are told, was Coel Hen, 'Coel the Old', a figure sometimes equated with the cheery 'Old King Cole' of the well-known nursery rhyme. The vision of continuity saw portions of Coel's kingdom being partitioned by his sons and grandsons to create a patchwork of smaller realms whose rulers competed with each other for wealth and territory, while the core domain of the *Dux* survived at York until it fell to the Anglo-Saxons in c. 580. Surprisingly, this imaginative reconstruction of fifth-century events proved to be quite popular and has appeared in a number of scholarly studies of post-Roman Britain. Because of this popularity it may be worthwhile to explore its origins.

Coel Hen appears in a group of medieval Welsh genealogical tracts purporting to show the ancestries of North British kings. He stands at the head of several royal 'pedigrees' as a forefather of figures who lived in the second half of the sixth century. A rough calculation of the generations listed in the pedigrees assigns Coel to the decades around c.400. Because his alleged descendants are shown in the pedigrees as a group of northern kings it was only a small leap for some historians to identify him as the first post-Roman ruler of the North. Coel was duly perceived as an ancestral figure who once held the entire frontier zone under his control. This in turn led to his identification as the last *Dux Britanniarum*. In the decades after World War II a number of respected scholars expressed varying degrees of support for this scenario, culminating in 1973 with the publication of a book entitled *The Age of Arthur*. This was written by John Morris and represented an ambitious attempt to synthesise fragments of literary and archaeological evidence into a coherent narrative history of post-Roman Britain. Other writers had already seen Coel's name as a derivation from Latin *Coelius* or *Caelius* and this formed a key plank of the continuity argument in *The Age of Arthur*.[10] The apparent link between Latinity and continuity was neatly summarised by Morris when he first introduced his readers to Coel: 'The lands ruled by his heirs comprise the whole of the region garrisoned in Roman times by the troops of the *Dux Britanniarum*; and it is possible that Coel was the last regularly appointed *dux*'[11]. Among the North British pedigrees Morris found the obscure figure Garbaniaun, a son of Coel, whose name does in fact seem to derive from Latin *Germanianus*. However, personal names of Latin origin were not uncommon in fifth-century Britain and merely reflected native pretensions to imperial prestige or *Romanitas*. There is thus nothing particularly remarkable about Garbaniaun, nor do we know anything about him. In *The Age of Arthur*, however, he became a fifth-century Roman soldier, 'an officer commanding a force permanently detached by Coel or his successor to hold the north-west coast'.[12] Fundamental to the entire hypothesis was the notion that the territories of the *Dux Britanniarum* remained intact until the end of the fifth century. This in turn rested on a belief that the North British royal genealogies, especially those linking back to Coel, provide an accurate picture of the political situation between c.400 and c.600. A more realistic approach to the pedigrees treats them not as genuine records of post-Roman history but as literary products of a much later era. Far from showing a remarkable longevity for the Roman frontier command, the pedigrees instead reflect the 'antiquarian' interests of medieval Wales.[13] The ancestry of the so-called 'Coeling' kings of the sixth century was important to Welshmen of later times because those same kings were regarded as heroic figures. They were Britons, like the people of Wales, and their deeds were celebrated in poems and stories recited at the courts of medieval Welsh kings. Since the genealogical texts are examined in detail in Chapter 3 all that will be said here is that it is wiser to adopt a minimalist view of the historical value of the pedigrees, at least in their upper generations around c.400. Such a stance is consistent with the scant archaeological evidence for continuity. Large-scale collapse of the Roman garrison in northern Britain, rather than large-scale survival of its command structure, is a more likely scenario for the fifth century. In a time of crisis and upheaval, when the economic system that had formerly sustained the imperial garrison ceased to function, it is unlikely that any senior officer at York or elsewhere was capable of propping up the military hierarchy. If any such attempt had been made, it would surely appear in the archaeological record as a post-Roman occupation phase at numerous forts and would make Birdoswald the rule rather than the exception.

Padarn 'Red Tunic' and the Northern Foederati

The idea of a fifth-century *Dux Britanniarum* ruling a kingdom based at York is mirrored by similarly speculative theories relating to lands further north. As with Coel Hen the alleged evidence is found in the North British genealogical tracts, in a royal pedigree naming a certain Cunedda as the ancestor of later Welsh kings. Cunedda's pedigree seems to place him in the fifth century, in the lands of the Votadini of Lothian, and it is in this context that we will meet him again in Chapter 2. Here we focus instead on his immediate ancestors who bear names of Roman origin. His father Aetern, grandfather Padarn and great-grandfather Tacit respectively carry the Latin names Eternus, Paternus and Tacitus.[14] The pedigree gives Padarn the epithet *Pesrut*, a Brittonic nickname meaning 'Red Tunic'. It has been suggested that he may have received this garment from the Roman army in recognition of a formal military relationship.[15] This in turn has led to Cunedda's family being seen as *foederati*, 'federates', entrusted with the task of protecting the imperial diocese against Pictish raids. Granting federate status to one group of barbarians and paying them to fight another was a feature of Roman policy and may have been tried in Britain. Less feasible is the notion that a barbarian in a red tunic was necessarily an imperial *foederatus* rather than simply a man whose favourite colour was red. Padarn's *pesrut* in fact tells us nothing about political relations between the Votadini and the Empire, nor does his name necessarily mean that he or his kin were friendly to Rome. The bestowing of Latin names may have been a fashion among some sections of the Votadinian elite, especially among those to whom an air of *Romanitas* conveyed special value. Latinity undoubtedly had important social and cultural connotations among the Votadini, as among other peoples living outside the Empire, but it says little about their relationship with Rome. Padarn may have been no more pro-Roman than his Pictish neighbours across the Firth of Forth.

One group of barbarians who do seem to have held federate status in Late Roman Britain were the German warbands hired by the imperial administration. These were the forerunners of the 'Saxons' whom Gildas identified as mercenaries recruited by native leaders of the fifth century. In Roman times the German hirelings, accompanied by their wives and children, were placed in areas regarded as vulnerable to attack by other barbarians. Their first colonies were established as early as the fourth century when raids by Picts, *Scotti* and 'Saxons' demanded a military response by Rome. Manpower shortages made the recruitment of barbarian *foederati* a convenient solution, but, being little more than a quick fix, it healed a short-term problem with a long-term one whose effects – according to Gildas – could only prove disastrous. In the military zone of Britannia Secunda the German warbands were mostly settled east of the Pennines, especially in the fertile Vale of York or on the exposed North Sea coast. This region included the *civitas* of the Parisi, one of the few northern *civitates*, and the military headquarters at York itself. In the early fifth century the end of Roman rule heralded the collapse of the *foederati* system and deprived the hirelings of their pay. The scenario offered by Gildas saw the newly independent Britons inviting more mercenaries to sail over from Germany. Eventually these warriors rose in rebellion. In so far as the revolt affected northern areas we may imagine Anglo-Saxons in the Vale of York attacking their British employers and seizing control. If this is an accurate reconstruction of events, a major casualty must have been the *civitas* of the Parisi or whatever political entity had succeeded it. Native elites in the affected districts, unless they had already thrown in their lot with the mercenaries, would have been driven from their lands. Similar scenarios of violent insurrection and dispossession would have erupted all over the eastern parts of Britain, from the Thames to the Tyne. So began a long era of conflict and assimilation, a process that would eventually bring large tracts of territory under permanent Anglo-Saxon control. The fifth-century revolts reported by Gildas signalled to the Britons that the Anglo-Saxons or 'English' were no longer content to remain as hirelings. Tales of the uprising appear in later English legends where prominent rebel leaders are identified by name. In the South, for instance, we meet the brothers Hengist and Horsa fighting in Kent against their former paymaster Vortigern.[16] Similar traditions identify the northern *foederati* as Angles and name their leader as Soemil, a figure roughly datable to the mid-fifth century. The Welsh *Historia Brittonum* asserts that Soemil 'first separated Deira from Bernicia', a statement carrying no political relevance in fifth-century terms but referring instead to two northern English kingdoms not established until after c.500. What this statement probably means is that the territory later represented by Deira, a realm corresponding roughly to Yorkshire, was 'separated' by Soemil from the authority of its British rulers. English genealogical tradition regarded Soemil as the ancestor of Deira's later kings and as a founder of their dynasty, but his historical existence cannot be verified.[17]

North of Hadrian's Wall we would not expect to find Germanic mercenary colonies in Roman times. The region between the Wall and the Forth–Clyde isthmus had not been part of the Empire since the third century. It would seem, however, that a colony was installed on the north-eastern coastlands after the end of Roman Britain. In one obscure source of English origin and pre-dating the middle of the ninth century we are told of an early Anglo-Saxon presence between Tyne and Tweed on the southern fringe of Votadinian territory. The central figure here is Oessa or Eosa, a man listed in the *Historia Brittonum* as an ancestor of Anglo-Saxon kings. His chronology according to the *Historia* suggests that he was active at the end of the fifth century, in which case he and his warband may be envisaged as mercenaries hired by local Britons – perhaps by a sept of the Votadini – for coastal defence. His historical existence remains unproven, but, in the absence of other clues about post-Roman military strategy in the intervallate region, he represents one of the few scraps of data we possess.[18] From the west of this region, in the lands between Solway and Clyde, no similar traditions are known, despite a suggestion that a group of Frisian warriors might be remembered in the place-name Dumfries. Early forms of the name, such as *Dunfres* in the twelfth century, allow the possibility of an original meaning 'Fort of the Frisians', but the second element seems more likely to be a Brittonic word related to Welsh *prys*, 'copse'.[19]

Kings and Kingdoms

There was little difference between the Early Historic kingdoms of the British Isles in terms of social organisation. In this regard they were not markedly different from other realms elsewhere in post-Roman Western Europe.[20] In Gaul, for instance, the imperial administration broke down in the decades after c.450 and barbarian warlords seized the reins of power. Franks, Burgundians and other Germanic peoples carved new domains from the ruins of Roman Gaul to establish vibrant kingdoms which collectively laid the foundations of medieval France. These kingdoms were essentially barbarian in character, but differed from their British counterparts in two important aspects. First, they were usually much larger, often encompassing groups of *civitates*. Secondly, their elites adopted Latin speech and absorbed many elements of Roman culture. The fifth-century Burgundian kings even assimilated entire regiments of the imperial army into their own military forces.

In northern Britain the Roman army disappeared in the early decades of the century, probably before c.420. Britannia Secunda, the region formerly under military jurisdiction, passed to native elites who divided it into smaller units. Some of the latter may have evolved into small kingdoms, such as the Pennine realm of Elmet, but we should also keep in mind the possibility that this did not happen, or happened only rarely. Three and a half centuries of Roman oppression may have broken the spirit of the native population in some areas, leading them to despise their 'Britishness' and making it difficult for them to support a new, home-grown leadership.[21] A sustainable kingdom like Elmet might have been extremely difficult to establish in places where weak elites failed to impose their authority. It is not known if any of the kingdoms north of Hadrian's Wall exploited the situation by launching a grab for territory on the southern side, but such expansion seems unlikely. The great barrier remained largely intact for many centuries and continued to exert a huge visual impact on the landscape. Despite being no longer manned by a permanent garrison, the Wall posed an obstacle to communication and continued to funnel travellers towards its ancient crossing-points or to newer gaps formed by the ravages of Man and Nature. Although there is no certain evidence that it served as a political barrier in post-Roman times, its presence undoubtedly influenced social interaction among communities living on either side of it.

The kingdoms north of the Wall had been established long before the fifth century. They were fully-fledged barbarian realms of the kind previously seen among Rome's enemies and provided working models for the new elites emerging in the Pennines. The ancient monarchies of the Votadini, Damnonii and other intervallate peoples were drawn from powerful families who claimed royal status as an ancestral right. In each kingdom several families might claim a vacant kingship, vying with one another to install their own representatives on the throne. Rivalry among these kindreds sometimes grew into hostility which in turn might lead to bitter civil war. Such disputes could be settled by mutual agreement between two or more families, one option being an alternating kingship which rotated royal power by turn. This system was common in contemporary Ireland and may have been used by the North Britons too, perhaps during periods of dynastic strife or in cases where two or more families held equal claims on the kingship.

The British kingdoms of the fifth and sixth centuries are sometimes referred to as 'successor states' of Rome, but this is a misleading label. None fitted the criteria of 'states' in the modern sense: they lacked the bureaucratic infrastructures which enabled a central authority – the monarch and his close kin – to maintain tight control over large tracts of territory beyond a core domain. A king in Early Historic times held sway over his kingdom by demanding allegiance from the landowning aristocracy, an elite class whose members provided the manpower for his warbands. The leading aristocrats ruled their own ancestral lands as hereditary lords and maintained warbands of their own. Their allegiance to the king was conditional on his success as a protector and on his generosity in distributing loot – especially cattle and slaves – acquired in raids on neighbouring kingdoms. Failure to protect the borders against marauding bands of enemies or ineffectiveness in aggressive warfare placed a king in danger of being ousted by a more competent rival. Conversely, any king who earned a reputation as a successful warlord would be in a strong, secure position within his kingdom. If he was a man of ambition, he might extend his authority to other kingdoms, either by war or threats, and so bring these under his hegemony. The subjugated kings would then become his vassals or clients, while he himself would be elevated to the status of an overlord wielding great power far beyond his heartlands. However, with no bureaucracy to cement his rule in distant areas his extended 'overkingship' would be fragile and personal and impermanent, its cohesion relying on his continuing success and survival. An overking's hegemony normally dissolved upon his death, his clients and other vassals thereafter being free to reclaim their independence or seek a new patron.

Warfare played a central role in the life of a kingdom. Relations between king and aristocracy relied on mutual obligations, of which military service was the most important. In exchange for leading their warbands to fight under the king's banner the nobles expected to be rewarded with a share of the spoils. Unswerving loyalty to the king, and special valour in battle, might bring additional privileges such as favour at court and the possibility of marriage to a royal female. Young aristocratic warriors, the sons of senior lords, received rich gifts of land in return for deeds of martial renown. Such gifts were usually large agricultural estates within the kingdom or in lands subjugated by recent conquest. In peacetime the obligations of military service were replaced by renders of hospitality to the royal entourage whenever the king made a tour of his lands. It was partly because of these regular tours or 'circuits' that a king typically maintained several halls or palaces in different parts of his kingdom, each serving as a focus of royal business when he and his entourage were in residence. To these centres the lords of a province or district would come to pay homage, renewing oaths of allegiance at formal ceremonies conducted under the solemn gaze of the chief priests of the kingdom. Such rituals were fundamental to the relationship between king and nobleman, both parties thereby being brought together in a bond sanctified by the priesthood. The latter was itself drawn primarily from the aristocracy and was therefore an elite group on equal status with the secular lords. Prior to the fourth and fifth centuries the priesthood was a pagan clergy heading local cults of gods and goddesses. By c.500 this clergy had been replaced in many parts of Britain by a Christian one whose members brought new ideas about the duties and responsibilities of kings.

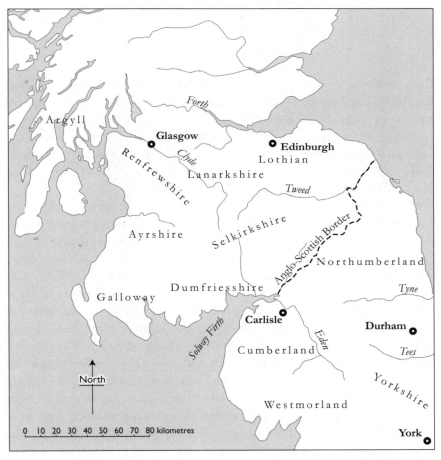

Southern Scotland and northern England, showing a selection of modern territorial divisions.

2

FORTH AND CLYDE

The Welsh Sources

The beginning of the sixth century brings the North British kingdoms into focus. They become visible in the literary sources and, in some cases, their geographical contexts can be placed on a modern map. How and when they were formed are important but largely unanswerable questions. It is generally accepted, however, that a number of kingdoms were flourishing in the lands on either side of Hadrian's Wall by c.500. The main focus of this chapter is the political history of these kingdoms and the activities of the kings who ruled them.

Most of what we know about the North Britons in the sixth century comes from texts written much later in Wales. To what extent these sources preserve genuine material of northern origin is a matter of frequent modern debate. Taken at face value, and setting aside all caution and scepticism, they appear to provide a rough narrative history of what medieval Welshmen called *Yr Hen Gogledd*, 'The Old North', a region today corresponding to southern Scotland with the northernmost parts of England. With little effort the Welsh texts can be employed to weave a more-or-less coherent picture of events in the North during the two or three centuries after the collapse of Roman Britain. This weaving has occasionally been attempted, with varying success, but the picture emerging from such reconstructions is seldom more than an illusion.[1] At best, the result is merely one possible view among others that can be devised from the same pool of data. At worst, it offers a plausible but misleading vision of North British history based on an uncritical acceptance of the Welsh texts. The fundamental problems with the latter are, firstly, that they were written not in the North but in Wales and, secondly, that their writers lived hundreds of years after the events they purport to describe.[2] This means that the most immediate context of these texts is Welsh rather than northern, a realisation that should make us wary of their testimony. We must suspect, at the outset, that a tenth-century Welshman writing about sixth-century northern Britain might choose to construct his narrative in ways appropriate to the literary or political needs of his own time.

The Welsh sources, then, constitute an imperfect body of information for the early history of the North. None can be shown to be as old as the events they claim to report. Some exist in manuscripts separated from the sixth century by nearly a thousand years of transmission, their surviving versions representing a lengthy process of copying and editing at the hands of numerous scribes. A small number of texts can be traced back to the eighth, ninth or tenth century and thus appear to be closer in time to their topic. Even these, however, are not contemporary records for sixth-century northern history, their immediate context being Wales in the era of their composition. Among the many problems arising from all of these texts is their tendency to depict the past as a mirror of their own present. Welsh kings of the ninth and subsequent centuries revered their ancient countrymen – the heroes of the Old North – as paragons of valour whose military campaigns against the English resonated with their own troubles along the Anglo-Welsh border. It was common for medieval Welsh rulers to claim North British descent to enhance their own status. Professional genealogists at the courts of Gwynedd, Powys and elsewhere devised royal ancestries showing kinship between their own kings and the renowned *Gwŷr y Gogledd*. Tales of old northern wars were incorporated into a new vision of Welsh royal origins to form an elaborate pseudo-history. The deeds of northern heroes were relocated to Wales and, by an inevitable two-way process, their Welsh counterparts were parachuted into genuine northern tales to transform these into pan-British sagas.

The Welsh material dealing with the Men of the North falls into two broad categories of literature: poetry and historical writing. Among the former are collections of verses attributed to Aneirin and Taliesin, two sixth-century bards, together with other poems supposedly created by their contemporaries. Little of this material can be assigned with confidence to an early period of composition. Some poems do exhibit linguistic features which appear to be archaic – that is, they contain elements of a Brittonic language spoken in a time before the creation of their surviving manuscripts – but this does not imply that they were originally composed in that language. Stray archaisms may simply reflect the 'antiquarian' interests of later Welsh poets who, by peppering compositions of their own with obsolete grammar and vocabulary, sought to create poems with a flavour of the Old North. Nevertheless, some poems attributed to Taliesin and Aneirin contain so many archaisms that they are generally seen as having a sixth-century origin.[3] Although such a broad assumption over-simplifies a wide range of literary and linguistic problems, it is cautiously accepted by most historians. Consequently, the poems attributed to these two bards are regarded as useful sources for the history of the *Gwŷr y Gogledd*. Using the poems for this purpose does, however, require great care, not least because their original sixth-century versions have not survived. Welsh scholarship is still scrutinising and analysing these poems and no firm consensus has yet been reached on how far they can be pressed into service as tools for the historian. In this book the poetry attributed to Aneirin and Taliesin is cautiously admitted as useful source material.

Far more northern poetry has been lost than has been preserved. Much of it probably never arrived in Wales or, having arrived, was subsequently discarded or forgotten. Some poems arrived in unwritten form, to be transmitted by recital before being copied into manuscripts. Other poems were never written down at all and eventually faded from bardic memory. Of the many that were lost a few scant traces survive, like faint footprints, among the 'mnemonics' known as the Welsh triads. Mnemonics were used by professional bards as a kind of indexing system in an age when poetry and other lore was recited from memory. Early medieval society in the British Isles was largely illiterate or pre-literate and relied on word-of-mouth transmission of knowledge, laws, news and saga. Thus, to a skilled bard in tenth-century Wales, the ability to recite a vast repertoire of verse without recourse to written versions represented the pinnacle of his art. Mnemonics or memory-triggers were an important bardic tool and, when grouped in threes or 'triads', provided a useful aid to recalling entire poems dealing with particular themes. The earliest collections of Welsh triads date to the ninth century, but many clearly refer to poems and stories of earlier times. Taken together as a single source they provide a bardic index or catalogue of poetic themes, among which are a number of unique references to northern Britain. It is in this collected form that they are most readily accessible today, in a compilation assembled through the painstaking scholarship of Professor Rachel Bromwich.[4] The triads give tantalising glimpses of what must once have been a substantial body of literature relating to the *Gwŷr y Gogledd*. In some cases a triad gives a genuine insight into North British history which can then be cross-referenced to a real person or event known from other sources.

The northern heroes of the poems and triads were kings, princes and aristocrats whom their later Welsh peers admired as fellow Britons. In seeking to forge artificial blood-ties with these renowned figures some Welsh royal families commissioned the creation of genealogies or 'pedigrees' to illustrate a fictional kinship. A necessary preliminary to this process was the devising of pedigrees for the Men of the North themselves, based in some cases on authentic tradition but in others on invention. To these lines of descent were attached the royal genealogies of kingdoms such as Gwynedd or Powys, whose kings thus received a heroic ancestry designed to legitimise their right to rule. Three major collections of northern pedigrees have survived. The oldest – commonly called the 'Harleian Genealogies' – is a compilation of c.950 preserved in an early twelfth-century manuscript designated Harley

3859. This lists thirty-two lines of descent, of which nine trace the ancestry of North British figures who lived in the late sixth century.[5] Of the other two collections the most useful is found in a Welsh text of the thirteenth century as a single page under the heading *Bonedd Gwŷr y Gogledd*, 'The Descent of the Men of the North'. Its original compilation can be dated no earlier than c.1150. The 12 pedigrees in the *Bonedd* partly overlap with those in Harley 3859, but there are enough discrepancies to suggest that the information came from a different source.[6] One obvious dissimilarity is the truncation in *Bonedd Gwŷr y Gogledd* of the royal pedigree of the Clyde Britons which appears in full in the Harleian collection. This pedigree is generally accepted as an authentic genealogy compiled in the ninth century by a North British scribe or by a Welshman using northern information. Of related interest is the third collection, preserved in a fourteenth-century manuscript held at Jesus College, Oxford. Four of the five northern pedigrees in the Jesus College text derive from the Harleian, the fifth being an otherwise unknown item commonly regarded as a Welsh invention. In spite of the lateness of the manuscripts containing the genealogical tracts, their individual pedigrees are not always regarded with appropriate caution by historians. No pedigree can be considered an impeccable source of sixth-century history, nor should it be seen as a king-list. Groups of pedigrees linked together to show descent from a common ancestor do not represent real political relationships between royal houses. Deliberate manipulation by Welsh genealogists is a far more likely cause of such links. Acknowledgment of these limitations does not render the pedigrees unusable as historical sources, but should warn us against casually accepting their testimony.

Having discussed the poems and pedigrees, we turn now to the genre of historical writing and find ourselves facing the controversial *Historia Brittonum*, 'The History of the Britons'. This was written in Wales in the early ninth century by an author whose name is unknown. The oldest manuscript containing a complete version is the previously mentioned Harley 3859 of c.1100 which also contains the Welsh Annals and a collection of genealogies. Textual analysis of the *Historia* shows it to be a work of c.830. It was produced a hundred years after Bede's *Ecclesiastical History*, seemingly as a Welsh retort against the latter's Anglocentric vision in which the Britons are consistently portrayed in a poor light. There are few similarities between the two, for the Welsh author was no Bede and had little desire to create a *magnum opus* like the *Ecclesiastical History*. He produced instead a much shorter work, a brief chronicle of the deeds of the Britons compiled from a plethora of oral and written traditions. His aim was not to compile an authentic narrative of the past but to present his fellow Welshmen with an agreeable version of it.[7] Modern historians are no longer fooled by the author's claim that he made a casual heap of data from the ancient texts. The *Historia Brittonum* is a clever synthesis of data abstracted and manipulated by its author in line with his literary purposes. Its information is therefore difficult to assess in terms of historical accuracy and authenticity. This is an especially frustrating comment to make about one of the most important sources of North British history, but it has to be stated nonetheless. Like the poems and genealogies, the *Historia Brittonum* must be handled with appropriate caution.

The Kingdom of Gododdin

The people known to the Romans as Votadini emerged into the sixth century with their name unchanged and their core territory intact. In medieval Welsh tradition they were called Gododdin (pronounced *Go-dothin* with *th* as in *bathe*), a name representing a later form of an older term *Guotodin* (pronounced *Wo-todin*). Their heartland, as in pre-Roman times, lay south of the Firth of Forth in what is now Lothian.[8] In the Welsh poem *Y Gododdin*, 'The Gododdin', attributed to the sixth-century bard Aneirin, several verses indicate that the main centre of Gododdin power was a fortified settlement on the rocky height now occupied by Edinburgh Castle. Recent excavations have revealed traces of what seems to be elite occupation there in the Early Historic period.[9] In poetry this site is called *Din Eidyn*, 'Fort of Eidyn', a Brittonic name of which *Edinburgh* represents an English translation. The lords of Din Eidyn were the kings not only of the Gododdin people, the descendants of the ancient Votadini, but also of an eponymous realm. In this book the term 'Votadinian' is employed as a convenient adjective for the Early Historic kingdom and its people.

The geographical extent of Gododdin is unknown, but it clearly related in some way to the old tribal heartlands. On a second-century Roman map the name *Uotadinoi* seems to encompass a large swath of the eastern coastlands running south from the Forth estuary. In Roman times a Votadinian 'confederacy' or hegemony may have stretched as far as Hadrian's Wall and the River Tyne, or perhaps only to the Tweed. By the sixth century, when the Votadini reappear in our sources as the kingdom of Gododdin, their southern boundary perhaps ran along Lower Tweeddale. Here, in the coastal districts facing the tidal island of Lindisfarne, lay a territory called *Berneich*, 'land of the mountain passes'.[10] Formerly a part of the old Votadinian hegemony, Berneich at the end of the fifth century was either an independent kingdom or a client realm still under Gododdin overlordship. Its principal stronghold, and arguably its main seat of royal authority, was the imposing fortress of *Din Guayroi* whose site is now occupied by Bamburgh Castle. Other centres of power in Berneich included a coastal stronghold at *Din Baer*

(Dunbar) and another at Coldingham. It was in this region, on the exposed North Sea shorelands, that a colony of Germanic mercenaries was established in the fifth century to provide protection against Pictish raiders. Whether these were led by the mysterious Oessa or Eosa referred to in the previous chapter is unknown for both the date of this settlement of 'Anglo-Saxons' and its precise location elude us. Its instigators, however, were members of the British elite and it is tempting to identify them as the rulers of Berneich or of some part of the greater realm of Gododdin. Arriving initially as hired swords, perhaps from older Germanic colonies further south, the newcomers seemingly served their patrons well by repelling Pictish and other seaborne marauders. Inevitably, as the numbers of colonists increased, their ambitions began to expand. Intermarriage with local Britons gave them access to power and influence among the native elite of Berneich, gradually altering the contract between hirelings and paymasters. By the middle of the sixth century this had evolved into a different kind of relationship carrying profound implications for both sides. The nature of the new arrangement, together with the destinies of its participants, is looked at more closely in Chapter 4.

Calchfynydd, Yarrow and Goddeu

How far Berneich extended to the north, south and west can only be surmised in vague terms. Her northern frontier faced Gododdin and presumably followed a major natural boundary such as the Tweed.[11] Further south, in what is now Yorkshire, lay the Anglo-Saxon kingdom of Deira, perhaps the motherland of the colonists in Berneich. The border between Berneich and Deira is unknown, but a sixth-century divide along the River Tees seems plausible. Deira's elite was an English-speaking aristocracy led by kings who claimed to be of Germanic descent and whose ancestors had probably been hired as mercenaries in Late Roman times. Turning north again we find the western flank of Berneich nudging native realms on the River Tweed. One of these was probably *Calchfynydd*, 'Chalk Hill', the domain of a king called Cadrod whose pedigree appears in *Bonedd Gwŷr y Gogledd*. The belief that Cadrod's kingdom lay in Tweeddale arises from the suggested identification of Calchfynydd as Kelso, both names having the same meaning.[12] The earliest known name of Kelso is *Calkou*, recorded in the twelfth century, deriving from Old English *cealc hoh*, 'chalk height'. It has been objected that Welsh *mynydd*, 'mountain', the second element of *Calchfynydd*, is not an apt description of the *hoh* at Kelso.[13] However, the instances where *mynydd*, in its older Brittonic form *minit*, occur in the place-names of southern Scotland demonstrate that the term was applied to low hills as well as to mountains.[14] This removes the linguistic objection and allows us to cautiously accept the identification of Kelso as the realm of Cadrod Calchfynydd. The original 'chalk hill', known today as the Chalk Heugh, is an eminence of carboniferous limestone whose location is indicated by the street-name Chalkheugh Terrace. The

Chalk Hill itself need not have held an administrative function and might simply have been adopted as an iconic landmark symbolising the locality. In the sixth century the chief stronghold of Cadrod's family may have lain where the ruined Roxburgh Castle now stands, half a mile to the west of Kelso near the confluence of the Rivers Tweed and Teviot. This twelfth-century fortification was built on an elevated site in a strategic position guarding the river-meeting. Today its wider setting still has strong associations with status and authority: across the Tweed it faces Floors Castle, the residence of the Duke of Roxburghe. In searching for the main focus of Early Historic Calchfynydd it is worth noting the possibility that the visible ramparts of Roxburgh Castle may incorporate earthworks of earlier origin.[15]

Cadrod's father, named in *Bonedd Gwŷr y Gogledd* as Cynfelyn, has no territorial epithet linking him to a particular place. Above the generation represented by Cynfelyn the pedigree merges with others, suggesting that the names of Cadrod's earlier antecedents were not known to the Welsh gene-alogists. The kingdom ruled by his family may have evolved from a political entity of the Iron Age, perhaps from a sept or sub-group of a larger popula-tion. In Roman times the area around Kelso lay within the hegemony of the Selgovae and it is possible that the leaders of a Selgovan sept founded the kingdom of Calchfynydd in the fifth century.

To the west of Calchfynydd a different group, also nominally Selgovan, held sway in the Yarrow Valley near present-day Selkirk. Although the sources say nothing about this district a sixth-century elite is represented on a monument discovered in c.1803 in a field near Yarrow Kirk. Upon this stone is a Christian inscription, now so weathered as to be illegible:

> This is the everlasting memorial. In this place lie the illustrious princes Nudus and Dumnogenus. In this tomb lie the sons of Liberalis.

Neither Nudus nor Dumnogenus, nor their father Liberalis, 'The Generous One', are identifiable in the North British genealogical tracts. The name *Nudus* is a Latinisation of *Nud* or *Nudd*, evidently a not uncommon name in Early Historic times. In one northern pedigree a certain Nudd, son of Ceidio, appears as a descendant of Coel Hen, while another tradition refers to a Nudd Hael, 'Nudd the Generous', joining other northerners in an attack on Wales.[16] The occurrence of the name *Nudus* alongside a Latin synonym of *Hael* has prompted speculation that the Yarrow stone commemorates members of the kindred to which Nudd Hael belonged.[17] Dumnogenus has an otherwise unattested name, but he and his brother belonged to a family of high status which had sufficient wealth and influence to commission memorial stones inscribed in Latin. The commemoration of two princes

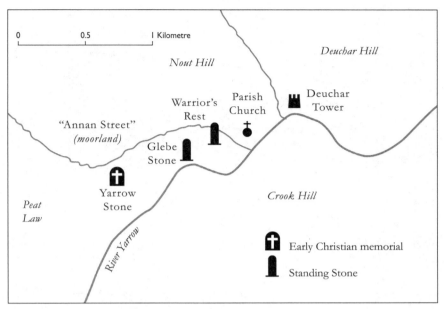

The Yarrow Valley: monuments and centres of power.

buried together in one grave suggests either simultaneous death in adulthood – perhaps in battle – or victims of childhood mortality. Stylistic features of the inscription date the memorial to the first half of the sixth century and have prompted speculation that the brothers died from the Yellow Plague which ravaged Britain at this time.[18] There were, however, many possible causes of untimely death, especially among children. In any case, the description of the deceased as 'illustrious princes' implies that they were old enough to perform deeds of renown with their father's warband. The fact that they were princes confirms their father Liberalis as a king. His family's Christianity would have required access to a place of worship, perhaps in the vicinity of the nearby parish church of Yarrow. The family's secular residence presumably lay in the same vicinity. Poor agricultural land prior to improvement in the eighteenth century made the Yarrow Valley unattractive for settlement in early times and this, in turn, reduces the number of possible candidates for an Early Historic centre of power. Our attention is nevertheless drawn to Deuchar, close to the stone's current location, where a late medieval tower-house implies a focus of authority which might be far older.[19]

Further west, towards the valley of the River Clyde, lay a district called *Goddeu*. Because the name means simply 'The Trees' or 'The Forest' it has been suggested that Goddeu should be identified as the ancient Wood of Celyddon

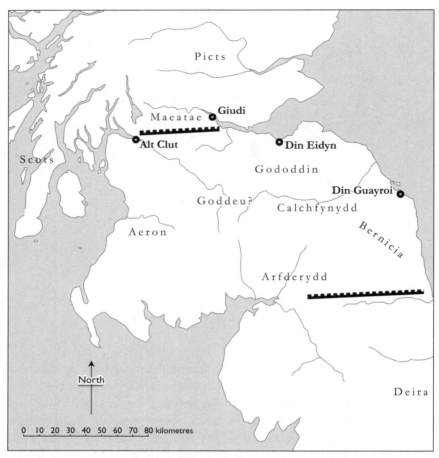

Early Historic kingdoms of northern Britain.

which once straddled the uplands from where the Tweed and Yarrow rise. In medieval times this area of tree-covered hills, much of it contained within the old county of Selkirkshire, was indeed known as 'The Forest'.[20] Heroic poetry attributed to the sixth-century bard Taliesin speaks of Goddeu as a distinct political entity, while the North British pedigrees refer to Gurycon Goddeu as the wife of Cadrod Calchfynydd. We therefore seem to be presented with a topographical name referring both to an area of woodland and to a defined unit of lordship. Are we, however, looking for Goddeu in the right place?

The *dd* in *Goddeu* is pronounced like *th* in *them*, as indeed is *d* in the older spelling *Godeu*. Both spellings have a similar sound to *Cadyow*, an old form of the place-name *Cadzow* formerly borne by the town of Hamilton in Clydesdale. The *z* in *Cadzow* arose from erroneous substitution of the medieval letter *yogh*, a mistake so pervasive that the incorrect spelling eventually

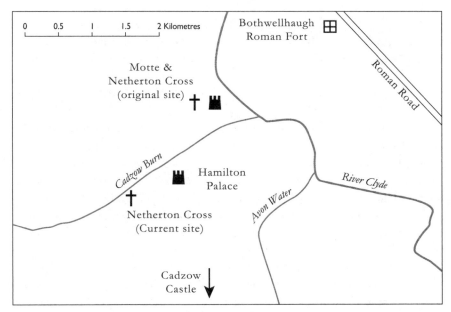

Cadzow: a focus of power in Clydesdale.

supplanted the original form of the place-name. The error was noticed in the nineteenth century by William Forbes Skene who suggested that the place-name *Cadzow* might preserve a memory of ancient Goddeu. Cadzow has a long history as a centre of power, its castle having been used by Scottish kings in the twelfth and thirteenth centuries.[21] This stronghold probably occupied the old motte on the north side of the Cadzow Burn above its confluence with the Clyde. In the sixteenth century the Hamilton family erected a new castle above the Avon Water a mile southward and the centre of lordship moved away from the older site. The latter, however, retained a semblance of its former status by continuing in use as a 'moot hill' where local justice was dispensed. Nearby stood an ancient church, of which no trace now remains, together with the original setting of the tenth-century Netherton Cross. Carved at a time when Clydesdale still lay under British rule, the cross testifies to Cadzow's antiquity as a focus of elite patronage. When the Scottish king David I began to use the earthwork castle as a centre of administration, he was probably continuing a long tradition of royal authority in the area north of the Cadzow Burn.[22] It seems likely that this tradition reached far back into the era of British rule, perhaps even beyond the time when the Netherton Cross was sculpted to an even earlier age. If *Cadzow* and *Goddeu* are indeed the same name in different forms, as Skene suggested, the twelfth-century residence of David I may have lain in the vicinity of an older royal settlement where Gurycon once dwelt as a princess. This would be a much neater hypothesis if a philological connection between the place-names could be proved beyond the superficial temptation of 'sounds-like' etymology.

Alt Clut

West of Gododdin lay the valley and estuary of the Clyde, a region inhabited in Roman times by a people called *Damnonii*. Unlike the Votadini, whose name survived the upheavals of the fourth and fifth centuries to reappear in the sixth, the Damnonii vanish from the documentary record. In onomastic terms their identity fades from history at the end of the Roman period. In reality, or rather in terms of human settlement, they remained in their ancestral lands and were still there when the sixth century began. A memory of their presence might be preserved in the place-names Cardowan (near Wishaw) and Dowanhill (near Milngavie).[23] The apparent diminution of the old name after c.500 suggests a significant change among the Damnonian elite, perhaps a shift of power which resulted in the discarding of ancient identities and the creation of new ones. By the late fifth century a vibrant kingdom held sway over former Damnonian lands at the eastern end of the Firth of Clyde. Its kings ruled from Alt Clut, 'Clyde Rock', from where they operated as a seafaring power capable of launching raids on Ireland. Textual evidence for one of these pirate-kings comes from the writings of Patrick, Ireland's patron saint, whose career as priest and missionary spanned the middle and later decades of the fifth century.[24] Patrick's death, which most probably occurred between 470 and 493, provides a chronological context for what he tells us about the Britons of the Clyde.

Patrick was himself a Briton, perhaps also a northerner, and a member of the landowning gentry. His family was Christian and both his father and grandfather had served the Church as deacon and priest respectively. In his teens Patrick was captured by pagan Irish pirates and spent time in their homeland as a slave. He eventually escaped and returned to Britain where he was later ordained into the priesthood. Resolving to bring Christianity to his former captors, he went back to Ireland as a missionary, preaching the Word among a largely heathen population and becoming their first bishop. The principal focus of his mission lay in the northern parts of the country, especially in County Armagh where he founded a *familia* or network of churches. His position was already well-established when news reached him of an attack by seaborne raiders in which a number of his followers – including novice monks and nuns – had been taken captive. The culprits were Britons, his own fellow countrymen, to whom he sent a stern letter of rebuke. The letter was addressed to the warriors who had taken part in the raid, but its real target was their king Coroticus. At Armagh in the seventh century it was believed that Coroticus ruled a kingdom called in Gaelic *Aloo* or *Ail*, 'The Rock', a place commonly identified as Alt Clut, the Rock of Clyde. The identification is accepted here and is discussed in more detail later. In expressing his anger at the raiders Patrick pulled no punches, as the following passage demonstrates:

> With my own hand I have written and composed these words to be given, delivered and sent to the soldiers of Coroticus – I do not say to my fellow citizens nor to fellow citizens of the holy Romans but to fellow citizens of demons, because of their evil actions. Like the enemy they live in death, as allies of Scots and of Picts and apostates. These bloodthirsty men are bloody with the blood of innocent Christians whom I have begotten for God in countless numbers and have confirmed in Christ.[25]

If Coroticus sent a response to Patrick, it has not survived and no source refers to it. It is possible that the saint's complaint never reached the royal court at Alt Clut or that, having arrived, it was greeted by the king with scorn and disregarded. Much depends on the nature of any previous contact or relationship between Patrick and Coroticus and this, in turn, touches on the question of the saint's own origins. In his own summary of his life he refers to a family estate near a place called *Bannavem Taburniae*, apparently a settlement with a church in which his father Calpurnius served as a deacon. Calpurnius was in turn the son of Potitus, a priest, and held the secular office of decurion as well as the ecclesiastical rank of *diaconus*. Patrick's mention of the Latin title *decurio* has prompted a suggestion that his family belonged to a district formerly under Roman rule where remnants of the old imperial administration still functioned at local level. This would place Patrick's childhood in an area south of Hadrian's Wall, in the erstwhile Roman part of Britain. An alternative explanation is that *decurio* represents an attempt by Patrick to translate into Latin a vernacular, Brittonic designation of secular rank. If pretensions of *Romanitas* indeed explain this terminology, we would have no need to imagine his family living south of the Wall. His narrative offers slight hints that he hailed from the same region as the soldiers of Coroticus.

In his letter of complaint, Patrick castigated the plunderers as unworthy of being called 'my fellow citizens' or 'fellow citizens of the holy Romans'. Here he was not suggesting that these men came from the Romanised areas of Britain, but was rather reminding them of their membership of a wider Christian community whose spiritual focus lay at Rome. They may have been his fellow citizens, his compatriots, in a literal rather than merely a spiritual sense. He may be speaking as a native of the Clyde when he says: 'If my own people do not recognise me, well, a prophet does not have honour in his own country. Perhaps we are not of one fold and do not have one God as father ....'.[26] Elsewhere he describes the rule of Coroticus as 'unjust', a remark which might indicate a particular concern for the king's subjects back home in Britain. We cannot, of course, press the theory of Patrick's Clyde origins too far, but nor should we regard it as any less plausible than suggestions that he hailed from Wales or Carlisle or elsewhere. In the sixteenth-century *Aberdeen Breviary*, a collection of hagiographical material relating to a plethora of saints, Patrick's birthplace is said to be Old Kilpatrick, 4 miles upstream from Alt Clut. Regardless of its origin this tradition was sufficiently well-known to attract pilgrims to the old parish church in medieval times.[27]

Of Coroticus we learn from Patrick that he was a Christian and – like the saint – a Briton. His co-operation with the Picts places him in a northern context, in some region where contact between Picts and Britons included a thriving cross-border trade in human captives, as does his raiding in northern Ireland. Patrick does not identify the king's domain, but we can assume that it was Alt Clut because of the later tradition, referred to above, which calls Coroticus *rex Aloo*, 'King of the Rock'. The place-name appears in the ninth-century *Book of Armagh* within a list of chapter headings for a *Vita* of Patrick written by the seventh-century priest Muirchu. *Aloo* is generally interpreted as a truncation of *Ail Cluaide*, an Irish form of *Alt Clut*. If the identification is correct, we should expect to find Coroticus in the ancestry of the Clyde kings at a point roughly corresponding to the mid-fifth century, and indeed we do. One of the Harleian pedigrees traces the royal line of Alt Clut backwards from the ninth century through many generations to a dim, prehistoric past. Coroticus appears as Ceretic Guletic, son of Cynloyp, in a position five generations earlier than a descendant who ruled in c.600. *Ceretic* is simply a medieval Welsh form of Latin *Coroticus*, but the epithet *Guletic*, a word related to *gwlad*, 'land', and seemingly denoting wide territorial power, testifies to a career of successful plundering and competent war-leadership. Aside from the slave-raids on Ireland nothing is known of Coroticus, nor can we say how far his authority extended beyond his primary stronghold at Alt Clut. He is likely to have ruled a domain of sufficient size to sustain the estates of a warrior-nobility from whom he received renders of food and hospitality as well as obligations of military service. We might envisage, therefore, a core territory comprising the vale of the River Leven, together with a narrow swath of land running east along the northern shore of Clyde as far as the Kelvin. How far the realm extended south of the firth is hard to say, but some northern districts of Renfrewshire, especially those actually visible from the summit of Alt Clut, should probably be included within its bounds. It may be that this fairly compact zone corresponds roughly to the heartland of the kingdom ruled by Coroticus and his heirs in the fifth and sixth centuries.

Patrick was dead before the end of the fifth century and might not have been long outlived by the king whom he castigated. The pedigree of Alt Clut identifies the son of Coroticus as Cynwyd who presumably succeeded him. Later traditions in Wales regarded Cynwyd as the eponymous founder of the Cynwydyon, one of three warbands grouped together in a triad inserted among the pedigrees of *Bonedd Gwŷr y Gogledd*:

> The three hundred swords of the Cynferchyn, the three hundred shields of the Cynwydyon and the three hundred spears of the Coeling, on whatever expedition they might go together they would never fail.

All three warbands take their names from figures listed in the pedigrees. The Coeling are associated with the mysterious Coel Hen, whom we encountered in the previous chapter. He was regarded by Welsh genealogists as the forefather of several northern dynasties including that of Cynfarch, the eponym of the Cynferchyn. If Cynfarch was a real person rather than merely an eponym for a warband, he can be tentatively placed in the mid-500s. His geographical context, and the deeds of his family, are discussed in Chapter 4. The usual interpretation of the triad sees each of the three warbands representing the ruling dynasty or royal army of a North British kingdom, or the combined forces of a number of kingships linked by ancestry. This has prompted suggestions that the triad reflects real political alliances of the sixth century and that the warbands or allied armies actually bore the names given above. There is no justification for attaching such meaning or significance to the triad. It merely reflects a desire in ninth-century Wales to portray the heroes of the Old North as capable of acting in unison against a common enemy. The latter, although unnamed, can be understood as the English, a people whose ascendancy posed a major problem for Welsh kings and whose earlier expansion in the North had been strongly resisted by the *Gwŷr y Gogledd*. It is unlikely that the triad has anything useful to say about Cynwyd or Cynfarch or Coel, still less about military co-operation among their respective heirs in the sixth and seventh centuries. In Cynwyd's case this means that he emerges from the Alt Clut pedigree as a mere eponym, a man without a history. It may be too severe a judgment to deny his existence but he certainly ranks among a long list of very obscure northern figures. In Wales he was perhaps selected randomly by the compiler of *Bonedd Gwŷr y Gogledd* as a suitable early figure to whom the creation of the army of Alt Clut could be attributed. A medieval Welshman is not likely to have known anything more about Cynwyd than we do today and probably would not have guessed that the king berated by Saint Patrick may have been Cynwyd's father.

In the Harleian pedigree Cynwyd is followed by his son Dyfnwal Hen, 'Old Donald', to whom two additional pedigrees were attached. Dyfnwal, like Coel, thus has a role as forefather to several dynasties of North British kings. The main royal line of Alt Clut continues through his son Guipno ap Dyfnwal, another obscure figure. One of the two attached pedigrees traces the descent through another son, Clinog ap Dyfnwal, of a king called Rhydderch Hael who reigned on the Clyde in the last quarter of the sixth century. The other is a short, two-generation pedigree for Clydno Eidyn, 'of Edinburgh', who was known to later Welshmen through heroic poetry. Clydno's epithet takes him away from the Clyde and associates him with the chief citadel of Gododdin. Although we might wonder why Welsh genealogists attached a figure with Votadinian connections to Dyfnwal Hen's pedigree, it would be unwise to suggest that this reflects political relations between the Britons of Clyde and Lothian. The attachment is more likely to be of later Welsh origin and therefore of little relevance to the sixth century. This has not deterred historians from using Clydno's epithet to devise a political scenario in which he plays the role of a Clyde prince who gained control of Din Eidyn.[28] Such speculation allows the pedigrees to dictate our ideas about relationships between kingdoms in a way they were never intended to do. Clydno is in fact an obscure character and we cannot really say much about him. In poetry attributed to the northern bard Aneirin the fame of Clydno Eidyn derives chiefly from that of his son Cynon, a Votadinian hero of high repute, rather than from his own deeds. Clydno also appears in what is most probably a fictional account of a raid on Wales by forces from the Clyde, a campaign in which his allies included other northern figures such as the aforementioned Rhydderch Hael and Nudd Hael.[29]

The main royal line of Alt Clut is by far the longest of the North British genealogies, tracing the descent through many generations of a king called Rhun ab Arthgal whose father died in 872. Its extraordinary length sets it apart from the other pedigrees and suggests that it had a different origin. Between the fifth and ninth centuries its testimony is frequently confirmed by the Irish annals and other independent sources, thereby giving it an unusual aura of authenticity. It probably originated in the North as a formal statement of Rhun's ancestry. In the hands of Welsh genealogists it later served as a useful anchor to which the real or invented ancestries of Rhydderch Hael and Clydno Eidyn could be attached and around which a bundle of other pedigrees could be arranged and manipulated. We can probably assume that the Harleian genealogy of Alt Clut was already in existence in written form on the Clyde in the late ninth century, at which point it was brought to Wales. The shorter pedigrees were probably compiled at that time by Welsh genealogists for whom the main sources of data were written versions of the northern poems or lists of names already abstracted from them. Some of these short pedigrees were then linked to the line of Alt Clut.

Even without Rhun's long pedigree we would still guess that a powerful elite resided at Alt Clut in the fifth and sixth centuries. Archaeologists from Glasgow University undertook small-scale excavations at Dumbarton Castle in the

1970s and found clear signs of high-status occupation from the Roman period onwards.[30] Such evidence prompts us to consider how much power was wielded by these people and how far their authority extended beyond their heartlands around the Firth of Clyde. Until the reign of Rhydderch in the late sixth century we find no answers to these questions in the textual sources. We have already seen Coroticus depicted as a ruler who commanded considerable military resources – warriors and ships – with which to launch raids in the western seaways. We can see this king's ambitions reaching out in other directions via his commercial dealings with the Picts. He or his descendants may have nurtured territorial ambitions westward along the Firth of Clyde or southward into Ayrshire, or perhaps upstream via Clydesdale into what is now Lanarkshire. To the east lay the realm of Gododdin where the mysterious Clydno Eidyn perhaps held some kind of authority in the sixth century. At that time the western flank of present-day Lothian may have been a contested borderland between the rulers of Gododdin and Alt Clut. North of it lay an even more troubled region whose name in Early Historic times became a byword for conflict.

Manau

Topography suggests that the north-east frontier of the kings of Alt Clut was defined by the Campsie Fells, an area of upland rising to heights of a little under 2,000 feet. Campsie forms the western buttress of a larger network of hills surrounding the upper courses of the River Carron and nestling between the firths of Forth and Clyde. To the Britons the eastern end of this upland mass was *Bannauc*, a name corresponding to modern Welsh *bannog* meaning 'peaked' in the sense of 'the peaked hills'. On the high moorland rises the Bannock Burn whose waters flow down towards Stirling and to the famous battlefield of 1314. South of the burn lies the Carron and, further south again, the River Avon on the western boundary of Lothian. In ancient times the Avon marked the southern border of Manau, a territory encompassing much of what are now Stirlingshire and Clackmannanshire. The town of Slamannan on the Avon has a name deriving from Gaelic *Sliabh Mhanainn*, 'Hill (or Slope) of Manau', which probably supplanted an earlier Brittonic name conveying a similar meaning. The northern part of Manau straddled the head of the Forth estuary and stretched east beyond present-day Clackmannan, a town whose Gaelic name means 'Stone of Manau'. The stone itself, an unshaped whinstone boulder, can today be seen in the town centre alongside the seventeenth-century Tolbooth. Neither the stone's current location nor the pillar-like plinth on which it stands are original: the stone formerly lay 600 metres to the south at the curiously named Lookabootye Brae.[31] Other possible examples of 'Manau' place-names are Cremannan on the outskirts of Balfron in Stirlingshire and Dalmeny a mile east of Queensferry in Lothian.[32] Early forms of Dalmeny include *Dunmanyn* which seems, at first glance, to incorporate the Gaelic genitive of Manau, although a more likely derivation might be a Brittonic word similar to Welsh *meini*, 'stones'. In any case, the position of Dalmeny is perhaps too far east of the presumed frontier of Manau on the River Avon. Cremannan might derive from Gaelic *crioch Manann*, 'boundary of Manau', if its origin is not simply *Crò-meannán*, 'goats' fold'. The *crioch* derivation seems plausible if we imagine Manau encompassing the entire Forth Valley between Stirling and Loch Lomond.

In Roman times the inhabitants of this region were the Maeatae, a people whose leaders were regarded by the imperial authorities as allies of the Picts. It is sometimes thought that the Maeatae themselves were Picts, but their location south of the Pictish heartlands makes it far more likely that they were Britons.[33] The ethnic distinction need not be pressed too far. Differences between 'Pictish' and 'British' cultural groups are likely to have emerged gradually over several centuries and may not have been recognisable at all before c.400. It is nevertheless possible that the Maeatae and their territory were divided into northern and southern parts, the former perhaps becoming more receptive to 'Pictish' influence as cultural distinctions became more marked, while the southern group remained 'British'. This, at least, is one inference to be drawn from the story of a warlord called Cunedda who allegedly hailed from Manau. Our source for this controversial tale appears in the *Historia Brittonum* as a foundation-legend for the royal dynasty of Gwynedd in North Wales.

> King Maelgwn the Great was reigning among the Britons in Gwynedd, for his ancestor Cunedda (*Cunedag*) with his eight sons had come here from the North, from the region called Manau Gododdin, 146 years before Maelgwn reigned, and expelled the Irish from these countries with immense slaughter so that they never again returned to inhabit them.[34]

Maelgwn ruled Gwynedd until his death in AD 547. The darker aspects of his character were criticised by his contemporary and former acquaintance Gildas who called him *insularis draco*, 'Dragon of the Island'. From the Welsh Annals we learn that Maelgwn died of the Yellow Plague in his palace at Rhos but little else is known about his reign. His genealogy echoes the *Historia Brittonum* in tracing his ancestry back to Cunedda but since both sources appear in the same manuscript they are unlikely to be independent. Neither the genealogy nor the foundation-legend can be confidently assigned a date earlier than the tenth century when both were combined with the Welsh Annals in the manuscript Harley 3859. The claim of a northern origin for the Gwynedd dynasty arouses suspicion, not least because of the great fame of the *Gwŷr y Gogledd* among tenth-century Welshmen. Equally suspicious is the 146-year interval given in the *Historia*

Brittonum which, if taken at face value, should place Cunedda's expulsion of the Irish from Gwynedd around c.400. This seems to strain the genealogy which, in making Maelgwn a great-grandson of Cunedda, should assign the latter to the period 450 to 500.[35] Much ink has been expended on reconciling the chronological problems, with various ingenious theories being proposed to find a better 'fit' between Cunedda and Maelgwn. Some historians point to the Irish settlers allegedly expelled by Cunedda and propose that the Irish colonisation of Wales should be dated several decades after the collapse of Roman Britain in the early fifth century. Cunedda's migration from the North in the second half of the century, rather than sometime around c.400, seems then to fit rather neatly. An alternative and simpler solution is to reject both the genealogy and the foundation-legend as propaganda designed to create a northern heroic origin for Gwynedd's royal family. Cunedda himself cannot, however, be dismissed so easily and, if we choose to reject the Welsh material, we must explain the very early form of his name as given in the *Historia Brittonum*. There seems little doubt that *Cunedag* is an archaic form of the mid-eighth century or perhaps even earlier.[36] This should warn us against dismissing the person so named as a fictional character invented by the propagandists of Gwynedd. If Cunedda was indeed a historical figure, we ought to place him in some kind of context. To this end, albeit with some caution, he can tentatively be envisaged as a North British leader of the fifth century, one of the earliest of the *Gwŷr y Gogledd* to find fame in Welsh lore. If this lore is correct in associating him with Gododdin, he was perhaps a member of the Votadinian aristocracy. His primary association was with Manau, an area northward of the Votadinian heartlands, and specifically with Manau Gododdin, a district whose compound name means 'Votadinian Manau' or 'Manau of Gododdin'. From this we might infer that a unit of territory beyond the Avon was regarded as being part of Gododdin in the fifth century. Alternatively, Manau as a whole may have been frequently described as 'of Gododdin' to distinguish it from the other Manau, the Isle of Man. The first inference suggests a north–south division of Manau, with the southern part being considered 'Votadinian' in terms of cultural or political allegiances while the northern part may have been 'Pictish'. The second inference imagines all of Manau as 'Votadinian' and contradicts Roman perceptions that Stirlingshire belonged not to the Votadini but to the Maeatae. There is, however, no reason to believe that the latter were anything other than a distinct people, or that the Votadini ever conquered Stirlingshire. Cunedda might nonetheless have been based in a southern district of Maeatae territory where Votadinian authority was acknowledged. As a lord of 'Manau of Gododdin' his allegiance probably lay with the Votadinian king at Din Eidyn. With the story of his journey to Wales disregarded as fiction he becomes, like many other northern heroes, an elusive figure stranded on the edge of history.

If Cunedda really existed, he may have been a Votadinian by blood as well as by political allegiance. Alternatively, his roots may have lain among the Maeatae, a people whose identity survived into Early Historic times. Two place-names in Stirlingshire appear to preserve a memory of them: Dumyat in the Ochils and Myot Hill above the south bank of the Carron. The former has a name derived from an earlier *Dun Myat*, 'Fort of the Maeatae', and is borne by a distinctive outlier of the Ochil Hills upon which traces of ancient ramparts are visible. These earthworks enclose a large settlement of Iron Age type whose size, location and name suggest that it may have been a pre-Roman tribal centre or *oppidum* of the Maeatae. In the absence of detailed archaeological survey we can do no more than draw analogies with similar sites to make informed guesses about the date and purpose of Dumyat. Like other large hillforts or *oppida* it was probably abandoned long before the fifth century AD, its usefulness having dwindled in a time of social change or political upheaval. Abandonment may have been related to Roman aggression in the period when the Maeatae first came to the notice of Latin writers. In the fifth and sixth centuries the Maeatae elites are likely to have adopted smaller elevated sites as their centres of power and it is to this context that Myot Hill and its summit fort may belong. The most plausible candidate for an Early Historic 'capital' of Manau lies between Dumyat and Myot Hill at Stirling, where the towering Castle Rock dominates a wide tract of lowland at the head of the Forth estuary. The topography and character of the Rock are reminiscent of other imposing sites such as Din Eidyn and Alt Clut, both of which unquestionably held royal status in Early Historic times. It is almost inconceivable that Stirling was not utilised in a similar way, even if the foundations of the medieval castle have obliterated any trace of older structures. Literary references confirm the presence of kings at Din Eidyn and Alt Clut, but can the same be said of Stirling?

Giudi

In the early eighth century Bede described two major strongholds of the North Britons guarding the western and eastern ends of the isthmus between Forth and Clyde. He called the western site *Alcluith*, adding that this name 'in their language means Clyde Rock because it stands near the river of that name', and referred to the eastern site as *urbs Giudi*, 'the city of Giudi', which he perceived as lying *in medio*, 'in the middle of', the Firth of Forth.[37] Historians have long debated the location of Giudi but are unable to reach agreement on the issue.[38] Some identify the place as Stirling while others propose the Roman fort at Cramond, the island of Inchkeith or other places along the firth. At the heart of the debate lies Bede's use of the term *in medio* which, if taken at face value, could be seen as a description of an island in the middle of the firth itself. Alternatively, Bede may have used the term in this instance to convey the meaning 'in the midst of', a description which fits the character of Stirling when viewed from the east. To an eighth-century traveller coming by boat from the North Sea the most prominent geographical feature visible after reaching the narrows of the firth would indeed have been the mighty Castle Rock looming like a sentinel above the lower lands. Neither Inchkeith nor Cramond, nor any of the other suggested alternatives such as the promontory of Carlingnose, can realistically compete with Stirling in terms of sheer physical dominance of the area. In Irish tradition the Firth of Forth was called *Miur nGiudan*, 'the Sea of Giudi', a name incorporating the English orthographic form *Gi-* and possibly derived from Bede's reference. This 'sea' surely received its Irish name from the most prominent feature in the shorelands at the head of the estuary.

The Scots

Until recently it was commonly believed that a group of migrants from Antrim in northern Ireland established a colony on the coastlands of Argyll at the beginning of the sixth century. This image of Irish migration to Britain has long been accepted as the traditional origin-tale of the Scots. It seemed to explain why the Early Historic inhabitants of Argyll spoke Gaelic, the language of Ireland, at a time when their neighbours – the Picts and Britons – spoke languages of the Brittonic group. The migration theory has a long and distinguished pedigree, its earliest mention appearing in Bede's *Ecclesiastical History*:

> In course of time Britain received a third tribe in addition to the Britons and the Picts, namely the Scots. These came from Ireland under their leader Reuda and won lands among the Picts either by friendly treaty or by the sword. These they still possess. They are still called Dalreudini after this leader, *dal* in their language signifying a part.[39]

A similar tale appeared among the Scots themselves in the early tenth century. This took the form of a foundation-legend tracing the ancestry of three principal dynasties back to Fergus Mór, 'the Great', who came from an Irish kingdom called Dál Riada sometime around AD 500. Because *Dál Riada* (or *Dalriada*) was the name applied to the land of the Scots in Britain it seemed logical to deduce that the 'colony' took its name from an original homeland across the Irish Sea. The combined testimony of the Scottish and Bedan versions of the legend has persuaded generations of historians that the origins of the Scots lie in Ireland rather than in Britain. Other literary evidence has often been used to support the migration hypothesis. The Irish annals, for instance, refer to campaigns fought in Antrim by Argyll kings of the sixth and seventh centuries. Through the lens of a traditional, migration-centred view of Scottish origins these campaigns look like wars waged by the rulers of Argyll in defence of ancestral domains in northern Ireland. It was only when archaeologists began to look for physical evidence of migration and colonisation that the traditional theory was called into question, for the evidence is simply not present. If the early Scots had arrived from Ireland in large numbers, we would expect them to have lived in houses of similar type to the ones they left behind. Houses of recognisably Irish type are not, however, a major feature in the archaeology of Argyll, nor do the place-names of the area suggest that a mass of Gaelic-speaking immigrants supplanted an indigenous population of Brittonic speakers. Remnants of a displaced or obsolete language should be visible among place-names devised by a dominant incoming group, but this is not what we find in Argyll. The expected traces of Brittonic place-name elements are not there at all. Gaelic names are in fact so prevalent that they appear to be an indigenous feature of the landscape. This should make us wonder if Scottish Dál Riada was founded by an Irish immigrant group rather than by a people who had always lived there.

The Romans called the inhabitants of the Argyll coastlands *Epidii* and noted this name on their maps. They gave the name *Epidium Promontorium*, 'Cape of the Epidii', to the Mull of Kintyre and regarded the entire peninsula as Epidian territory. Isolated in the far north-western seaways, Argyll lay far beyond the frontier of Roman Britain and had little formal contact with the Empire. Like much of the unconquered North it was a region peopled by barbarians who posed an ever-present threat to imperial interests. Thus, any information about the Epidii probably reached Roman ears not through direct contact with the inhabitants of Argyll but via the less-hostile Britons of the Clyde who lay between. The name *Epidii* is of British origin and was formerly seen as evidence that the indigenous population of Argyll were themselves Brittonic-speakers whom Fergus Mór and his Gaelic-speaking Scots displaced. An alternative proposition is that it represents a Brittonic translation of an original Gaelic name like *Echidi*, both names conveying the same meaning: 'Horse Folk'.[40] By this reasoning *Epidii* would be the name used by the Romans and their British informants on the Clyde, while the people of Argyll called themselves *Echidi*, a name coined in their own Gaelic tongue. *Epidii* can therefore be disregarded as linguistic evidence for Argyll being a Brittonic-speaking area in Roman times. This leaves us with the likelihood that Gaelic had been the main language long before the alleged arrival of Fergus Mór in c.500.

An issue connected to the migration theory is the question of how many immigrants would have arrived from Ireland. One scenario imagines an elite migration of kings and aristocrats rather than a large influx of ordinary folk. There is certainly no archaeological evidence for a mass-migration of peasants, but nor are there any hints that a small group of Irish nobles imposed themselves on a native British population.[41] If this had happened, we might expect objects such as decorated brooches, the ubiquitous emblems of wealth and status among barbarian peoples living outside the Roman Empire, to be of similar type in Ireland and Argyll. Instead, we find that the brooches worn by the early Scots were of British rather than Irish design.

What, then, are the implications of all of this for the traditional foundation-legend? Bede's reputation as a scholar is so high that historians are reluctant to dismiss his testimony outright. Moreover, as the earliest known proponent of the migration theory, he clearly cannot be ignored. The problem with Bede's account of Scottish origins is that it is not early enough: it has no precursors in Ireland or Britain, nor does it appear in contemporary Irish texts of the eighth century. The obvious inference is that Bede gleaned his information from a legend recently devised by the Scots themselves, a fictional tale of Irish ancestry which subsequently evolved into the story of Fergus Mór. Artificial foundation-myths of this sort were common in early medieval Europe and usually began as political propaganda created to provide dramatic or grandiose origins for a dominant royal dynasty. They cannot be taken literally or at face value.

The alternative hypothesis to the migration theory imagines a process of cultural change rather than of political or demographic upheaval. Far from being a fifth- or sixth-century phenomenon, the Gaelicisation of Argyll may have begun much earlier, perhaps even before the Romans came to Britain. It is not difficult to think of social and economic links being forged across the narrow straits between Antrim and Kintyre, nor is it hard to see how Gaelic could have been adopted as a *lingua franca* for trade and social interaction. Argyll's archaeology suggests that, although the native people abandoned Brittonic in favour of Gaelic, their material culture – as expressed by the designs of their jewellery and houses – remained an important part of their ancient identity and did not fall prey to Irish influence. Who, then, were these 'Scots'? The ethnic term *Scotti*, formerly applied by Roman writers to groups of seafaring marauders in the Irish seaways, may have originated as a collective term for all speakers of Gaelic regardless of whether they came from Ireland or Argyll. This was certainly its usage in later times: people of Irish origin were still being referred to as *Scotti* as late as the twelfth century.

EARLY CHRISTIANITY

Memorial Stones

The northern part of Roman Britain supported Christian communities as early as the beginning of the fourth century. In 314, soon after Constantine the Great became Rome's first Christian emperor, a bishop was in residence at York, the city where the northern frontier army had its headquarters.[1] Evidence of early Christianity is more plentiful from the towns and *civitates* of southern Britain where Romanisation and Continental influences had taken a stronger hold, but the presence of a bishop at York shows that the North was not entirely pagan at this time. Christian objects of fourth-century date have been found west of the Pennines in the vicinity of Carlisle, where a large *vicus* associated with a military settlement had grown into a sizable town, and also at Maryport on the shore of the Irish Sea. As yet there is no archaeological evidence for Christianity beyond the imperial frontier at this time. While the absence of evidence is not conclusive, we may infer that the Britons living north of Hadrian's Wall had not embraced the new religion in sufficient numbers to warrant the appointment of a bishop.

In the fourth century, then, the people living between the Hadrianic and Antonine walls mostly still worshipped their own gods. Christianity first appears in the archaeological record of this area around the time of the collapse of Roman Britain in the early fifth century. Our attention is drawn to Whithorn in Galloway, on the northern side of the Solway Firth, where a memorial stone commemorates a man called Latinus and his unnamed daughter. At the top of the stone is a *chi-rho* symbol, formed from the first two Greek letters of Christ's name, with a Latin inscription below. The inscription begins with a characteristically Christian phrase *Te laudamus Dominum*, 'we praise you, Lord', and continues by giving the ages of the deceased. It refers to Latinus as *nepus Barrovadi*, 'grandson (or descendant) of Barrovadus', and is therefore not merely a tombstone but a statement of kinship.[2] It was erected in the fifth century as a grave-marker, its original setting being either a religious site such as a cemetery or, no less plausibly, a secular residence associated with the family of Barrovadus. As the oldest known Christian object from Scotland it has a special status among historians, but its relationship to other archaeological features at Whithorn is uncertain, not least because we do not know where it originally stood. Nonetheless, some important observations can be made with regard to this stone. It shares similarities with a number of other monuments found in various parts of Britain, all of which are Christian and of fifth-century date. One aspect shared in common by these stones is their imitation of Roman inscriptional styles, a feature suggesting that the wealthy folk who commissioned them were keen to display a 'Roman' aspiration and thus a claim to high status. Despite the outwardly sacred nature of such memorials, they served an additional purpose as statements of power by prominent local families. If this was true of the Latinus stone, its commemorative inscription had some special significance in the locality, perhaps in relation to a claim of ownership over lands formerly held by an ancestor.

Somewhat later than the Latinus stone, but from the same part of Britain, are three sixth-century memorials from Kirkmadrine in the Rhinns of Galloway. The oldest of these commemorates Viventius and Mavorius, two *sacerdotes* or senior clerics, and has a prominent *chi-rho* carved in the upper portion. It belongs to the first half of the sixth century and is the finest of the Kirkmadrine monuments in terms of the quality and legibility of its inscription. Viventius and Mavorius were *sancti et praecipui sacerdotes*, 'holy and chief priests', a description indicating that they were men of high ecclesiastical rank renowned for their piety. The stone was clearly commissioned by a prosperous, well-organised religious community whose leaders in the sixth century wished to honour two notable predecessors, perhaps the founders of the settlement. Slightly later, in the second half of the century, another stone was carved to commemorate a man called Florentius who was presumably another high-ranking cleric. His monument bears a *chi-rho* identical in design to the one on the *sacerdotes* stone but scaled down to fit the narrower area available to the carver. Like Latinus at Whithorn, Florentius bore a name strongly reminiscent of the Roman past and perhaps reflecting his family's aspirations. This does not mean that he and Latinus were not Britons, nor does it necessarily suggest that they came to Galloway from a more Romanised region further afield. The likelihood of parental aspirations to *Romanitas* should not blind us to the probability that both men, together with Viventius and Mavorius, came from the area where they lived and died. It was once believed that the inscriptions honouring these four individuals showed influence from Gaul, especially with regard to the style of lettering, but this has recently been challenged.[3] There are good reasons now to think of the scripts and motifs on the Galloway stones as native to the British Isles, in the sense that they belong to stylistic traditions developed in British and Irish contexts rather than imported from Continental Europe. Communication with Gaulish Christianity was certainly maintained by the Insular clergy and sculptural techniques were undoubtedly exchanged. However, as these contacts were probably frequent and unremarkable we need not attribute to them the founding of Kirkmadrine or of any other religious settlement around the western seaways. The establishment of an early church or monastery in the Rhinns of Galloway was more plausibly undertaken by native Britons under the patronage of a local lord.

Turning to the third Kirkmadrine stone we find that it was once thought to be of seventh-century date, but is now regarded as being not much later than the other two. Unlike them, it refers to no specific individual, but instead carries the words *Initium et Finis*, 'the Beginning and the End', a uniquely Christian phrase echoed by the Greek letters alpha and omega inscribed above the *chi-rho* on the *sacerdotes* memorial. It shares with the other stones a *chi-rho* of identical design and a distinctive style of lettering. All three stones formerly stood outside the present-day church at Kirkmadrine but are now in the care of Historic Scotland and reside behind protective glass in an alcove at one end of the building. The church itself, sited on a small natural mound in low-lying farmland, succeeded a medieval building which in turn replaced an older structure as yet unidentified. That this earlier feature was a monastery is strongly suggested by the commemoration of an ecclesiastical hierarchy, the patronage of skilled stonemasons and the curvilinear shape of the churchyard. The place-name itself has the Norse prefix *kirk-*, 'church', but the second element is more obscure and could represent either a personal name such as *Mathurinus* or a compound of Gaelic *mo*, 'my', with a personal name *Drine*. Many old religious settlements in Ireland and Scotland incorporated the element *mo* in their names, as a prefix to the name of a holy figure who was usually the patron saint or founder. In such instances 'my' has the affectionate, devotional sense of 'dear' or 'beloved'. If Kirkmadrine is not simply the church or monastery of an otherwise unknown Saint Mathurinus, its name might mean 'Church of (my dear) Saint Drine'. The latter name seems to occur without any prefix at Kirkdrine near the southern tip of the Rhinns peninsula, barely 10 miles from Kirkmadrine, and the two places are perhaps connected in some way. Who 'Drine' was, and where he (or she) originally came from are matters of speculation. One obscure Irish tradition mentions a Saint Draighne, pronounced *Droyn*, a male Briton of royal blood whose name seems to be echoed in *Kirkmadroyn*, an older form of modern *Kirkmadrine*.[4] Although we cannot draw any useful insights from this, we may pause to wonder if Drine or Droyn bore the same name as Dreon ap Nudd, a sixth-century North British warrior whose context is discussed in Chapter 5.

Christianity established a firm presence on the northern shore of the Solway Firth in the fifth and sixth centuries, but this was not its only early foothold beyond the old imperial frontier. Away to the north and east, on the southern side of the Forth estuary, stands the Cat Stane. This famous monolith on the boundary of Kirkliston parish marks the grave of Vetta, the son or daughter of

Victricius. The inscription is contemporary with that on the Latinus memorial at Whithorn, but the monument upon which it is carved has the character of a prehistoric standing-stone. It rises from an early Christian cemetery close to an ancient highway which crosses the River Almond at a nearby ford. Just as the kin-group to which Latinus belonged gave Roman names to their children so the family of Victricius displayed similar aspirations, both names on the Cat Stane being of Latin origin. If Victricius commissioned the inscription, he must have been a person of wealth and status, most likely a member of the local aristocracy. While apparently keen to display his Christian credentials, he chose to bury his child in a place where the tombstone would be a prominent feature. Vetta's grave may have served some specific landholding purpose on the margin of a family estate whose western limit was the river. The opening words of the inscription are *in hoc tumulo iacet*..., 'in this mound lies...', which to fifth-century travellers may have conveyed a message of ownership as clear as a modern sign saying 'This land belongs to the family of...'

Also from the intervallate region comes a stone found in the uplands north of the Hadrianic frontier bearing a Latin inscription and Christian stylistic features. It commemorates Carantius, son of Cupitianus, and was erected in the sixth century in what seems a remote and isolated setting. The stone was sited near Brox in Liddesdale, the long valley of the Liddel Water running south-west from the hills above Upper Tweeddale to meet the River Esk near Carlisle. Cupitianus and his son belonged to a local Christian elite, a powerful and wealthy aristocracy, some of whose members clearly chose to erect tombstones of their kin in prominent positions in the landscape. Both Cupitianus and Victricius wanted people to know that Carantius and Vetta were honoured and not forgotten. The two monuments perhaps served an additional purpose as statements of social class. What better way for a nobleman to display his status than to erect a 'Roman' monument carved in the style and language of the imperial past and espousing the religion of the emperors? From the same region as the Carantius stone comes the gravestone of Coninia, formerly located at a cairn near the ruins of St Gordian's Chapel.[5] This carries no inscription other than the name, but its Latin script indicates that the deceased was a Christian. Other Christian memorials were undoubtedly set up across the territories of the North Britons, but most, we can assume, were lost or destroyed in the ensuing centuries. A few may yet await rediscovery beneath farmland or as building-material in later structures, but the majority will never be found or have not survived.

The stones described here were commissioned by Christians who presumably attended Mass at places of worship presided over by Christian priests. At Kirmadrine the association between monuments, church and clergy is explicit, but the picture is less clear elsewhere. The church which ministered to the family of Cupitianus, for instance, has not yet been identified in the vicinity of his son's memorial. At Kirkliston on the Firth of Forth the Cat Stane dominates what appears to be a sixth-century cemetery of local Christians, but the community's place of worship remains unknown. Coninia's grave lay near an ancient chapel, now ruined, but little is known of its history. Its dedication to Saint Gordian, a fourth-century martyr, is unique in northern Britain and may have had special meaning for the community to which Coninia belonged.[6] All of the people commemorated on these stones must have had access to the rites of their faith through the medium of a professional clerical class, who in turn would have built churches where those rites could be performed and where the patronage of local elites could be received. If we knew where these churches lay, we might gain a greater insight into the evolution of North British Christianity than we currently possess. A distribution map of early ecclesiastical sites could then illustrate, for example, how they relate to known centres of secular power. It might also reveal the major concentrations of organised Christianity, perhaps even allowing us to identify the places where the new religion made its first significant inroads among the North Britons. No such map can be created from the meagre amount of data currently available, forcing us therefore to rely on a combination of guesswork and inference to form a picture of Christian beginnings in the region south of the Forth–Clyde isthmus. Our guesses must also take account of one very old tradition which places the enigmatic figure of Saint Ninian at the heart of the picture.

Ninian and Whithorn

In the early eighth century, much of what is now southern Scotland formed part of the English kingdom of Northumbria. Monasteries populated by English monks thrived all over this area, while English bishops held spiritual sway in districts formerly ministered to by a native British clergy. It was at this time that Bede, by then an elderly monk at Jarrow in the Northumbrian heartlands further east, wrote his *Ecclesiastical History*. In the book he asserted that the northern Picts, those living beyond the Grampian Mountains, had been introduced to Christianity by the Irish saint Columba who arrived in Britain in 563. Bede believed that the southern Picts, those of Fife and Perthshire, had long before received the Faith from Bishop Nynia, a Briton whose training for the priesthood had allegedly taken place at Rome. According to Bede, the diocese over which Nynia was bishop lay not in Pictish lands but at Whithorn in Galloway where a church dedicated to Saint Martin had been built of stone. Bede added that Whithorn was known by an alternative name *Candida Casa*, 'The White House', and that it was constructed 'using a method unusual among the Britons'.[7] Nothing more is said of Nynia in the pages of the *Ecclesiastical History*, although Whithorn is mentioned again in Bede's summary of the state of the English Church in the year 731. At that time the episcopal see was headed by Pehthelm, a Northumbrian whom Bede regarded as the first bishop.

Until fairly recently Bede's information about Nynia was accepted by historians as accurate and factual. It seemed to fit rather well with the evidence for early Christian activity at Whithorn as revealed, for example, by the Latinus stone. The dedication to Saint Martin also fitted neatly into the chronological picture of an early mission to the Picts pre-dating the Columban mission, Martin having been a major ecclesiastical figure in fourth-century Gaul. Historians suggested that a Martin dedication pointed to a church foundation of the early fifth century, within a generation or two of his death in 397, rather than of the sixth. Columba's preaching among the Picts is not precisely dated, but it occurred between his foundation of Iona in 565 and his death in 597. For Nynia's mission to have occurred, in Bede's words, *multo ante tempore*, 'a long time before', the Columban venture it could feasibly have happened at any time up to the middle of the sixth century. The traditional view, in which Nynia's activities belong to the fifth century, has been heavily influenced by Bede's mention of Saint Martin and by information presented by two other writers. Of the latter, the first was an anonymous Northumbrian monk at Whithorn who wrote a poem entitled *Miracula Nynie Episcopi*, 'Miracles of Bishop Nynia', in the eighth century. This fleshed out Bede's brief summary by adding extra details such as identifying the Picts converted by Nynia as an otherwise unknown group called *Naturae*, and naming a British king of the Whithorn area as Tudwal. The second additional source is the *Vita Niniani*, 'Life of Ninian', a formulaic work of hagiography attributed to Ailred of Rievaulx in the twelfth century. This gave Nynia's name as Ninian, the form most readily recognisable today, and pushed his chronological context back into the fourth century by making him a contemporary and acquaintance of Saint Martin. Like the author of the *Miracula*, Ailred used material produced by the Northumbrian brethren at Whithorn and gave several details not offered by Bede. Ailred claimed to have drawn most of his information from an earlier Life, presumably a Northumbrian work of the eighth century, which unfortunately has not survived.

The traditional view of Nynia or Ninian as a fifth-century figure who preached to the Picts 'a long time before' the Columban mission of 565–97 held sway until quite recently, its main points largely unchallenged by excavations at Whithorn in the 1950s. In the past 20 years an intensive programme of excavation has allowed a rather different view of the data to emerge. The archaeological evidence now indicates that the earliest religious settlement was established around the year 500 and may have had little or no fifth-century existence.[8] If the archaeological background for a fifth-century bishopric at Whithorn is lacking, then so is the evidence for Nynia being its first incumbent. The Life attributed to Ailred, the only text in which Nynia appears as a contemporary of Martin, is a purely hagiographical work designed as a promotional tool for the cult of 'Ninian' established at Whithorn in the Norman period. Neither Bede nor the author of the *Miracula* place Nynia's chronological context at such an early date or with such precision, nor do they necessarily imply that he lived before the sixth century. All three sources are nevertheless consistent in presenting Nynia as a missionary to the heathen Picts, with the *Miracula* naming the target community as *Naturae*. No group or place-name corresponding to this ethnonym is identifiable today, despite an ingenious modern attempt to equate it with a district of Fife.[9] The alleged Pictish connection in fact arouses suspicion, especially when viewed alongside the ecclesiastical milieu of eighth-century Northumbria to which both Bede and the author of the *Miracula* belonged. At that time, the Northumbrian clergy was exerting a strong influence on the Picts and had recently helped the Pictish churches to become independent of their mother-church on Iona. Bede's mention of Nynia immediately follows a reference to Columba and might reflect deliberate efforts by Northumbrian Whithorn to downplay Iona's role in the conversion of the Picts. By claiming that a Whithorn cleric – albeit a Briton rather than an Englishman – had preached among the Picts long before Columba's mission Bede may have been disseminating anti-Ionan propaganda current in his own time.[10] The factual core of Nynia's story was presumably compiled by Christian Britons at Whithorn before their church fell prey to the Northumbrian conquest of Galloway in the late seventh century. After c.700 this story's basic elements were embellished by English clerics and presented as ecclesiastical propaganda to diminish Columba's role in Christianising the Picts. The fictional adornments – Nynia's clerical training in Rome and his mission to the Picts – formed part of the Life of Nynia used as a source by Ailred of Rievaulx in the twelfth century. They fitted with the literary needs of the medieval cult-centre at Whithorn. The dedication of the church to Saint Martin may likewise have been a Northumbrian innovation. There remains, however, the fundamental question: who was Nynia? This cannot be answered satisfactorily and remains a somewhat frustrating puzzle. Few historians doubt that a historical figure lurks beneath the layers of clerical fiction and propaganda. Some accept him as a Briton – a monk or bishop – who had a formal connection with the early Christian community at Whithorn. An attempt has been made to equate him with Saint Uinniau, a priest of British origin who laboured in Ireland in the sixth century. Uinniau is more commonly known as Finnian, an Irish form of his name, or by the later British form *Winnin* and its variants. In northern Britain he is commemorated in many places, especially in the lands between the Firths of Clyde and Solway where early church sites such as Kilwinning and Chapel Finnian preserve his name. A *Vita* of this saint, probably written in the twelfth century, places him at Whithorn as a novice monk in the sixth century, a hundred years before the monastery fell into Northumbrian hands. It has been suggested that a later scribal error, made when this *Vita* was being copied by an incoming English cleric, amended the initial U of Uinniau to N, thereby producing an incorrect form *Ninniau* which in turn produced Bede's Nynia and Ailred's Ninian.[11] Although this hypothesis is ingenious, it relies on the unlikely scenario that the conquered Britons around eighth-century Whithorn were unaware that their Northumbrian conquerors had made a fundamental error regarding the name of a famous local cleric. Even the most casual conversation on religious topics between an English priest and a British peasant would surely have corrected the mistake. Perhaps no such correction would have occurred if usage of the incorrect *Nin-* forms of the name had been confined to the literary exchanges of a narrow circle of Northumbrian churchmen but it is hard to imagine nobody among this group discovering the error or, having discovered it, keeping such knowledge to himself. An alternative scenario is that Nynia-Ninian and Uinniau-Finnian were two distinct individuals, both of them Britons, who were separately associated with Whithorn in the sixth century. If Bede is to be believed, the former pre-dated Columba by some years and was most probably active in the period before c.550. He was presumably buried at Whithorn where his tomb subsequently became a focus for Christian Britons and the nucleus of their cemetery. A century later, after the English conquest of Galloway, the Northumbrian clergy took control of the Whithorn monastery and tried to promote Nynia-Ninian as a precursor of Columba in converting the Picts. The attempt produced some literary propaganda but ultimately failed to establish a viable cult. Later still, when the Whithorn bishopric was revived by Scottish kings in the twelfth century, a second attempt to promote a cult was more successful and Whithorn became a centre of pilgrimage. In Irish tradition Uinniau or Finnian died in 579, in Ireland, and may have belonged to the generation after Nynia. He presumably trained at Whithorn at a time when the monastery was attracting students from both sides of the Irish Sea. There is even a hint that the two men may have met: in the *Vita* of Finnian the saint's mentor at Whithorn is a senior cleric called 'Nennius'. Could this be Nynia?

Kentigern

Forty miles east of Whithorn another Early Christian settlement arose at Hoddom on the north bank of the River Annan. Excavations in the 1990s revealed traces of a large monastic complex which reached its zenith in the late eighth and early ninth centuries.[12] Its personnel at that time were Northumbrian Englishmen, but they were using a site established much earlier by native British clergy. Later medieval tradition attributed the founding of Hoddom to Kentigern, the patron saint of Glasgow, whose ecclesiastical career seems to lie around the end of the sixth century and the beginning of the seventh. According to Welsh tradition of the ninth or tenth centuries, Kentigern died in 612, or perhaps more correctly in 614.[13] This date is consistent with the chronological context assigned to him in two *Vitae* written in the twelfth century, both of which make him a contemporary of individuals who are known to have lived around c.600. The *Vitae* were produced in support of a medieval cult centred on Glasgow Cathedral, itself the hub of a newly established diocese whose first bishop was appointed by the Scottish king David I in 1114.[14] The earlier *Vita* was commissioned by Herbert, bishop of Glasgow from 1147 to 1164, but its author is unknown and only its first few chapters have survived. Historians generally refer to it as the Herbertian Life. Slightly later, and commissioned during the episcopate of Jocelin between 1175 and 1185, is a much more complete work written by the bishop's namesake Jocelin, a monk at Furness Abbey. We may assume that Jocelin of Furness had access to sources used by the anonymous author of the Herbertian Life, but he used the information in a different way and omitted various details, especially the names of persons and places. An examination of the two texts allows us to compile a basic summary of Kentigern's career as understood by the bishops and brethren of Glasgow Cathedral in the twelfth century. The story begins with the saint's parentage, his mother being identified as Teneu (or Thaney) the daughter of 'King Leodonus' of Lothian. Kentigern's conception is due to Teneu's rape by Owain, son of Urien, who assaults her whilst disguised as a woman. All of the characters mentioned thus far are Britons, and all are of royal blood, although only Owain and his father Urien are attested by other sources as genuine historical figures. Leodonus looks like a fictional eponym for Lothian, while Teneu seems to have no independent existence beyond the traditions relating to her son.[15] The story continues with a brutal punishment meted out to the pregnant princess by her father: she is thrown from a hill but survives the fall before being cast out alone on the North Sea in a small boat. After another miraculous survival she comes ashore at Culross on the southern coast of Fife and there gives birth to Kentigern. Mother and child are then rescued by Saint Serf or Servanus, abbot of the Culross monastery, who adopts Kentigern as his disciple and pupil. Kentigern eventually leaves Culross, travelling south-west to a place called *Kernach* where he meets Fergus, an old man on the brink of death, whom he buries at *Cathures* in a cemetery consecrated by Saint Ninian. Curiously, and for reasons unstated, Fergus is the first person to be interred there, the cemetery not having been used until that time. Kentigern, with the assistance of two disciples, decides to settle in the vicinity as a hermit before his appointment by King Rhydderch as first bishop of Glasgow. Rhydderch Hael, like Owain ab Urien, is attested independently outside the Kentigern traditions. He ruled from Alt Clut, the Rock of Clyde at Dumbarton, and was active as a northern warlord in the late sixth century. In the North British pedigrees and in Adomnán's *Vita Columbae* his father is named as Tudwal. A king of this name appears in the literature surrounding Nynia of Whithorn and might be the same man, unless the two Tudwals are merely namesakes and contemporaries. On Kentigern himself there is no reason to question the basic picture which sees him as a royal bishop on the Clyde, either at Glasgow or – perhaps more plausibly – at a site further downstream nearer to Rhydderch's citadel of Alt Clut. It is in the context of Rhydderch's reign that Jocelin of Furness associates Kentigern with Hoddom, a place whose location far from Clydesdale presented no geographical problems to the hagiographer. Hoddom certainly existed as a religious site before the Northumbrian takeover, as the recent excavations have shown, but its alleged status as an ecclesiastical centre for the sixth-century kings of Alt Clut is doubtful. Kentigern may have visited the place while serving as bishop of the Clyde but, if so, he might not have held any formal authority there. Jocelin depicts Rhydderch's authority reaching as far south as Annandale, a not unfeasible scenario in an era of ambitious warlords, and a wide hegemony is not inconsistent with other traditions about this king. However, the inclusion of Hoddom within Kentigern's alleged orbit might have a wholly different origin, perhaps in fiction devised by later ecclesiastical propaganda. Twelfth-century Scottish interests may have gained from the forging of a retrospective link between Glasgow's patron saint and the former Northumbrian monastery at Hoddom. Alternatively, the link could have been made in the tenth century, by Britons of the Clyde, at a time when their kingdom was extending its political sway to the Solway. On current evidence there is nothing to connect the 'real' Kentigern with Hoddom, but nor is there unequivocal evidence to rule out the possibility that he spent part of his career there. Some other elements in his story, such as an alleged sojourn in Wales and a meeting with Columba, are almost certainly fictitious and can be traced to common hagiographical motifs found in the *vitae* of several saints. To these literary inventions we may add the episodes featuring Teneu, Leodonus, Owain and Servanus. When the fiction is stripped away, we seem to be left with a historical figure, a British priest called Kentigern who became a bishop on the Clyde during Rhydderch's kingship and who died, presumably at Glasgow, in the early seventh century.

Other Saints and Centres of North British Christianity

Archaeological and literary evidence suggests that Whithorn, Kirkmadrine, Hoddom and possibly Glasgow were important early Christian centres among the North Britons. Three of these were associated in later tradition with the saints

Nynia and Kentigern, while the fourth, Kirkmadrine, was clearly a site of high ecclesiastical status. This is not to say that these places were necessarily regarded in the sixth century as the four most important Christian sites north of Hadrian's Wall. Rather they seem especially significant to modern eyes because of the quality of their archaeological remains, their contribution to our knowledge of Scotland's Christian beginnings or their links to famous saints. Other sites in the region whose profile is not so high today might have had equal prominence with these four in the eyes of early Christian communities. The literary sources refer to a number of monasteries housing English clergy during the seventh, eighth and ninth centuries when a large part of the area south of the Forth–Clyde isthmus lay under Northumbrian rule. Some, if not all, of these may have originated as British foundations whose personnel fled the English advance. Hoddom and Whithorn provide models for this kind of continuity, even if archaeology does not reveal the violence which must have preceded the change of ownership. At both Hoddom and Whithorn we should probably imagine British clergy departing in fear of Northumbrian armies, seeking refuge in lands further west and abandoning their churches to English monks who arrived in the wake of the warriors. If the same model is extended to the seventh-century Northumbrian monasteries at Melrose and Abercorn, we might surmise that these also were native foundations. In Bede's time both sites bore names of Brittonic origin – respectively *Mailros* and *Aebbercurnig* – and both were located in districts formerly under native rule. On the other hand, not all Northumbrian monasteries succeeded British ones, even if Britons dwelt nearby. At Coldingham on the North Sea coast, for example, a religious community headed by the English abbess Aebbe dwelt on the site of a fortress which had once been the home of a British aristocrat.

At the other end of the scale we find sites where a single fragment of sculpture or a distinctive place-name raise the possibility that a British church or monastery once flourished nearby. A medieval Scottish chronicler reported the discovery at Peebles in 1261 of a finely carved cross, beneath which lay a stone allegedly bearing the inscription *locus sancti Nicholae episcopi*, 'the place of the holy bishop Nicholas'. This stone is now lost, but whoever commissioned it clearly intended *locus* to be interpreted in the ecclesiastical sense of 'sacred place' or 'consecrated ground'.[16] Chronological reasons make it likely that the late form 'Nicholas' is a misreading of some other, less intelligible name, but the rest of the inscription suggests a British Christian milieu. The person commemorated may have been a senior cleric at a monastery in the Peebles area holding a position of spiritual authority like the *sacerdotes* at Kirkmadrine. Unfortunately, the disappearance of this mysterious monument means that it exists solely as an artifact of literature rather than as something tangible that can be studied by art historians and archaeologists. Unlike the Kirkmadrine stones it tells us little about early North British Christianity and merely suggests Peebles as an area for future research.

Another type of signpost is found in place-names which have the ability to highlight sites where archaeological investigation may yet reveal evidence of early Christian activity. The place-name elements *eccles* and *eagles*, for instance, sometimes derive from Latin *ecclesia*, 'church', via a Brittonic form that subsequently evolved into modern Welsh *eglwys*.[17] In southern Scotland an example is *Ecclefechan* in Dumfriesshire, a place-name meaning 'little church' or, less probably, 'Saint Fechan's church'. If the first meaning is preferred, it might hint at Ecclefechan's status in relation to a more important centre of which it was a dependent foundation. The pre-Northumbrian monastery at nearby Hoddom is an obvious candidate as a mother-church and may have been the original *ecclesia* of the district before the creation of a satellite at Ecclefechan. A religious foundation of similarly grand stature seems to underlie the place-name Paisley, earlier Passelek, which derives from Latin *basilica* via an intermediate Brittonic form. The name indicates that a foundation of considerable importance, perhaps containing the relics of a famous saint, once stood on the site now occupied by the great medieval abbey.[18] Tradition associates Paisley with Mirin or Mirren, supposedly a disciple of the sixth-century Irish saint Comgall of Bangor.

Dedications to North British saints, or to Irish saints labouring as missionaries among the North Britons, are found in many places. In some cases Hiberno-Norse *kirk-* or Gaelic *kil-* when prefixed to a personal name suggest the existence of an early Christian church. Kirkmadrine is a prime example of a dedication supported by firm evidence of sixth-century activity by Britons. Other names of this type commemorate major figures of Gaelic tradition such as Brigid, Patrick or Columba and generally indicate a late dedication or re-dedication by Gaelic-speaking immigrants. In former British lands around the Clyde estuary we find the place-names *Kirkbride*, *Kilpatrick* and *Kilmacolm*, none of which bear dedications pre-dating the ninth century. In the same area we also find the name *Inchinnan*, a site with tenth-century sculpture of British origin and a name perhaps deriving from an early dedication to Finnian or Uinniau. Inchinnan is also the traditional burial-place of Saint Conval, an obscure figure associated with Kentigern of Glasgow.[19] Traditions preserved in the *Aberdeen Breviary* identify Conval as an Irishman who became Kentigern's disciple. However, although Conval is arguably a genuine historical figure, his alleged link with Kentigern should be viewed within the context of attempts by the twelfth-century bishops of Glasgow to subordinate the church at Inchinnan to their authority. Kentigern himself has numerous dedications all over northern Britain, but few, if any, can be assigned to a period before the vigorous promotion of his cult by the monks of Glasgow Cathedral in the twelfth century. Another of Kentigern's alleged disciples was Constantine, to

whom the old parish church of Govan was dedicated. A Christian cemetery at
this church was in use in the sixth century, but whether Constantine himself was
associated with the site at such an early date is uncertain. His identity is likewise unknown.[20] If he is not an obscure Cornish namesake allegedly martyred in
Kintyre, he might have been a North Briton, perhaps even a native of the Clyde.
His association with Kentigern, like Conval's, is almost certainly a fiction devised
much later at Glasgow. Finally, the monastery supposedly founded by Saint Blaan
or Blane at Kingarth on the Isle of Bute should be mentioned. This was either
an Irish foundation or, less probably, a British one taken over at an early date by
a Gaelic-speaking clergy. Its location on a large island in the Firth of Clyde has
prompted a suggestion that it may have provided an important link between the
kings of Alt Clut and their peers in neighbouring Cowal.[21] The Cowal kings were
Gaelic-speaking Scots, but it is possible that they developed a political friendship
with the Clyde Britons in the sixth and seventh centuries. In such circumstances
the brethren at Kingarth might indeed have played a key mediating role.

FOUR KINGS

Bernicia

Bernicia was the name given by Bede and later writers to the most northerly of the Anglo-Saxon kingdoms. The precise origins of the kingdom are unclear, but it grew out of the native realm of *Berneich* during the sixth century and was recognisably 'English' by c.550. The Bernician elite claimed descent from Anglo-Saxon immigrants who had arrived in the previous century. That these incomers were Germanic mercenaries hired to defend the British rulers of Berneich from Pictish raiders seems a likely scenario in the light of later English and Welsh traditions. The mercenaries either seized control of the kingdom by force or were invited to do so by native factions opposed to an indigenous regime. The coming of Christianity and the possibility of resistance by pagan Britons in Berneich may have created conditions which facilitated the Anglo-Saxon takeover.[1] Adherents of British and Anglo-Saxon paganism perhaps found common cause with each other in the face of the new religion.

Although the bulk of Bernicia's population were Britons, it became clear as the sixth century progressed that the adoption of an Anglo-Saxon identity was the key to social advancement. It is even possible that a sense of 'Britishness' might no longer have seemed desirable and that it was discarded by certain elements among the native elite. A similar process may have occurred in other parts of Britain during the social and economic upheavals of the fifth-century when the earliest Anglo-Saxon kingdoms were forming.[2] In such circumstances the English language would have rapidly displaced Brittonic as the medium of aristocratic discourse. By the middle of the sixth century new cultural affiliations and a new ethnic identity were being willingly embraced in Berneich as the British elite became the 'Anglo-Saxons' of Bernicia.

The history of Bernicia's relations with her British neighbours begins with a king called Ida, a shadowy dynastic forefather like Coel Hen or Fergus Mór. Bede says little of Ida beyond noting that his 12-year reign commenced in 547 and that he was the king 'from whom the Northumbrian royal family trace their origin'.[3] It seems likely that Bede calculated the dates of Ida's reign from a king-list and that no other written sources dealing with the origins of Bernician kingship were available to him in the monastic library at Jarrow. In the absence of additional material of English origin we are obliged to turn instead to British traditions of uncertain provenance and dubious accuracy. This inevitably brings us to Wales and to the *Historia Brittonum* whose author had access to various regnal lists and royal genealogies relating to the early English kingdoms. From these he constructed a framework on which small details about the kings of the northern English could be hung. After naming Ida's father as Eobba, the *Historia* gives Ida an impressive progeny of twelve sons, six of whom were born legitimately of a queen called Bearnoch.[4] We are also presented with the following information:

Ida, son of Eobba, held the countries in the north of Britain, that is, north of the Humber Sea, and reigned twelve years, and joined Din Guayroi to Bernicia.[5]

This in turn sets the scene for one of the most famous passages in the *Historia*:

At that time Outigirn fought bravely against the English nation. Then Talhaearn Tad Awen was famed in poetry; and Aneirin and Taliesin and Bluchbard and Cian, known as Gueinth Guaut, were all simultaneously famed in British verse.[6]

Nothing more is said of the mysterious Outigirn, nor is he mentioned in any other source, but the implication of this brief reference is that he and Ida were contemporaries and adversaries. Bede's belief that Ida was the progenitor of later Northumbrian kings has led historians to create a picture of Bernician origins in which Ida appears as the first of the dynasty. This may be taking Bede's statement too far. We cannot, on present evidence, casually dismiss Eobba as a non-royal figure, nor do we have grounds for denying his historical existence. He appears in our source-material as Ida's father and may have held the kingship before him. The statement that Ida 'joined' Din Guayroi to Bernicia is often regarded as making little sense. *Din Guayroi* is a form of the Brittonic name for Bamburgh, the great citadel of Bernicia's English kings, a name supplanted by English *Bebbanburh* in the early seventh century. The place is commonly regarded as Ida's original stronghold and as the power-base from where he seized or otherwise obtained the Bernician kingship. This might prompt us to reverse the statement about Din Guayroi to give a different meaning, namely that Ida joined (or annexed) the British realm of Berneich to his own domain centred on Bamburgh. An alternative interpretation, requiring no meddling with the testimony of the *Historia Brittonum*, envisages Bamburgh not as Ida's original centre of power but as a key target of his ambitions. In 'joining' the great citadel to adjacent lands already under his control he may have ousted its existing incumbents to secure overall authority over Berneich. The ethnic identity of his opponents at Din Guayroi is immaterial – they were either 'British' or 'English' or some mixture of the two – but we might cautiously place Outigirn among them.

To understand how and why a group which identified itself as English took control of what had once been native British territory requires us to consider Ida's ultimate origins. Looking back through his genealogy as presented in the *Historia Brittonum* we find, in the sixth preceding generation, the name *Beornec*. Like the name of Ida's queen Bearnoch, this looks suspiciously like an eponym for Berneich rather than the name of a genuine historical figure. The possible presence of fictional characters in the upper portion of Ida's genealogy casts suspicion on all of his alleged ancestors. None of them, with the possible exception of his father Eobba, can be accepted as real figures of early Bernician history. Their necessary exclusion deprives Ida of a valid ancestry, leaving him rootless and isolated as a king without background or context. This need not trouble us too much, for it is possible that his status as the first king was created retrospectively as part of a revised foundation-legend.[7]

In our ignorance about Ida's origins we are not alone. Neither Bede nor any other literate Englishman of the eighth century possessed more than a vague chronology of early Bernician kingship. It is inconceivable that Bede, himself a member of the Northumbrian elite, knew less about Ida than the author of the *Historia Brittonum*, but neither Eobba nor the eponymous Beornec appear in the *Ecclesiastical History*, nor does Bede mention Ida's connection with Bamburgh. We must assume that he was aware of the same oral or written traditions which eventually found their way into the *Historia Brittonum*, but that he chose to exclude them from his narrative. Perhaps he regarded them as spurious tales of little worth? On the other hand, he may have had no desire to burden his readers with too many reminders of their pagan past.

The true story of Ida is irretrievable, but a more-or-less plausible context for his career can be envisaged. Later Northumbrian tradition identified him as English and we should assume that this was his preferred cultural affiliation. He no doubt claimed descent from real or imagined forefathers in the Anglo-Saxon homelands across the North Sea, but his immediate ancestry lay among the English-speaking elite in Berneich. We may envisage him as belonging to an ambitious family who sought authority over the whole kingdom by neutralising rival factions. Their opponents would have included British royal families together with other elements of the native aristocracy and rival English kindreds. Eventually Ida's group secured a dominant position and subjugated its competitors to become the new ruling dynasty. Overall sovereignty was sealed by the capture of the iconic royal fortress of Din Guayroi, an event which traditionally marks the birth of English Bernicia.

Ida's sons ruled after him as warrior-kings, holding sway over a predominantly British population which comfortably wore the mantle of 'Englishness'.

The foregoing scenario is necessarily speculative and relies largely on connecting a number of possibilities. Alternative theories could be offered, among them the suggestion that English rule in Bernicia originated with a military unit based at Bamburgh. This sees Ida leading a roving group of Germanic warriors who seized Din Guayroi with the intention of using it as a pirate base for raids on neighbouring British territory. In this scenario the rise of English power in Berneich is seen as a swift process unfolding from a single event: the sudden, violent seizure of Bamburgh by a small band of Anglo-Saxon adventurers. It offers a different interpretation of the sources from the one proposed above, but each has its own merits and both eventually meet at the point of takeover when Berneich became an English kingdom.

The Lindisfarne Campaign

If Outigirn, then, was a king of some part of Berneich in the time of Ida's rise to power he may have been the lord of Din Guayroi. Although later tradition recalled that he 'fought bravely against the English nation', he was ousted or slain or otherwise removed. According to the generally accepted chronology, Ida's reign ended in 559 and his son Adda succeeded him. Of Adda and his successor Aethelric – another of Ida's legitimate offspring – nothing is known apart from the lengths of their reigns. A more detailed picture begins to emerge during the reign of their brother Theodoric who attained the kingship in 570 or 571. The *Historia Brittonum* identifies Theodoric as the enemy of a renowned North British king called Urien. The passage in question follows a reference to Hussa who ruled Bernicia from c.585 to c.592, but the context seems to encompass all the sons of Ida:

> Against them fought four kings; Urien, and Rhydderch the Old, and Gwallawg, and Morcant. Theodoric fought vigorously against Urien and his sons. During that time, sometimes the enemy, sometimes the citizens (i.e., Britons) were victorious, and Urien blockaded them for three days and three nights in the island of Lindisfarne. But, while he was campaigning, Urien was murdered at the instigation of Morcant, from jealousy, because his military skill and generalship surpassed that of all the other kings.[8]

The conventional interpretation of this passage is that it describes four British kings joining forces to launch a unified attack on Bernicia.[9] The alliance is often seen in ethnic terms as an anti-English coalition under Urien's overall leadership.

However, the widespread popularity of the conventional view should not blind us to its flaws.[10] At its heart is a twentieth-century perception of sixth-century warfare in which 'Celtic' Britons on one side fought 'Germanic' Bernicians on the other. It shows an unfortunate modern tendency to imagine Urien, Hussa, Theodoric and their contemporaries going to war for reasons of ethnicity. A closer examination of the passage reveals no hint of ethnic conflict, nor indeed any mention of a British military alliance. This becomes apparent as soon as the constituent elements in the passage are identified. Phrases such as 'sometimes the enemy, sometimes the Cymry . . .' and 'three days and three nights' are drawn from a standard repertoire of medieval literary devices and can be disregarded. We are left with four segments, each of which conveys a single item of information: four British kings, including Urien, fought wars against Ida's sons; Theodoric, son of Ida, fought against Urien; in one campaign Urien besieged a Bernician force on the island of Lindisfarne; in the same campaign, or another, Urien was killed at the instigation of a British king who resented his prowess. From this deconstruction it is clear that the main focus of the passage is Urien's military career. The other British kings play no role in the narrative beyond being paraded as less competent than Urien. Rather than reading the passage against an imagined backdrop of coalitions and ethnic warfare a more objective interpretation can be offered. In the period c.559 to c.592 the English of Bernicia fought a number of wars against the Britons. Among their enemies during this period were Urien, Rhydderch, Gwallawg and Morcant. During one of these wars an attack by Urien included a noteworthy event: a siege of Bernician forces on Lindisfarne. Urien was killed at the instigation of Morcant while on a military expedition.

With no additional sources referring to the Lindisfarne campaign, we are left to speculate on its political context. The author of the *Historia Brittonum* used the Latin term *conclusit*, translated above as 'blockaded', to describe Urien's action. Since the term has a broader range of meanings we could alternatively translate it as 'confined', 'enclosed', 'besieged' or even 'imprisoned'. Whatever the meaning intended here, we can probably envisage Urien launching a direct assault against a Bernician stronghold on Lindisfarne. His advance would not have been thwarted by the tidal waters that separate the island from the mainland for at low tide the strait can be crossed on foot. The main action of his campaign might therefore have occurred on the island itself, at a fortified settlement or some other centre of power. The obvious location is the prominent rocky height on which the modern castle now stands, an eminence known as Biblaw or Beblowe.[11] That this was a key target of Urien's aggression seems a strong possibility. By comparing the Bernician reign lengths in the *Historia Brittonum* with Bede's dates for Ida we can date the campaign to the final quarter of the sixth century. Precise dating is impossible because we lack an accurate chronology for Urien. It is often assumed that the siege occurred during Theodoric's reign, but the *Historia* does not actually say this. The most we can deduce is that it occurred within a period defined by the reigns of Ida's sons.

We have seen that there is no justification in imagining Urien as the leader of a coalition of British kingdoms in a joint war against a common English foe. Contrary to a widespread belief, the *Historia Brittonum* does not associate Rhydderch, Gwallawg and Morcant with the Lindisfarne campaign. Military alliances in this period were in any case quite rare, chiefly because kings were individual competitors in a relentless contest for wealth and status. If one king joined forces with another, he generally did so through obligations of clientship to an overlord. Urien was a powerful figure in the northern political arena and various lesser rulers may have been subjected to his authority, their obligations as clients requiring them to answer his summons when he called them to war. If Rhydderch, Gwallawg and Morcant recognised Urien as their overlord at the time of his Bernician campaigns, no surviving source hints that this was the case. In the *Historia Brittonum* their war-leadership was depicted as inferior, but this opinion was not necessarily held by anyone outside the limited circle of Urien's admirers in ninth-century Wales. The passage simply says that Urien and three other kings fought the Bernicians, perhaps in separate campaigns, either in pursuit of their own ambitions or in defence of their kingdoms. Where were these kingdoms located? This question will be addressed in the following sections, each of which examines one of the four British kings mentioned in the passage.

Urien Rheged

The verses attributed to Taliesin are our main source of information on Urien, who appears therein as the poet's royal patron.[12] Taliesin indicates that the heart of Urien's kingdom was *Rheged*, a territory known only from texts preserved in Wales. Rheged makes no appearance in English or Irish sources, nor indeed is it mentioned in the *Historia Brittonum* or the Welsh Annals. Outside the Taliesin poems it appears in the triads and in a group of ninth-century verses attributed to Llywarch Hen, a North British figure whom later Welsh tradition regarded as Urien's cousin. Despite this lack of a broad arc of reference, nearly all historians imagine Rheged as a major Early Historic kingdom extending over a very large area straddling the Solway Firth. It is generally seen as encompassing Galloway, Dumfriesshire, Cumbria and parts of Yorkshire. How has this widespread belief arisen?

Taliesin does not say where Rheged lay. Neither the Welsh triads nor the Llywarch poems offer any clear signposts. We are thus presented with a lost North British kingdom bereft of a specific geographical context. Its name seems to have existed for a brief time before disappearing without trace. Remarkably, such grave uncertainties have not disturbed the consensus that Rheged lay in the Solway area. This is because of a theory that has evolved into something of a 'factoid', a fact-shaped object. It has been repeated so often that its origin as an unproven hypothesis is barely remembered today. At its core stand a few lines of Welsh verse composed not in the sixth century but in the twelfth. These appear in a poem by Hywel ab Owain, a prince of Gwynedd, and translate into English as follows:

> How far from Ceri is Carlisle?
> I mounted my bay from Maelienydd
> to the land of Rheged, by night and day.[13]

The usual interpretation of these lines is that Hywel envisaged Carlisle as being in Rheged. This may indeed have been his perception, but it adds little to our understanding of sixth-century political geography. The verse or *awdl*, 'ode', in which these lines appear is not concerned with northern Britain. Together with other *awdlau* it forms part of Hywel's poetic *gorhoffedd*, 'boasting', and deals with matters close to his heart. Its primary themes are romantic love and patriotic devotion. Hywel's reference to a journey on horseback 'to the land of Rheged' should therefore be regarded as rhetorical.[14] It is unlikely that he ever rode to Carlisle. If he had done so, he would surely not have begun the journey in Maelienydd, in south-east Wales, but in his homeland of Gwynedd further north. Rhetorical and literary considerations likewise explain his mention of Rheged, a place already famous in the lore of twelfth-century Wales. Reverence for Taliesin's poems had made the name of Urien's kingdom a byword for native resistance against the English. Hywel's own father Owain Gwynedd was a namesake of Owain of Rheged, the most famous of Urien's sons, whom Taliesin praised in verse as the slayer of an Anglo-Saxon king. To medieval Welshmen struggling to protect their lands from English aggression Owain ab Urien had the status of an iconic hero and had already become a figure of Arthurian romance. This adulation can be seen in Hywel's choice of words at the closure of the *awdl*, four lines after his mention of Rheged: 'May my God have regard to my death.' Here he echoes *Marwnad Owain*, 'The Death-song of Owain', Taliesin's best-known poem, which has a similar ending: 'The soul of Owain ab Urien, may the Lord have regard to its need.'[15] Owain Gwynedd's own wars against the English, coupled with the heroic heritage of his forename, perhaps explain why his son's poem made reference to Rheged: Hywel may have wanted his audience to imagine contemporary Gwynedd as a twelfth-century manifestation of Urien's kingdom.[16] Beyond such speculation on the literary aspects of the *awdl* nothing more can be gleaned from its rather tenuous connection with North British history. Hywel was as far removed from

Urien's time as we are today from the age of Bruce and Wallace. He lived in Wales and, like most of his countrymen, would have had little need to visit Carlisle. In his poetry he alludes to a period of exile, but, if this is not merely metaphorical, there is no reason to connect it with northern Britain. His only known years of exile were spent in Ireland from where, in 1170, he embarked for a fatal showdown with his half-brothers at a battle on Anglesey. It is inconceivable that Hywel alone among medieval Welsh bards had an accurate perception of the geography of Rheged. The kingdom served a useful literary purpose in epitomising a land of heroes, but neither he nor his contemporaries knew where it lay. His poem, for all its vivid imagery and rhetoric, tells us nothing useful about the sixth century. If it provides what Professor John Koch has recently described as 'our best evidence' for the location of Rheged, then the conventional theory of Urien's geographical setting rests on shaky ground indeed.[17]

Historians locate Rheged around Carlisle and the Solway Firth chiefly on the basis of Hywel's *awdl*. Various additional arguments are employed in support of this view, most of them relying on guesses drawn from the Taliesin poems or from place-names allegedly preserving the name of the kingdom. Most of the arguments proceed from an unspoken assumption that Hywel possessed a clear understanding of North British political geography. A glance at the place-name data shows it to be based largely on 'sounds like' etymology, a random technique which rarely yields useful results. This point is usually ignored when the question of Rheged's location is raised because the 'factoid' of the Carlisle–Solway theory holds an almost unassailable status. The theory nevertheless remains unproven. Rather than supposing that the location of Urien's realm is adequately indicated by a twelfth-century poem, we should approach the topic from a position of little knowledge. Only by doing so can we hope to find an objective answer to the question: Where was Rheged?

Supporters of the consensus point us to the northern shore of the Solway Firth, to the village of Dunragit in Galloway. This is situated at the head of Luce Bay on the now-disused railway between Dumfries and Stranraer. Here, according to 'sounds like' etymology, we have a place-name meaning 'Fort of Rheged'. This occurs in records of the sixteenth century as *Dunregate*, but no earlier forms are recorded, nor is there any hint that a major stronghold once stood in the locality. Centres of power known to have been used by the Men of the North are usually associated with imposing rocky heights such as Alt Clut or Din Eidyn. The same trend is seen in the kingdoms of the Picts and Scots and in Anglo-Saxon Bernicia at sites like Dunbar and Bamburgh. But in the vicinity of Dunragit no such feature exists, our attention being directed instead to the only viable candidate: the Round Dounan, a small knoll lying some 200 metres north of Dunragit House.[18] This unimpressive eminence stands only a dozen feet high and seems an improbable residence for a renowned warrior-king. Visible remains include traces of an enclosing ditch or earthen bank and, on the summit, another bank or collapsed drystone wall.[19] Archaeologists are extremely sceptical that this was a site occupied in Early Historic times, still less that it was a royal residence.[20] Such scepticism raises serious doubts about the usual derivation of the place-name *Dunragit* which may in fact be a red herring. It has been suggested that the second element could be Gaelic *reichet* rather than Old Welsh *Reget*, and that the place was so named by the *Gall Gáidhil*, 'foreign Gaels', who colonised Galloway in the Viking period. It is worth noting the occurrence in Ireland of a place called Dun Reichet which obviously has no connection with Urien. Another possibility is that the second element represents a Brittonic term similar to Welsh *gwaragedd*, 'women'.[21]

We turn now to a poem composed in Wales long after the era of Taliesin but erroneously attributed to him. Here the phrase *tra merin reget* incorporates the Old Welsh words for 'beyond, sea, Rheged' and is usually taken to mean 'beyond the Sea of Rheged'. This was the interpretation proposed by Sir Ifor Williams, one of the most eminent scholars of early Welsh literature, in a detailed study of Taliesin's poems.[22] Sir Ifor quoted two other poetic occurrences of *tra merin*, namely *tra merin llestyr*, 'foreign vessel', and *tra merin llu*, 'foreign host'. These, he concluded, demonstrate that *tra merin* meant 'transmarine'. To this we might add the synonymous term 'overseas' in the sense of 'foreign'. Having reached this conclusion, Sir Ifor then went on to say:

> and so we may take *tra merin reget* to mean 'beyond the Sea of Rheged', or, in other words, 'beyond the Solway Firth', and this proves that Carlisle was definitely in the land of Rheged and that the northern shore of the Solway may also have been included in it.[23]

Sir Ifor's reasons for replacing his earlier interpretation of *tra merin* as 'foreign' or 'transmarine' with 'beyond the Sea of' remain unexplained. A few lines earlier he drew an analogy between *merin Reget* and *merin Iddew*, the latter occurring in the poem *Y Gododdin* in the phrase *tra merin Iddew*. Sir Ifor interpreted this as meaning 'Sea of Giudi' and considered it to be synonymous with *Muir nGiudan*, an Irish name for the Firth of Forth. Elsewhere in the *Gododdin* we find instances of Merin being used as a personal name, and of *tra merin* being used in the sense of 'foreign, overseas'.[24] Is it not possible that both Iddew and Merin were names of people, and that *tra merin Iddew* refers to a 'foreign' warrior called Iddew rather than to the Firth of Forth? In the case of *tra merin Reget* we find no supporting evidence that the Solway Firth was ever known as 'The Sea of Rheged'. We should therefore consider the possibility that *tra merin Reget*, like *tra merin Iddew*, might mean something other than 'across the sea or firth of . . .'. Perhaps it meant 'foreign Rheged', 'transmarine Rheged' or the more literal 'Rheged beyond the sea'? Here the geography of Wales in relation to the ancient lands of the North Britons might be relevant: to a medieval Welshman looking out from his own country the long-vanished kingdoms of the *Gwŷr y Gogledd* would indeed lie 'beyond the sea'. Rheged, Gododdin and other lost realms lay far away in a distant region beyond the northern horizon. In geographical terms the phrase *tra merin Reget* might be nothing more than a vague signpost pointing northward from Wales.

The most unlikely example of a supposed 'Rheged' place-name is Rochdale in the present county of Greater Manchester. This town, formerly in south-east Lancashire, was recorded in 1086 as *Recedham*, a name whose first element seems to contain a word similar to Rheged. Given the traditional placing of Urien's kingdom around the Solway, it might seem strange to think of Rochdale, a place more than 100 miles away, being included within it, but the suggestion has been made nonetheless.[25] Towards the end of the twentieth century few historians supported this scenario, chiefly because it assigned to Urien an unfeasibly large area stretching from the Rhinns of Galloway to the Mersey Estuary, but it has recently reappeared.[26] A more likely origin of *Recedham* lies in the name of the River Roch on which the place stands. The river was first recorded as Rached in the thirteenth century. It is clearly the main element in *Rachetham* and *Rachedal*, two variant names of Rochdale recorded in c.1195. Rochdale, then, seems to take its name from the river, which in turn seems to derive from a Celtic compound incorporating *coet* or *cet*, 'wood'.[27] An alternative suggestion sees Old English *reced*, 'hall or house', as the source of *Recedham*, with the name of the river being a back-formation derived from the name of the settlement, but the absence of *reced* as an element in other place-names renders this unlikely.[28] The uncertainties about Rochdale's origins make any firm connection with Urien's kingdom impossible.

Sir Ifor Williams believed that the River Eden, which flows through Carlisle on its way to the Solway Firth, is mentioned in a line of poetry attributed to Taliesin.[29] In the fourteenth-century manuscript containing the Taliesin poems the line in question appears in *Gweith Gwen Ystrat*, 'The Battle of Gwen Ystrat', a poem praising Urien's war-leadership. This poem was regarded by Sir Ifor, and by his distinguished former tutor Sir John Morris-Jones, as a genuine composition of the sixth century. Other scholars of Old Welsh literature, and several generations of historians, have tended to follow the opinions of these two eminent figures. The line allegedly referring to the River Eden appears in the manuscript as *kyfedwynt y gynrein kywym don*. In a recent study of *Gweith Gwen Ystrat* Graham Isaac commented that 'this line is the most difficult in the poem, and still defies satisfactory analysis'.[30] Sir Ifor amended the final words to *rywin idon*, 'the plentiful wine of Idon', and suggested that Idon might have been a name applied by sixth-century

Britons to the River Eden. The emendation was rejected by Dr Isaac on metrical grounds and seems to have no special merit above others that might be proposed. Less radical amendment is required, for instance, by Isaac's own cautious suggestion *kywydon*, 'ranks'. This would give the following meaning to the line: 'May the ranks of his chiefs feast together.'

In addition to rejecting *Idon*, Dr Isaac dismissed a sixth-century date for *Gweith Gwen Ystrat* and instead advanced a strong case for seeing it as a composition of the period 1050 to 1150. If we accept his views – and there is no reason why we should not – we must disregard this poem as a source of information about Rheged. This is an important point, for without *Idon* we have no reason to associate Urien with the Eden Valley. Having cast serious doubts on Dunragit and *merin Reget*, the consensus view of Rheged's geography already begins to look fragile. Another of its foundations collapses when we examine *Llwyfenydd*, a place-name associated by Taliesin with an estate or residence of Urien. This is commonly identified as the valley of the River Lyvennet in Cumbria, an area showing clear evidence of native settlement in Roman times.[31] The identification is based on nothing more than a resemblance between the two names, both of which seem to derive from a Brittonic term related to Old Welsh *llwyf*, 'elm'. Although originating as an etymological guess, the Lyvennet hypothesis has proved remarkably durable. It received a major boost from Welsh scholarship when Sir Ifor Williams offered his cautious support and, like much repetitive theorising about Rheged, it has since developed into a 'factoid'. Its resilience is demonstrated by its continuing ability to attract support despite potentially fatal doubts raised by a dearth of positive archaeological data. Excavation of ancient settlements in the Lyvennet Valley has produced no evidence of habitation in post-Roman times, nor has a suitable candidate for an Early Historic royal residence so far been found.[32] The only reason for an alleged connection between Urien and Lyvennet is the river's proximity to Carlisle and the Eden Valley, neither of which – as we have seen – can be confidently associated with his kingdom.

Rejection of the conventional, consensus view brings us no nearer to answering the question: Where was Rheged? We are left with a choice between tackling the question in an objective way or leaving it unanswered. Of these two options the first can only be chosen if we discard preconceived notions about sixth-century political geography. The second requires us to continue our study of the Men of the North without locating the realm of their most famous representative. This is not as defeatist as it sounds, for it may be sufficient for our purposes to say merely that Rheged lay 'somewhere in northern Britain'. Urien's political dealings with other kings, and the fate of his dynasty, can still be studied even if we cannot be certain of his precise geographical context. Fixing the exact location of Llywfenydd or other places is unnecessary. If, however, we take the first option, we might start by turning our original question on its head by asking: Where was Rheged *not* located?

On a map of northern Britain we can impose a rough outline showing the political geography of Urien's time. The estuary and lower courses of the River Clyde should be envisaged as the hinterland or resource-base of Alt Clut. Eastward in Lothian lay Gododdin with its great citadel at Din Eidyn. In mid-Clydesdale or Selkirkshire we might cautiously place the kingdom of Goddeu. West of the Clyde Valley and south of Alt Clut our map shows Ayrshire with its focus on the valley of the River Ayr. In the Taliesin poems and in others attributed to North British bards we find *Aeron*, a territorial name which might mean the Ayr Valley.[33] Moving eastward again we reach the realm of Calchfynydd with its likely focus at Kelso, and further east the marches of Bernicia and the North Sea coastlands. This is as far as our rough outline takes us. Areas left untouched appear as voids on the map and include huge tracts of territory that we know were inhabited in the sixth century. It is in these voids that Rheged and other lost kingdoms probably lay. One large void is Galloway and Dumfriesshire where we find a number of Early Historic forts, none of which can be linked to an identifiable figure among the *Gwŷr y Gogledd*. Another void occupies the uplands where both Tweed and Clyde begin their journeys, a region supporting an elite presence attested by inscribed stones but to which no named kingdom can be assigned with confidence. Further south in what is now Cumbria we do not know who ruled the Solway Plain and the Eden Valley, but someone established a centre of power at Carlisle after the end of the Roman period.[34] Into any of these blank spaces we could parachute Urien, simply by finding superficial modern equivalents for a selection of Taliesin's place-names. Assigning Urien to the Solway Firth could no doubt be achieved in this way, using 'sounds like' etymology, even without drawing on Dunragit, *Idon*, Lyvennet or Hywel's poem. Alternatively, we could make a good case for locating Rheged in the upper valley of Tweed, perhaps in the vicinity of Peebles where the River Lyne offers a possible origin for Taliesinic names such as *Llwyfenydd* and *Argoed Llwyfein*. At the confluence of Lyne and Tweed the Romans built a fort to guard an important east–west road and other indications of power and authority are found nearby. Taliesin portrays Urien as ruler of Goddeu, a district discussed in the previous chapter, whose possible modern form *Cadzow* is found in a place-name only 18 miles west of the Lyne at Kilncadzow. Elsewhere the poet describes battles waged by Urien at a ford near Alt Clut, at an unnamed site in Manau and possibly at the Roman fort of *Bremenium* in the Cheviot Hills. Warfare in these three locations, together with the siege at Lindisfarne, would not be inconsistent with a kingdom nestling in a central position relative to Alt Clut, Gododdin and Bernicia. This musing is not a serious attempt to locate Rheged in Upper Tweeddale, but merely an illustration of how easily a valid theory can be constructed by looking for Taliesin's place-names in a void area on our sixth-century map. Although advanced here in a fairly casual manner, this theory is no less plausible than the conventional one. Both rely to some extent on 'sounds like' etymology, but the Tweeddale alternative at least has the advantage of not being based on preconceived ideas about political geography. In this regard it may provide a more objective answer to the question *Where was Rheged?* than an elaborate hypothesis built around a twelfth-century poem. The simple truth is that we cannot deduce the location of Urien's kingdom from the data currently available. We can, however, dismiss the conventional placing of Rheged in the shorelands of the Solway Firth as an unproven hypothesis whose frailties need to be acknowledged.[35] The Solway hypothesis could yet be correct, but the arguments currently employed in its support rest on extremely weak foundations. Without a firmer basis the theory cannot sustain the complex tapestries of sixth-century political history so frequently woven around it.

Turning now to Urien's life and career, we find little in the Taliesin poems except references to battles and cattle-raids. No source hints at when or where Urien was born, nor can we be sure that he gained the kingship of Rheged by legitimate means. He may have been a usurper or pretender, seizing power by force during a time of crisis. In the pedigrees his father is named as Cynfarch, the eponym of the Cynferchyn warband. As noted in the previous chapter, the Cynferchyn appear in an isolated triad in *Bonedd Gwŷr y Gogledd* as one of three groups whom later Welsh tradition portrayed as allies. Cynfarch is not mentioned by Taliesin and has no independent existence outside the pedigree, his main roles in Welsh literature being to provide an eponym for the Cynferchyn and a patronym for his famous son. He may nevertheless have been a historical figure. The genealogy names his father as Merchiaun whose name derives from Marcianus, the name of an Eastern Roman emperor who ruled in the mid-fifth century. Urien's warfare against Theodoric of Bernicia, who ruled from 572 to 579, places him a hundred years after the reign of Marcianus. We might thus expect his grandfather Merchiaun to have been born during the final quarter of the fifth century, perhaps at a time when the imperial name *Marcianus* may have been popular among elite families in the barbarian West. Beyond Merchiaun the genealogy runs through Gwrwst to the ubiquitous ancestor Coel Hen. Urien's attachment to Coel seems to be confirmed by Taliesin in the poem *Gweith Argoed Llwyfein*, 'The Battle of Argoed Llwyfein', and might thus be regarded as historical. If so, then the attachment of other pedigrees to Coel should be regarded as manipulation by later Welsh genealogists. In Wales the creation of kinship links between North British heroes fulfilled literary or political purposes. Similar creativity produced Urien's alleged ancestor Ceneu who appears in a variant of the pedigree. Ceneu is nothing more than a genealogical 'ghost' arising from a Welsh misunderstanding of Taliesin's reference to Coel in *Gweith Argoed Llwyfein*. The reference appears in a pre-battle boast by Owain, Urien's son, who answers an enemy's demand for hostages with the retort:

> *a cheneu vab coel bydei kymwyawc*
> *lew kyn as talei o wystyl nebawt*

Sir Ifor Williams believed that the word *vab*, 'son of', was erroneously added to the manuscript by a Welsh scribe who here assumed *ceneu vab coel*, 'whelp of Coel', to be a personal name.[36] Thus, although Sir John Morris-Jones retained *vab* to give the meaning 'Ceneu, son of Coel', Sir Ifor offered a different version of Owain's boast. Translated into English, Sir Ifor's amended reading gives: 'And a whelp of Coel would be a hard-pressed warrior before he would hand over any hostage.'

Having dismissed the fictional Ceneu, we can return to Urien's pedigree and to his great-grandfather Gwrwst, earlier Gurgust, a son of Coel. *Gurgust* is a British equivalent of *Fergus* or *Urguist*, a name popular among the Scots and Picts, but apparently rare among the Britons. This particular Gurgust does not appear in any poems or tales, but the Welsh genealogists gave him an epithet *Ledlum*, meaning 'Bare', which may have come from a northern source. In the absence of contrary evidence we can cautiously accept him and his son Merchiaun as real ancestors of Urien in authentic genealogical traditions transmitted from northern Britain. The alternative, which must also be kept in mind, is that the generations above Cynfarch were invented in Wales to create a suitable pedigree where none existed before.

Taliesin's verses say almost nothing about Urien's family. Owain is mentioned in *Gweith Argoed Llwyfein* and is the subject of a *marwnad* or death-song, but no other close kin of Urien are identified beyond two references to unnamed 'sons'. A note added to an eleventh-century manuscript of an abridged version of the *Historia Brittonum* mentions that the text included 'excerpts made by the son of Urien from the Book of the Blessed Germanus'. This son is usually identified as Rhun, a mysterious figure to whom the *Historia* credits the baptism of an English king. Rhun's vague associations with literature and religion, together with his role in the later dynastic history of Rheged, are discussed further in Chapter 6. Neither he nor Owain appear in the pedigrees, despite their undoubted fame in medieval Wales.

Several of Urien's battles have already been mentioned in the context of locating his kingdom. If we could place these on a modern map, we might be able to reconstruct a rough picture of his military career, but the sources do not provide the necessary data. Taliesin refers to a number of battles, but only three – Manau, Rhyd Alclud and Cellawr Brewyn – can be located with any measure of confidence. *Manau* must mean the northern Manau rather than the Isle of Man, while *Rhyd Alclud* is 'Alt Clut Ford' which we should think of as a tidal crossing on the Clyde close to Dumbarton Rock. The name *Brewyn* has been equated with *Bremenium*, a Roman fort in Redesdale on the western fringe of Bernicia, where the *cellawr*, 'huts', were perhaps derelict buildings in the long-abandoned *vicus* outside the walls.[37] Taliesin calls Urien a 'defender in (or of) Aeron' which implies warfare in defence of domains in Ayrshire. Other battles in the poetry defy identification, because their names are either too obscure or – like *Argoed Llwyfein*, 'Next to the Elm Wood' – too general. Urien's campaign against the Bernicians at Lindisfarne is not reported by Taliesin, but a reference to it seems to be present among a group of poems known collectively as *Canu Urien*, 'Urien's Song'. This collection, although composed in Wales during the ninth century, apparently drew on earlier North British traditions of unknown provenance. One poem gives the site of Urien's death as *Aber Lleu*, a place-name meaning 'Mouth of the Lleu', and this has been identified as the estuary of the River Low on the Northumberland coast opposite Lindisfarne.[38] Curiously, *Lleu* appears not to be a name of Brittonic origin but rather a borrowing into Welsh of an English word *low* meaning 'tidal stream or pool'. If the equation Lleu = Low is correct, we may envisage Urien's career as ending in violence on the shorelands of his Bernician enemies, his nemesis being the jealous British king Morcant. He may have been advanced in years when he perished: in more than one poem Taliesin refers to him as an old man, an aged lord with white hair. The precise circumstances of his death are unclear, but Welsh tradition regarded Morcant as the instigator and Llofan Llaw Difro, 'Llofan of the Exiled Hand', as the killer. Other elements in the *Canu Urien* poems, such as the image of the old king's severed head being carried away, represent devices common in Celtic literature.

Finally, given the controversial nature of the source-material, what should be our assessment of Urien? Was he, for instance, a powerful overking who dominated his neighbours, or does his alleged superiority owe less to the sixth-century North than to ninth-century Wales? Our best response to these questions is to look at the historical king behind the literary hero. Whatever our opinions of the motives that regurgitated northern history and poetry to produce the triads, pedigrees, the *Historia Brittonum* and *Canu Urien*, we have no reason to deny Urien's status as an important figure of his time. The verses of his court-bard Taliesin immortalised him in medieval Welsh literature, but, when we cast this image aside, we see a typical barbarian warlord striving to enhance his wealth and status at the expense of his neighbours. Both Taliesin and the *Historia Brittonum* depict Urien as a competent commander and raider. Success in military campaigns brought territorial gains which expanded his kingdom beyond his core domain of Rheged. Like most overkingships, however, this enlarged hegemony depended on the fortunes of a single individual to maintain its cohesion. Thus, when Urien died at Morcant's instigation, his kingdom lost its dominant role and his hegemony almost certainly dissolved. The initiative was seemingly lost by his sons and passed instead to other ambitious warlords – including, no doubt, the rulers of Alt Clut and Gododdin – before being seized by the kings of English Bernicia. Rheged without Urien continued to function as a kingdom into the seventh century, its fortunes in the wake of his death being traced in Chapter 6, but its brief paramountcy was gone. In the meantime our attention turns back to Urien's contemporaries.

Rhydderch Hael

Of the three native kings named alongside Urien in the *Historia Brittonum* only Rhydderch Hael can be assigned a precise geographical context. Just as Urien is associated with the mysterious Rheged so Rhydderch is identifiable as king of Alt Clut, 'The Rock of Clyde'. Unlike Urien, however, Rhydderch is attested in a reliable source of non-Welsh provenance: he is briefly mentioned by Adomnán, abbot of Iona and hagiographer of Saint Columba. Adomnán wrote his *Vita* of Columba at the end of the seventh century, using texts in the monastic library at Iona as well as oral traditions handed down by the brethren. One story included in the *Vita* refers to 'the blessed man's prophecy concerning Roderc, son of Tothail, king of *Petra Cloithe*'.[39] The place-name is a Latin equivalent of Alt Clut, while *Roderc* is none other than Rhydderch. In the North British genealogies a pedigree attached to the main line of Clyde kings names Rhydderch's father as Tudwal, Adomnán's *Tothail*. Adomnán goes on to tell how Luigbe, a monk of Iona, took a secret message from Rhydderch to Columba. The king – described by Adomnán as a friend of the saint – wanted to know whether or not he would be slain by his foes. Columba answered with a prophecy, predicting that Rhydderch 'will never be delivered into his enemies' hands but will die at home on his own pillow'. Adomnán's motive for including this story was to highlight Columba's miraculous powers of foresight; Rhydderch's motive in seeking the saint's advice was surely to learn whether or not the Scots were planning to raid Alt Clut. Columba was not only a prominent cleric but also a man of high status in secular circles. His family in northern Ireland belonged to a powerful sept of the Uí Néill and in Argyll he served as high priest and spiritual mentor to the kings of Cenél nGabráin. The latter was at that time the dominant *cenél* or royal kindred of the Scots, wielding great power from a core territory in Kintyre. Columba was very close to the warlike king Áedán mac Gabráin, a role to which he was well-suited: even before his arrival in Britain he had acted as a mediator between kings and was an experienced diplomat. He was therefore an ideal point of contact for Rhydderch in any peace-making venture. Although reworked by Adomnán as a tale of miraculous prophecy, the story of messages passing between Iona and Alt Clut clearly had a secular aspect. What we are probably seeing is the negotiation of a truce between Rhydderch and Áedán in which Columba acted as facilitator.[40] We might additionally envisage the monk Luigbe acting as an interpreter between the Gaelic-speaking abbot and the British king.

The precise chronology of Rhydderch's life is unknown, but part of his reign coincided with Columba's abbacy of Iona which spanned the years 563 to 597. Adomnán has nothing more to say of Rhydderch, but, by sifting through a variety of other sources, we are able to draw a rough picture of him. The information is often of dubious reliability, deriving largely from texts of doubtful provenance and late composition. It draws on Welsh pedigrees and poetry, Scottish hagiography of the Norman period and various fragments of folklore. Looking first at the royal genealogy of Alt Clut in the Harleian collection we find Rhydderch and his immediate forebears not in the primary line of descent but attached as a branch. At first glance this seems puzzling, especially in the light of Adomnán's claim that 'Roderc' was a king of *Petra Cloithe*. However, Rhydderch's pedigree makes him a great-grandson of Dyfnwal Hen, a figure we have already encountered in the main Alt Clut line represented by the ancestors of the ninth-century king Rhun ab Arthgal. Rhydderch's separate pedigree can perhaps be reconciled by envisaging his family as an offshoot from the primary kindred, a branch which briefly held the kingship for one or more generations in the sixth century. Alternatively, his attachment to Rhun's pedigree could be artificial and fictional: he may have sprung from an unrelated family of usurpers who seized the kingship in a period of strife. Two or three centuries later, a Welsh genealogist who knew of Adomnán's reference to 'Roderc, king of *Petra Cloithe*' may then have linked his descent to that of the main Clyde dynasty. The usurpation theory can, of course, be reversed to portray Rhydderch's family as the legitimate line and the 'main' kindred as interlopers. We may note in passing that the pedigree gives Rhydderch no progeny. This should mean that his line had died out, or that his descendants in the ninth century were regarded as less important – in Wales and the North – than the family of Rhun ab Arthgal.

We can be fairly certain of Rhydderch's immediate ancestry: his father Tudwal is identified by Adomnán and can therefore be regarded as a genuine historical figure. Traditions surrounding the mysterious Saint Ninian mention a tyrannical King Tudwal who might be Rhydderch's father.[41] Outside the Harleian genealogies other Welsh texts link Rhydderch to various heroes of the Old North, usually with his epithet *Hael*, 'Generous'. Since these texts derive from heroic poetry or from fragments of saga preserved in the triads their validity is doubtful. One alleged kinsman of Rhydderch was Senyllt Hael, an obscure king famed for his hospitality. Another was Senyllt's son Nudd Hael who appears alongside

Rhydderch in the triad of the 'Three Generous Men'.[42] The pedigree of Nudd and Senyllt in the Jesus College genealogies attaches both men to the main Alt Clut dynasty, but the link is probably of Welsh rather than of northern origin and therefore fictional. In the *Bonedd Gwŷr y Gogledd* we find mention of Senyllt but not of his son. Nudd reappears in a curious tale preserved in a twelfth-century Welsh law code where he is shown as an ally of Rhydderch and the otherwise unknown Mordaf Hael. These three are depicted as joining the equally obscure Clydno Eidyn on a military expedition to avenge the murder of their kinsman Elidir by Rhun ap Maelgwn, king of Gwynedd.[43] The tale depicts the Men of the North leading an assault on Wales and burning the district of Arfon, thereby provoking Rhun to launch a counter-attack which brought his army to the River Forth. This story, like the tale of Cunedda's migration from Manau Gododdin, looks suspiciously like Welsh dynastic propaganda. It is almost certainly a product of the eighth to eleventh centuries and has a primary focus on the ruling house of Gwynedd. Rhun was a historical king who reigned in the second half of the sixth century. His portrayal here as a great warlord who fought the mighty heroes of the North gave him a powerful literary image which in turn reflected well upon his descendants. Whether the story of his march to the Forth has any historical value is extremely doubtful.

Of the three northerners who allegedly assailed Rhun's domain Rhydderch was the most renowned in Welsh lore, hence his presence alongside Urien as one of four kings who fought the Bernicians. Although this quartet is invariably seen as an alliance, we have suggested above that each king may have campaigned separately. In Rhydderch's case his conflict with one or more of Ida's sons probably arose at an interface of personal ambitions. Hostilities perhaps began with clashes in the Tweed Valley or in some other district on the southern fringe of Gododdin. Warbands from Alt Clut and Bamburgh may have raided such areas frequently, their objectives being portable loot – cattle and slaves – or the subjugation of local elites. Ethnic concerns are unlikely to have been a priority for the Clyde Britons or their English foes, nor indeed for any unfortunate community caught in the middle of their warring. The sources associate Rhydderch with only one other sphere of warfare, namely his dealings with the Cenél nGabráin dynasty of Kintyre. In a Welsh triad of unknown provenance one of the 'Three Unrestrained Ravagings of the Island of Britain' occurred when Áedán mac Gabráin 'came to the court of Rhydderch Hael at Alt Clut and left neither food nor drink nor beast alive'.[44] The same triad gives Áedán the epithet *Bradawc*, meaning 'wily' or 'treacherous'. How he earned this disparaging nickname is unknown, but it implies a belief among the Britons that he was not to be trusted. If this tradition has any validity, it might say something about the political relationship between Áedán and Rhydderch implied by the latter's approach to Columba. If the saint did indeed mediate a truce, it may have been treacherously broken at a later date by Áedán's 'unrestrained ravaging'.[45] Alternatively, the truce could have been forged after the raid at the instigation of a fearful and possibly submissive Rhydderch. Although the raid is unlikely to be the event commemorated in the lost Irish tale *Orgain Sratha Cluada*, 'The Slaughter of Strathclyde', it was probably not the only recorded conflict between Rhydderch and Áedán. They were, after all, close neighbours with common maritime interests in the Firth of Clyde. Scots from Kintyre and Britons from Alt Clut mounted major campaigns against each other during the Early Historic period, keeping alive a long tradition of rivalry perhaps reaching back into the time of the Epidii and Damnonii. Áedán was well-known as a belligerent warlord who campaigned as far away as Stirlingshire and Perthshire and also southward into Bernician lands. Rhydderch, too, was no stranger to long-range ventures, as his conflict with Ida's sons demonstrates. His bard at the royal court of Alt Clut would have celebrated these wars in heroic poetry and, although none of this literature has survived, a poem about Áedán and Rhydderch may lie behind the triad of the unrestrained ravagings. Another triad mentions Rhydderch's horse *Rudlwyt*, 'Dun-Grey', while his sword *Dyrnwyn*, 'White Hilt', was numbered among the 'Thirteen Treasures of the Island of Britain'.[46] Elsewhere he appears in a group of Welsh poems attributed to Myrddin, the precursor of the Arthurian Merlin, as an oppressive and vengeful tyrant.[47] The poems exist in a thirteenth-century manuscript in language not regarded as archaic so their relationship with sixth-century history is likely to be tenuous. In the poems Myrddin tells of his wretched existence in the forests after fleeing the Battle of Arfderydd, a historical event which took place at Arthuret near Carlisle in 573. He complains that since the death of his lord he is being pursued by 'the fierce Rhydderch Hael'.[48] In Welsh tradition Arfderydd was the most famous battle involving the Men of the North and it is discussed at length in the next chapter. Here we may simply note that Rhydderch is unlikely to have played any part in it.

Aside from the Welsh sources, the other main repository of information on Rhydderch is the hagiography surrounding Saint Kentigern. The twelfth-century *Vitae* commissioned by the bishops of Glasgow have already been mentioned in Chapter 3. In these controversial writings Rhydderch appears as 'King Rederech', Kentigern's patron and benefactor, in contexts where folklore and ecclesiastical legend are interwoven with genuine relics of the sixth and seventh centuries. Mention is made of a royal grant of land at Glasgow for Kentigern's new bishopric, thereby providing a foundation-legend for the twelfth-century cathedral. Another reference is to Rhydderch's estate north of the Clyde at *Pertnech*, Partick, which also happened to be royal land under Scottish kings of the twelfth century.[49] Rhydderch's queen appears as *Languoreth*, a Brittonic name unlikely to have been invented by the hagiographers. She may have been a real person, but, if so, we cannot prove her existence. The sixteenth-century *Aberdeen Breviary* does not name Rhydderch's wife, but calls her the queen of *Cadzow*, a district corresponding to the area around Hamilton and possibly to be equated with the Early Historic kingdom of Goddeu. If the Aberdeen information has any historical validity, it suggests that Languoreth, like Rhydderch, was a Briton of Clydesdale. The hagiographer Jocelin of Furness names Rhydderch's son and successor as Constantine, a prince who entered the clergy.[50] There is no record of this son outside the Kentigern material, nor does he appear in the royal genealogies. Current scholarly opinion sees Constantine, son of Rhydderch, as an invention of the clergy at Glasgow Cathedral, his creation being prompted by the earlier dedication of the nearby church of Govan to a 'Saint Constantine'. The new Glaswegian vision of early Christianity on the Clyde had no room for two patron saints so Constantine was subordinated to Kentigern with Rhydderch providing a convenient link between them. Aside from Constantine no other sons are credited to Rhydderch, but the Welsh triads assign him a daughter, Angharad *Ton Velen*, who appears as one of the 'Three Lively Maidens of the Island of Britain'. Her epithet or nickname has the literal meaning 'Tawny Wave' in the sense of 'Blonde Curls', an interesting physical detail which hints at some poem or story about her.[51] There is no compelling reason to deny that she existed, but she nevertheless remains caught in a hazy limbo between Welsh literature and North British history.

According to Jocelin of Furness, Rhydderch Hael died in the same year as his saintly bishop. Kentigern's death is entered at 612 or 614 in the Welsh Annals and this seems a plausible date for the passing of the king. Columba's prophecy that Rhydderch would end his life in his own bed finds some corroboration in Jocelin's belief that the death occurred at the royal estate of Partick. The Welsh and Glaswegian death-notices may be independent of each other, in which case we can cautiously accept both at face value. Any final summary or assessment of Rhydderch should begin with the most significant observation that can be made about him: he is not only the most securely dated North British king of the sixth century but also one of only two whose kingdoms can be located with certainty. He was probably the royal patron of Saint Kentigern, but whether the main focus of this patronage lay at Glasgow rather than Govan or elsewhere is open to question. Rhydderch's other activities are less clear. Welsh references to his involvement at the Battle of Arfderydd are spurious, but his wars against Bernicia were presumably real. His communication with Iona suggests that he was held in high regard by his peers, or at least by the secular and religious elites of Cenél nGabráin. This is perhaps unsurprising, given that he ruled a long-established kingdom located in a position of strategic importance. His principal centre of power, as Adomnán explicitly states, was Alt Clut, one of the most imposing fortresses in Britain. In an age where a king's status was measured by prowess in war it is inconceivable that Rhydderch could have maintained his authority without proving himself on the battlefield. Whatever the results of his encounters with the Scots and Bernicians, and no matter how many 'unrestrained ravagings' his realm endured, there must have been victories as well as defeats. Setting aside the allusions to warfare given by Adomnán and the Welsh sources, it is likely that Rhydderch's most frequent adversaries were his British neighbours.

Gwallawg

This enigmatic figure, although famed as a great warrior-king in Welsh poetry, can neither be securely dated nor firmly located. Two early poems about him are attributed to Taliesin, but both are corrupt and difficult to interpret.[52] Because they underwent significant alteration in Wales their information cannot be accepted at face value and must be viewed with caution. This means that Gwallawg's conventional identification as ruler of a kingdom called Elmet, an idea derived from a single line in one of the poems, is open to serious doubt. He appears in the *Historia Brittonum* alongside Urien and Rhydderch as an enemy of the sons of Ida, but this is his only appearance in that text. Later Welsh poets celebrated his martial deeds, presumably using material derived from authentic northern tradition, and in the Harleian pedigrees he is attached to the Coeling kindred via a branch descended from the mysterious Ceneu: *Gwallawg map Lleenawg map Masguic Clop map Ceneu map Coel*. We have already accepted Ceneu as a fictional 'ghost' created by a misreading of Taliesin's phrase *cheneu vab Coel*, 'whelp of Coel'. The generation concerned can thus be removed from the pedigree. Gwallawg's grandfather Masguic is otherwise unknown and was either invented by a Welsh genealogist or drawn from poetry and folklore that no longer survive. His existence outside literature is therefore questionable. Lleenawg, on the other hand, is usually regarded as a historical figure, chiefly because there is little reason to doubt the accuracy of Gwallawg's patronym as given by the pedigree. Lleenawg's name appears in one of the two Gwallawg poems attributed to Taliesin: 'He [Gwallawg] defended gentle Llan Lleenawg'. Here, the reference is to a place-name *Llan Lleenawg*, 'Lleenawg's Enclosure' or 'Lleenawg's Church'. If the *llan* was a real place, it evidently held special significance for the family. An analogous example of an ancestor's name being attached to a *llan* is Llangadwaladr in Anglesey, a church founded by the seventh-century king Cadwaladr of Gwynedd to which he eventually retired. If Lleenawg really was Gwallawg's father, and if Llan Lleenawg was a real place associated with him, he may have chosen a similar 'opting out' from the kingship. The key issue is the question of how much genuine North British material appears in the two Gwallawg poems. Even if, as seems likely, both were composed in Wales in response to Gwallawg's fame in heroic literature, they may have been constructed around a core of authentic northern tradition. Although they mention a number of Welsh locations, other references might be to places in the North. One poem offers what is commonly seen as a key geographical hint about Gwallawg:

> Everyone can judge the man who would be judged,
> Gwallawg, who was named a judge over Elvet.[53]

The above translation incorporates a particular interpretation of the second line as deduced by Sir Ifor Williams. Not all scholars agree with Sir Ifor's version which, according to Kenneth Jackson, rests on 'a doubtful interpretation of a doubtful line in a difficult poem'.[54] Historians usually identify *Elvet* as Elmet in West Yorkshire. Several modern place-names in the modern county incorporate *Elmet* as a suffix, their distribution indicating that they fall within the bounds of a geographical entity of this name. All of them are near the present-day conurbation of Leeds and it has long been assumed that this was the heart of an Early Historic kingdom of Elmet.[55] Elmet is also mentioned in the *Historia Brittonum* in a note relating to the seventh-century English king Edwin of Deira:

> Edwin, son of Aelle, reigned seventeen years. He occupied Elmet and expelled Certic, king of that country.[56]

Bede refers to *silva Elmete*, the 'wood of Elmet', and mentions elsewhere a King Cerdic, but draws no explicit connection between the two.[57] It seems possible, however, that Bede's Cerdic was indeed the Certic of Elmet whom Edwin dispossessed. Bede refers to Cerdic giving sanctuary to exiled members of Edwin's family after the Bernician takeover of Deira. One of these was slain with poison and, although the circumstances are not described by Bede, Edwin's later actions in the *Historia Brittonum* have led to the idea that he blamed Cerdic for the death. However, the name *Cerdic* or *Certic* (with variants such as *Ceretic* and *Ceredig*) was fairly common among the Britons so we cannot be absolutely certain that Bede and the *Historia* are here referring to the same man.[58] Nor should we assume that the 'Ceredic, son of Gwallawg' who appears in a Welsh triad necessarily has any connection with Cerdic of Elmet.[59]

The controversial Welsh poem *Moliant Cadwallon*, allegedly composed in the seventh century but possibly from a later period, refers to Gwallawg as the cause of a sorrowful battle at *Catraeth*.[60] The latter event is discussed in the next chapter, where its usual identification with Catterick in Yorkshire is challenged. Catraeth was very famous among the poets of medieval Wales and this might explain Gwallawg's association with the place in *Moliant Cadwallon*, a poem about a North Welsh king who fought the Bernicians. Given recent doubts about the date of this poem, together with uncertainty about the Catraeth = Catterick theory, the line referring to Gwallawg cannot be used as firm evidence for his alleged association with the Yorkshire Elmet.

Another figure usually associated with Elmet is Madog *Elvet* who appears in the *Gododdin* verses as a sixth-century warrior fighting alongside, or as a member of, the Votadinian army. Given the possible contemporaneity of Madog and Gwallawg, it has been suggested that they may have been rivals for the kingship of Elmet.[61] This is interesting but unnecessary. In the *Gododdin* the association between Madog and *Elvet* is asserted unambiguously. It is as strong as the links between Urien and Rheged or between Cadrod and Calchfynydd, whereas Gwallawg's sole connection to the place is merely as a 'judge', whatever this term implies in a sixth-century context. The ruler of *Elvet* was surely Madog, not Gwallawg. Another Madog in the *Gododdin* is usually seen as the same individual.[62] It is worthwhile noting that this namesake seems to be of Votadinian rather than Elmetian stock.

Did the Madog Elvet of *Y Gododdin* come from Elmet in Yorkshire? It is often assumed that he did, and that he joined the Votadinian army as an ally or mercenary. The assumption relies on a belief that *Elvet* always refers to the Yorkshire Elmet. However, both forms of the name occur in Welsh contexts far from the boundaries of Yorkshire. A Christian gravestone from Caernarvonshire, erected probably in the fifth century, commemorates Aliortus *Elmetiaco*, 'from Elmet', while the name Elfed is borne today by a district of Carmarthenshire.[63] Unless these two occurrences derive from the Pennine kingdom, we may infer that the name *Elmet*, or its later variants *Elvet* and *Elfed*, applied to several different places in Britain. One of these might have lain much further north than the Pennine *silva Elmete* known to Bede. If so, then Madog Elvet may have come not from Yorkshire but from a district closer to Votadinian territory, perhaps from the same Elvet where Gwallawg exercised a judicial role. The correct geographical context for both men might therefore be Lothian or Tweeddale.

The Cerdic whom Edwin expelled need not be connected with Gwallawg. Cerdic may indeed have been a seventh-century ruler of the Pennine Elmet, but Gwallawg's domain seems more likely to have lain north of Hadrian's Wall. Conflict with the Bernicians suggests that Gwallawg's kingdom – whatever it was called – lay under immediate threat from their warbands, or that the territorial interests of Ida's sons clashed with those of Gwallawg. The name of Gwallawg's realm is unknown, but the district over which he was apparently a 'judge', and likewise the home territory of Madog Elvet, perhaps lay in the borderlands of Gododdin.

Morcant

If the *Historia Brittonum* identifies any British king as a client or subordinate of Urien, the likeliest candidate is Morcant. This obscure figure has an interesting dual role as enemy of Ida's sons and instigator of Urien's death. In a Welsh literary context he is thus both hero and villain: a king who fought the English but whose jealousy brought the downfall of the greatest of the Men of the North. Morcant's special position in the *Historia* is second only to Urien's: of the four kings named as foes of Bernicia the only explicit link is made between these two. This close association in the narrative suggests a parallel association elsewhere, presumably in Welsh heroic poetry derived ultimately from North British tradition. Whatever poems or stories conveyed this information to Wales or were created there to disseminate it, none have survived, their absence condemning Morcant to obscurity. As in the case of Gwallawg, the name and location of Morcant's kingdom are unknown. It has been suggested that he may have ruled on the east coast, in a territory near Bernicia and perhaps adjacent to Gododdin. Some historians propose him as a king of Gododdin, mainly because the latter realm is otherwise unrepresented in Urien's 'Lindisfarne coalition' and partly due to the apparent absence of the Votadinian royal line in the pedigrees.[64] The simple truth is that we have absolutely no idea where Morcant's kingdom lay.

We are told that Morcant's reason for arranging Urien's demise arose *pro invidia*, 'from envy', of his military achievements. This need not imply an unequal political relationship, as between client and overlord, but nor can such a scenario be ruled out. If he was not a vassal, Morcant might simply have been a rival or neighbour who begrudged Urien's success. He perhaps feared Urien as the most immediate threat to his own territorial ambitions. Lacking the military resources to mount a full-scale challenge on the battlefield, he seemingly devised instead an alternative solution to the problem. The slaying is sometimes seen as a spiteful or treacherous assassination, but in a political context it may have been Morcant's best or only option. In the *Historia Brittonum* Rheged's renowned monarch *jugulatus est*, 'was murdered', while on a military campaign in some unspecified region. The terminology hints at an act of guile or trickery, perhaps undertaken during an ambush in a place of Morcant's choosing. A scenario involving a skirmish between royal warbands seems no less plausible than the rather more dramatic image of masked assassins creeping into Urien's encampment.

In the North British genealogies there are two Morcants, either or neither of whom could be Urien's rival. They appear as grandfather and grandson in a pedigree attached to the mysterious Coel Hen. The elder Morcant has the epithet *Bulc*, 'Gap', which describes either a physical feature such as missing teeth or a harelip or even a territory with which he was associated. If the latter is more apt, his kingdom was perhaps defined by an important mountain pass. Maybe his primary residence controlled access through one of the major routes in the uplands around Tweeddale? In so far as the pedigrees provide any useful chronological guide the sequence of generations seems to make Morcant Bulc a contemporary of Urien. He might then be the instigator of the latter's death, although we should note that it is his grandson and namesake who occupies the more significant position at the end of the pedigree. Either or neither of the two Morcants could be the tyrannical King Morken who, according to the Kentigern hagiography, was a malicious opponent of the saint. The geographical context assigns this tyrant to Clydesdale and associates him with a royal settlement called *Thorp-Morken* where he eventually died.[65] A place-name formed from the Scandinavian element *thorp*, 'farm' or 'hamlet', looks out of place in a sixth-century milieu and is probably a hagiographer's invention. The identification of Morken as a ruler on the Clyde likewise seems suspicious, especially as he is depicted as an otherwise unknown predecessor of Rhydderch Hael. On the other hand the hagiography might preserve authentic traditions connecting a king called Morken with some part of Clydesdale not subject to the Alt Clut dynasty. Beyond this vague suggestion it would be fruitless to speculate further.

TWO BATTLES

The four British kings discussed in the previous chapter were well-known in the poetry and lore of medieval Wales, but they were not alone in receiving such attention. Other members of the *Gwŷr y Gogledd*, the Men of the North, were similarly famed, even if all that now remains of their renown are fragments of lost saga preserved in the Welsh triads. Of people such as Cadrod Calchfynydd, Nudd Hael and Clydno Eidyn we know so little that they barely emerge into the light of history. The same can be said of almost every North British warrior mentioned by name in the *Gododdin* verses, despite their collective fame as an army of heroes pitched against English enemies. The battle of Catraeth, the event commemorated in *Y Gododdin*, is studied in the second part of this chapter. It lies at the heart of modern perceptions about the political history of the *Gwŷr y Gogledd* and has special relevance to the question of where Urien's kingdom lay. The reverence accorded to *Y Gododdin* as a Welsh literary monument gave the battle of Catraeth a special status, but, in the eyes of the bards, it was not the greatest battle fought by the Men of the North. That accolade was reserved not for a heroic clash between Britons and Anglo-Saxons but for a grim encounter between the Britons themselves.

Arfderydd

The Welsh Annals contain the following entry under the year 573:

> *Bellum Armterid inter filios Elifer et Guendoleu filium Keidiau in quo bello Guendoleu cecidit. Merlinus insanus effectus est.*
> The battle of Armterid between the sons of Eliffer and Gwenddoleu the son of Ceidio in which battle Gwenddoleu was slain. Merlin became mad.

This event, the battle of Armterid or Arfderydd, appears to have enjoyed considerable fame in medieval Wales, partly because of its association with the Arthurian wizard Merlin. It came to the notice of Welsh bards via a large corpus of earlier northern poems of which none have survived.[1] Brief allusions and residual fragments of this lost poetry are nevertheless preserved among the Welsh triads. Several triads mention the battlefield – using the variant name-forms *Arfderydd* or *Arderydd* – or the kings who took part. Cumulatively the triadic references suggest that the battle and its literature were well-known in Wales by c.900. Four triads allude directly to the battle, each listing an Arfderydd-related mnemonic as one of three sharing a common theme. The title of each triad and the relevant mnemonic are given below:

Three Faithful Warbands

'The warband of Gwenddoleu son of Ceidio at Arfderydd, who continued the battle for a fortnight and a month after their lord was slain.'

Three Noble Retinues

'The retinue of Dreon the Brave at the Dyke of Arfderydd.'

Three Horses Who Carried The Three Horse-Burdens

'Corvan, horse of the sons of Eliffer, bore the second Horse-Burden: he carried on his back Gwrgi and Peredur and Dunod the Stout and Cynfelyn the Leprous, to look upon the battle-fog of Gwenddoleu at Arfderydd. And no one overtook him but Dinogad, son of Cynan Garwyn, riding upon Swift Roan, and he won censure and dishonour from then till this day.'

Three Futile Battles

'The action at Arfderydd which was brought about by the cause of a lark's nest.'

As well as the triads, a group of poems allegedly composed by Merlin imply that he had been King Gwenddoleu's court-bard, that he had fought at Arfderydd and that he had escaped the battle to hide in the 'Wood of Celyddon'. There in the depths of the forest he adopted the guise of a wild man and mystic prophet, but lived in dread of capture by Rhydderch Hael whom he feared as a cruel tyrant. A flavour of this poetry can be gleaned from the following extract, in which the fugitive bemoans his unhappy fate.

Now that Gwenddoleu is gone no king respects me, teasing is no pleasure, no woman comes to look me up. And in the battle of Arfderydd I wore a golden torc.[2]

Analysis of the Merlin poems shows them to be ninth-century compositions incorporating older material of uncertain date and provenance.[3] Their inclusion of supernatural elements sets them apart from potentially older works such as the heroic poetry of Taliesin and places them rather with the imaginative tales of the Arthurian cycle. When the Merlin references are added to the triad information, we find ourselves dealing with a bundle of cryptic, often outlandish, data relating to Arfderydd. In none of this material do we meet any useful geographical or political contexts for the battle. It is only when we turn to the Welsh genealogical tracts that the picture becomes clearer. There, among the pedigrees of the Men of the North, we find many of the battle's participants listed alongside famous contemporaries such as Urien Rheged and Rhydderch Hael. We can thus assume that the conflict of 573 reported in the Welsh Annals occurred somewhere in northern Britain. But can a more specific geography be deduced?

At the beginning of the nineteenth century, the Scottish antiquary George Chalmers proposed Airdrie in Lanarkshire as *Arfderydd*, on the basis of a superficial similarity between the names.[4] With no supporting evidence the suggestion failed to gain much ground. The matter was finally settled later in the same century by William Forbes Skene whose research placed the location of the battle beyond reasonable doubt.[5] Skene had a keen interest in ancient Welsh literature and was familiar with the bardic references to Arfderydd. He was also aware that an objective search for the battlefield would find no answer in these enigmatic sources. Setting aside the Welsh texts, he turned instead to the chronicles of medieval Scotland and in particular to the *Scotichronicon* of Walter Bower. Skene was already acquainted with this fifteenth-century work whose narrative deals with a broad swath of early Scottish history. He knew, too, that it was a controversial and unreliable text whose testimony frequently strays into the realm of imaginative fiction. Bower's main source was the fourteenth-century *Chronica Gentis Scottorum* whose author, John of Fordoun, claimed to have had access to arcane texts written in much earlier times. In the *Scotichronicon* – although not in Fordoun – Skene found a curious passage relating to Saint Kentigern.[6] In this passage the saint meets a forest-dwelling wild man who had fought in a terrible battle. The wild man gives his names as Merlin and Lailoken and claims to possess the gift of prophecy. He describes the battle as 'well known to all inhabitants of this country' and adds that it took place 'in the field that lies between Lidel and Carwanolow'. On reading this passage Skene remembered the Welsh Merlin poetry and was convinced that he had found a reference to the battle of Arfderydd. He felt that the precise location might be identifiable from the information provided by Bower. The name *Lidel* posed no problem, being a medieval form of *Liddel*, the river of Liddesdale that runs along today's Anglo-Scottish border to join the Esk near Carlisle. But Skene was intrigued by the name *Carwanolow* and began to wonder if it preserved some echo of Gwenddoleu, the king whose defeat and death was lamented so bitterly in the Merlin poems. Perusal of maps soon yielded the place-name *Carwinley*, a hamlet overlooking the junction of the rivers Esk and Liddel near the site of the Roman fort of Netherby. A search of medieval charters and other documents enabled Skene to trace the name *Carwinley* back to the thirteenth-century forms *Kaerwyndlo* and *Karwindelhou*, to which we can now add the variants *Carwyndelaue* and *Carwendelowe*.[7] Skene regarded these early forms as clear evidence that the modern name *Carwinley* and Bower's *Carwanolow* both derive from an original Brittonic name *Caer Gwenddoleu*,

'Gwenddoleu's Fort'. In addition, he observed that Carwinley lay on the northern edge of an ancient parish called *Arthuret*, a name he interpreted as the *Arfderydd* of Welsh tradition. The variants *Artureth*, *Arturede* and *Arrthured* in landholding documents of the twelfth and thirteenth centuries supported the identification.

Armed with his theories, Skene made a visit to the area in the 1870s. Not far from the parish church of St Michael's he noticed two glacial mounds known as the Arthuret Knowes. Upon the crown of one he found traces of a small earthen rampart, some 16 yards square, which he enthusiastically associated with the battle of 573. This mound, the higher of the two, has since been demolished by quarrying. After leaving the Knowes, Skene travelled 2 miles northward to Carwinley, where, to his delight, a farmer directed him to an old earthwork known locally as the 'Roman Camp'. On reaching the 'Camp', Skene quickly dismissed any Roman connection and identified the place as *Caer Gwenddoleu*. The farmer mentioned local traditions of a battle fought at the site between a Roman army and 300 Picts. The latter had bravely defended the stronghold before being slaughtered in a bloody massacre, after which they were buried in a mass grave in a nearby orchard. To Skene this seemed a garbled but genuine folk-memory of the battle of Arfderydd, with the defenders of Gwenddoleu's *caer* emerging from centuries of oral storytelling in the guise of 'Picts'. Another detail noted by Skene was the figure of 300, this being the typical strength of a warlord's *teulu* or personal retinue in Welsh heroic poetry.

Skene believed that the site of the battle lay among the ramparts of the 'Roman Camp'. He had no hesitation in identifying these earthworks as the remains of a sixth-century royal fortress. What he had actually found were the remains of Liddel Strength, otherwise known as the Moat of Liddel, the chief stronghold of an English barony established in Norman times. The place appears in twelfth-century documents as the residence of Turgis Brundos, a Flemish knight installed in the newly created barony of Liddel after the Norman conquest of Cumberland in the 1090s.[8] Turgis built a motte-and-bailey castle which served as the baronial centre for several centuries before passing through the hands of various noble families – the de Stutevilles, the Wakes, and finally the Grahams. It survived the Anglo-Scottish wars and the troubled era of the Border Reivers before eventually being abandoned by the Grahams in favour of a new residence at Netherby where, on the site of the Roman fort, they erected a mansion. The barony of Liddel thereafter became known as the Netherby Estate and the older residence at Liddel Strength fell into decay.[9] Only one notable event is known to have occurred at the 'Moat': a siege in 1346 by David II, king of Scotland, in which the original wooden tower was destroyed. Later, a small stone keep was erected in the inner bailey rather than on the motte-mound itself. Traces of this were apparently still visible as recently as the 1930s, but today the most impressive features are very substantial earthworks surrounding the central mound. Also worthy of note is the site's commanding position at the end of a low ridge overlooking the confluence of Esk and Liddel, its dominance of an important north–south land route at the head of the Solway Firth and its command of a ford.[10] Despite its strategic potential, its candidacy as an Early Historic centre of power remains uncertain until additional evidence comes to light. The earthworks still await archaeological investigation to unravel their history and to identify older features which might lie underneath. Any search for *Caer Gwenddoleu* must therefore admit Skene's identification as a possibility, while allowing the candidacy of other sites to be considered. One alternative is the Roman fort at Netherby, a place known to the Romans as *Castra Exploratorum*, 'The Fort of the Scouts'.

Netherby was excavated by archaeologists in the mid-twentieth century, but no evidence of Early Historic habitation was found.[11] Nevertheless, although the final phase of Roman activity seems to end in the fourth century, a hitherto unrecognised phase of later occupation by native Britons cannot be ruled out. The matter might be settled by a new excavation, but, until such time, we must regard Netherby as an open case. We can, however, make a number of relevant observations about the fort's significance as a centre of power within the locality. First, we may note that the discovery of two Roman altars dedicated to a god Huetris or Vitris suggests a nearby cult-centre. A possible analogy is the fort at Bewcastle, 11 miles to the east, whose Latin name *Fanum Cocidii*, 'Shrine of Cocidius', suggests that the Romans deliberately established a military presence at an ancient place of ritual. Something similar could have led to Netherby being chosen as the site of a fort, with links subsequently being forged between soldiers and natives via shared veneration of a local Celtic deity. This would have made the fort important in the eyes of the Britons and, after the Romans had gone, such importance could have been exploited by local elites.

Another fort providing a possible analogy with *Castra Exploratorum* lies south of Bewcastle at Birdoswald on Hadrian's Wall. Birdoswald shows clear evidence of post-Roman occupation by an elite group who built a timber building identified by archaeologists as the hall of a king or chieftain. Something similar could have happened at *Castra Exploratorum* if it indeed later became Gwenddoleu's *caer*. A different kind of analogy is found much further afield at a Roman site in North Wales. Here, the fort of *Kanovium* in the Conwy Valley is known today as *Caerhun*, a name deriving from *Caer Rhun*, 'Rhun's Fort'. Rhun was a contemporary of Gwenddoleu and likewise also a king, having ascended the throne of Gwynedd after the death of his father Maelgwn in 547. Why his name became attached to a Roman fort is something of a mystery, especially as no clear evidence of sixth-century occupation was found at *Kanovium* during excavations in the 1920s.[12] On the other hand, the archaeologists were not actively looking for a post-Roman phase and might not have recognised it. Coins unearthed at

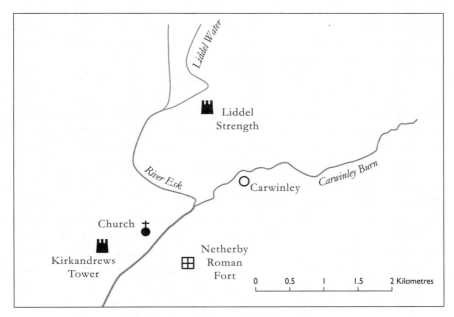

Gwenddoleu's kingdom: centres of power around Carwinley.

Caerhun include worn and well-used examples from the reigns of the early fifth-century emperors Honorius and Arcadius. These finds have prompted speculation that the fort was inhabited as late as the 420s. Caerhun's main significance for Netherby and *Caer Gwenddoleu* is its association with a sixth-century king famed in Welsh medieval lore: as we saw in the previous chapter, Rhun was the ruler of Gwynedd who allegedly fought a war against Rhydderch Hael and other Men of the North. We should remain open to the possibility that *Castra Exploratorum* by a similar association became known as *Caer Gwenddoleu*, especially if stories about the battle of Arfderydd circulated in the area long after the event took place.[13] The tenth and eleventh centuries saw a revival of Brittonic speech when the Solway region fell under the rule of Clyde-based kings and to this period we might assign a renewed interest in local heroic saga. Residual folk-memories associating Gwenddoleu with the district around Netherby may have led to his name being attached to the ancient Roman ruins. If, then, the hamlet of Carwinley owes its name to the Roman fort rather than to Liddel Strength, the latter would probably become irrelevant to discussions about the battle. At the present time we are in no position to disregard either site. Both are situated within a mile of the Carwinley Burn, the main topographical feature associated with the place-name, so neither has any special claim on the grounds of proximity. Elsewhere in the vicinity we seek other credible alternatives in vain, even if we widen our search to a 2-mile radius of the stream. The only places with early connotations of secular high status are Netherby and Liddel Strength. Having discussed the former, we now turn our attention back to the latter, and to Skene's belief that it had once been the stronghold of a warrior-king.

A first impression of Liddel Strength is that its habitable area is very small. Its summit is even smaller than that of the Mote of Mark, a diminutive hillfort on the Solway coast known to have been occupied in Early Historic times.[14] The dimensions of Liddel were measured and recorded by Skene when he visited the site. He observed that the north side, where a sheer rocky bank overlooks Liddesdale, rises to a height of 160 feet above the river. A massive earthen rampart 30 feet high encloses a space measuring 38 yards on an east–west axis and 55 yards north–south, within which lie a small 'inner citadel' and a well. A second great rampart is visible on the west side. Skene's findings were supplemented by a survey conducted in 1931 during a visit by members of the Dumfriesshire and Galloway Natural History and Antiquarian Society. The visit was reported in the Society's *Transactions* by T. Thornton Taylor who noted that Liddel Strength was unusual in that it seemed to consist of an inner and outer bailey, an uncommon character-istic in the Border area.[15] Commenting on the motte-mound, Taylor considered it sufficient to have supported a small wooden castle of the type depicted in the Bayeux Tapestry. He mused on the possibility that the presumed inner bailey and not the mound itself might have been the original 'motte', with the outer rampart marking the perimeter of a single-bailey stronghold more typical of the region. An alternative interpretation is that the inner rampart was simply the defensive wall of a single bailey which contained at its centre a small mound and tower. If this was the only Norman contribution to the defences of Liddel Strength, then the outer rampart may be much older. An archaeological investigation could perhaps reveal its age and purpose to confirm or reject Taylor's belief that the site had 'almost certainly been fortified from very early, possibly prehistoric, times'.[16]

It is interesting to note that the Anglo-Scottish border, which consistently follows the course of Liddel Water, briefly diverts from its direct line below Liddel Strength to follow instead the curve of a 'river cliff' cut into the base of the ridge. This cliff is a product of erosion caused by a long-vanished bend in the river's former course. It suggests that a portion of the ridge has fallen prey to the river, taking with it a section of the stronghold above. The size and shape of the area enclosed by the cliff – a patch of land known locally as 'Moat Cove' – point to a considerable landslip which destroyed part of the northern side of Liddel Strength. In the absence of a scientific survey, the date when this damage occurred can only be guessed, but it had already occurred before the mid-nine-teenth century when railway engineers laid a trackbed at the foot of the ridge. A lesser landslip on the eastern side removed part of the motte-mound, but neither this event nor the major erosion on the north can be dated with any measure of accuracy. However, since the lesser damage plainly occurred after the construction of the Norman defences at a time when the river flowed very close to the ridge, it is tempting to assign the larger landslip to the same era. What we now see at Liddel Strength may be the surviving portion of a much larger stronghold which partially collapsed before the modern period. If this is indeed the chronology of the erosion, we come a little nearer to Skene's idea of a major Early Historic citadel, in this case a promontory fort of somewhat greater size than the feature we see today. We might cautiously envisage a compact settlement enclosed by a single defensive earthwork – the rampart of the presumed 'outer bailey' of the Norman castle – with a gateway on the west or south. Aerial photography and antiquarian sketches not only suggest that the circuit of the rampart was originally far more extensive but also highlight the dramatic effect of the erosion. We begin to wonder if Skene's enthusiastic claim that he had discovered a fortress of the *Gwŷr y Gogledd* might not be wide of the mark.

Leaving the matter of *Caer Gwenddoleu* aside, we return to the battle of 573. In the Welsh triads Arfderydd appears as one of the Three Futile Battles, but this sheds no real light on its political context. Welsh tradition regarded the battle as futile because it pitched Briton against Briton at a time when they should have been uniting against the English invaders. Such a view represents political 'spin' in eighth- or ninth-century Wales among kings and nobles whose lands were threatened by Mercian and West Saxon warbands. Whether the combatants at Arfderydd paused to consider the intra-ethnic aspect of their contest is rather more doubtful. The victors who toppled Gwenddoleu would not have regarded their venture as futile, especially if his domains offered rich pickings like cattle and slaves. What, then, were their reasons for attacking, and how did the outcome affect the wider political picture?

The triad of the Three Futile Battles gives the cause of the battle as a lark's nest. One theory interprets this as a reference to Caerlaverock in Dumfriesshire, a place more famous today for its impressive thirteenth-century castle. This idea rests on the notion that *Caerlaverock* means 'Fort of the Lark' via the fusion of Brittonic *caer*, 'fort', with Old English *lawerce* (later *laverock*).[17] A more likely explanation of the name is that it is wholly Brittonic in origin, with *caer* preceding the personal name *Llywarch* to give the meaning 'Llywarch's Fort'.[18] Llywarch Hen, as we saw in the previous chapter, was associated by Welsh tradition with Urien Rheged and seems to have been a historical figure. Either he or a namesake presumably had some connection with Caerlaverock in history or folklore. In seeking a possible sixth-century residence in the vicinity our attention moves away from the low-lying castle to the hillfort of Wardlaw 1 mile northward. Wardlaw is a bivallate stronghold guarding the mouth of the River Nith, its strategic location prompting the Romans to build a fortress of their own alongside it. The hillfort has not been excavated and its history is unknown, but traces of prehistoric earth-works are still visible and it is possible that these were re-used in post-Roman times. This site is arguably the original *caer* of Caerlaverock, but, given the prob-able meaning 'Llywarch's Fort', there is no reason to connect it with the 'lark's nest' of the triad. Given also that the triad's main theme is pointless conflict, we should regard the 'lark's nest' as a bardic metaphor for futility and pettiness rather than as an etymological clue to the cause of the battle.

One popular hypothesis, first advanced by Skene, sees Arfderydd as a religious conflict between pagan and Christian factions. The alleged supporting evidence draws on triadic references to magical items owned by Gwenddoleu together with allusions in the Merlin poetry to practices reminiscent of shamanism.[18] Coupled with the likelihood that Gwenddoleu's opponents were Christian kings, this evidence seems, in some quarters, to be credible and compelling. As a contribu-tion to sixth-century history the entire scenario has little value, chiefly because it requires uncritical acceptance of vague details in the triads as historical facts rather than as literary themes. Triadic references to Gwenddoleu's magical posses-sions – an enchanted chessboard and man-eating birds – are not indicators of pagan beliefs but of his transformation into a figure of legend. It is unwise and misleading to confuse his literary development in Wales with his career as a North British warlord. Nor is there any reason to suppose that Christian kings of the sixth century were motivated by a crusading spirit or that the burden of royal duties allowed the luxury of religious warfare. Indeed, if the monarchs castigated by Gildas are a representative sample, the Christian zeal of some British kings extended no further than giving token allegiance to the Church. Others may have displayed genuine piety, while a few perhaps continued to embrace the pagan-ism of their ancestors as stubbornly as did their Pictish contemporaries further north. However, even allowing for the survival of heathen enclaves among the Britons, we have no warrant for placing Gwenddoleu's kingdom among them, nor for believing that this would have made him a target for religiously motivated aggression.

Setting aside the larks' nests and Christian crusades, we can search more objec-tively for the causes of the battle. A combination of factors may have provided the real motive for the campaign, especially if – as later tradition believed – several kingdoms were involved. The immediate geographical context was the district of Arfderydd where Gwenddoleu maintained a *caer* as his primary residence. No doubt his enemies came seeking plunder or conquest, but whether their plans included the destruction of Gwenddoleu himself is less certain. Success in war enhanced personal status and the victors at Arfderydd would have emerged with their military reputations greatly increased, especially if their opponent had been a mighty warlord in his own right. The genealogies of the Men of the North trace the ancestries of Gwenddoleu and his foes back to Coel Hen, but, as previously noted, such kinship should be regarded as artificial and retrospective. Thus, although the Arfderydd campaign is sometimes viewed as 'a clan skirmish among the Coelings',[20] the protagonists were probably not inter-related.

Of the kings associated with the battle only Gwenddoleu can be located with any measure of confidence. Arthuret and Carwinley may have lain at the heart of his realm, but how far his power extended beyond this zone is a matter of conjecture. Eskdale and Liddesdale presumably lay under the authority of whoever controlled their confluence and both valleys may be regarded as subject to Gwenddoleu. Various other districts around the head of the Solway Firth may have been similarly answerable to him, especially if he was a renowned war-leader from whom lesser lords sought protection and patronage. His core territory perhaps corresponded in some form with the later barony of Liddel, an administrative unit established by the Normans after their conquest of northern England in the last decade of the eleventh century. In many areas the conquerors created baronies on a pre-existing framework of territorial divisions consisting of agricultural estates and centres of power formerly held by English lords.[21] Among these units were some of great antiquity whose origins may lie in the period of British rule before the English takeover in the seventh century. The barony of Liddel might be one such unit, its eleventh-century focus of power at the junction of two mighty rivers perhaps overlying an earlier stronghold situated near a Roman fort. Across the Anglo-Scottish border the English barony was eventually mirrored by a Scottish counterpart, the barony of Liddesdale.[22] In the late sixth century, long before the medieval Border came into being, the area later represented by the two baronies possibly formed a single unit of lordship ruled by Gwenddoleu.

None of the other kings at Arfderydd in 573 can be located on a modern map, despite several attempts to identify their realms. Gwrgi and Peredur, the sons of Eliffer, appear in the sources as Gwenddoleu's chief foes, but neither they nor their father can be assigned a precise geographical context. The brothers are not mentioned in the Merlin poetry, but Welsh tradition added a hero named Peredur to the legends of King Arthur. The father of the Arthurian Peredur was *Efrog Iarll* who bears a name meaning 'Earl of York'. This has prompted speculation that the sixth-century Peredur actually hailed from York, despite the annals and triads consistently naming his father as Eliffer *Gosgorddfawr*, 'Great Warband'. There is in fact no need to conflate the two Peredurs and no reason to connect the historical one with York. The latter was a major northern earldom in the period when the medieval romance of Peredur came into being and may have seemed a suitably high-status base for the Arthurian hero. A better approach to the question of where the sons of Eliffer came from is to accept that their precise geographical context cannot be retrieved from the data available to us. Acknowledging this gap in our knowledge liberates us from the need to search for vague clues among sources that fail even the most basic tests of historical reliability. Of Gwrgi and Peredur the most we can say is that they were active in North Britain in the third quarter of the sixth century, that they were capable of launching a military venture against a kingdom whose focus lay at the confluence of Esk and Liddel, and that they were sufficiently powerful to defeat the ruler of that kingdom. Although the annals and triads usually mention the brothers as if they represent a single political entity, we should be wary of assuming that they ruled jointly. They may have ruled separate portions of their father's kingdom, uniting only for specific events such as the Arfderydd campaign. In literature they are nevertheless consistently depicted as close allies, their names being linked even in death. According to the triad of the 'Three Faithless Warbands' they were killed in battle at *Caer Greu* after being abandoned by their soldiers. Their opponent was Eda *Glinmawr*, 'Big Knee', a man bearing what appears to be an English forename, whom the author of the *Historia Brittonum* wrongly equated with Eata, a Bernician prince of the eighth century. The location of *Caer Greu* is unknown, but the simultaneous demise of Gwrgi and Peredur is entered in the Welsh Annals at 580, a date broadly consistent with military activity in the early 570s. It may be unduly speculative to wonder if their success at Arfderydd fed their ambitions too richly, bringing them into conflict with mightier foes who eventually destroyed them. It is interesting to note that neither they nor Gwenddoleu, nor indeed any of the Arfderydd participants, are connected in early Welsh tradition with Urien Rheged or other northern heroes. The seventeenth-century poet Robert Vaughan numbered Rhydderch Hael among Gwenddoleu's enemies at Arfderydd, but he was evidently the first to do so. Vaughan's sole warrant for this was Rhydderch's presence in the Merlin poems as a tyrannical king who terrorised Gwenddoleu's exiled bard.

The Welsh Annals note the death, in 595, of King Dunod. This entry may mark the passing of Dunod the Stout, one of the allies of Gwrgi and Peredur at Arfderydd. His kingdom likewise defies identification. In the North British pedigrees his father is Pabo *Post Prydein*, 'Pillar of Britain', whose lineage goes back to Coel Hen. Another group of pedigrees, the twelfth-century collection *Bonedd y Seint*, 'Descent of the Saints', attaches several Welsh and Irish saints to Dunod's family. This has prompted the notion that he and his kinsmen had important ecclesiastical connections. One of these saints is Sanctan or Santan, a name commemorated at Kirksanton in the modern county of Cumbria. In the same area lies the Roman fort of Papcastle, a place bearing a name apparently derived from Old Norse *papi*, 'hermit', but seen in some quarters as preserving a memory of Dunod's father Pabo. These place-names have led to a suggestion that Dunod ruled in some western district of Cumbria.[23] In the east of the same county Dent has been seen as a modern form of the Old English place-name *Dunutinga* which appears in a seventh-century *Vita* of Saint Wilfrid. Because *Dunutinga* might mean 'Land of Dunod's people' the area around Dent has been proposed as yet another domain of Dunod the Stout. Cardunneth in the north of the county seems to mean 'Dunod's Fort' and we could additionally bring this place into the discussion.[24] Taking all of these ideas together would assign Dunod a large kingdom comprising the whole of the former county of Cumberland. An alternative view is that the alleged ecclesiastical connections of his family are extremely tenuous and that *Dunutinga* might merely mean 'People of Dent'.[25] Setting all this speculation aside allows us to acknowledge that we lack a precise geographical context for Dunod. He therefore joins Urien, Gwallawg, Morcant and the sons of Eliffer as a North British hero whose kingdom remains unlocated.

The remaining Arfderydd participants listed in the triads are Cynfelyn the Leprous, Dreon ap Nudd and Dinogad, none of whom can be placed in a specific geographical context. Cynfelyn appears in the pedigrees as a brother of Cadrod Calchfynydd who, as we have seen, may have ruled a domain near Kelso. Perhaps Cynfelyn ruled in the same area, either in his own separate kingdom or at Calchfynydd as Cadrod's predecessor or successor? Dreon is absent from the genealogical texts, but, if his father is the Nudd listed there as Gwenddoleu's brother, we might place him among the defeated faction at Arfderydd. The memorial stone at Yarrow, previously mentioned, commemorates a prince called Nudd, but the name was not uncommon in the North and the stone probably has no connection with the combatants of 573. Dinogad, named in the triad as a son of Cynan Garwyn, is a puzzling addition, his father being a king of Powys in Wales. One of Cynan's sons apparently perished at the battle of Chester in 615 and it is not impossible that an older son, perhaps born of a different mother, participated in a northern war 40 years earlier. Nevertheless, Dinogad looks like an intruder into the Arfderydd lore, a Powys prince attached to the triad of the 'Three Horse Burdens' by a later Welsh scribe who favoured Cynan's dynasty. Alternatively, his father might have been a different Cynan, perhaps a northern namesake whom later Welsh tradition conflated with Cynan Garwyn of Powys. Further speculation about Dinogad adds little to our understanding of the Arfderydd campaign. We must place him alongside other heroes whose realms we cannot identify. That this group includes all but one of the battle's participants is a sober comment on the limitations of our sources. The lone exception is Gwenddoleu whom we can fairly confidently assign to a kingdom near the junction of Eskdale and Liddesdale.

Catraeth

Taliesin, the court-bard of Rheged, includes among Urien's domains a district called *Catraeth*. This is conventionally identified as Catterick in the modern county of North Yorkshire, a place known today as a major garrison town. The identification presents an obstacle for supporters of the theory that Rheged lay around the Solway Firth, for Catterick is 80 miles from the Solway and the Pennine hills lie in between. Acknowledgment of this problem is surprisingly rare, but its essence was neatly summarised by Ian Lovecy who wrote: 'Rheged seems a very large area in sixth-century terms to have been administered by one man living in its north-western corner'.[26] In other words, how can we envisage Urien as a king on the Solway while at the same time ruling a district on the eastern side of the Pennines? Various theories have been put forward to explain away this geographical difficulty. It has been suggested that the references to Catraeth in the Taliesin poems are later Welsh interpolations designed to promote Urien as a sovereign of wide-ranging power.[27] This finds less favour than a general acceptance that the Catraeth references are original and genuine, and that they relate to the actual extent of Urien's kingdom. Reconciling Catraeth's usual identification as Catterick with Rheged's traditional placement on the Solway is not, however, straightforward. Dr Lovecy saw Catterick as a south-eastern 'outpost' of Urien's kingdom, although we might wonder what this term might mean in a sixth-century context.[28] Urien and his peers lived in an age of aristocratic warbands who fought as the personal retinues of their lords, an era when the notion of military units manning frontier strongholds belonged to the Roman past. An alternative theory sees Urien's original domain lying not west but east of the Pennines and that from here he perhaps took control of Rheged at a time of uncertainty, striking westward from his main centre of power at Catraeth.[29] Such a view contradicts Taliesin's emphasis on Rheged as Urien's most important territory: Catraeth appears only twice in the poems whereas Rheged is mentioned eight times. There seems little justification for placing Urien's primary domain at Catraeth.

It is instructive to note that the identification of Catraeth as Catterick was not made by Taliesin, nor by any other sixth-century poet. It originated in 1853 in a paper delivered to the Abergevenny Eisteddfod by the respected Welsh scholar Thomas Stephens, reaching a wider audience 35 years later when the paper was published.[30] Since then, the Catraeth = Catterick equation has been endorsed so often by successive writers that its origin as a nineteenth-century guess has been forgotten. There is not, as Stephens correctly deduced, any linguistic obstacle to the theory – Catraeth and Catterick *could* be variant forms of the same name – but this merely confirms the philological validity. It does not confirm the geographical identification.

Taliesin is not our only early source of information on Catraeth. The place takes a far more prominent role in *Y Gododdin*, 'The Gododdin', a long poem or collection of verses attributed to Taliesin's contemporary Aneirin.[31] As its title suggests, the *Gododdin* commemorates the people anciently called Votadini whose heartland lay in Lothian. The verses praise a warband of 300 horsemen who rode from Din Eidyn to a battle at Catraeth. They fought on behalf of a Votadinian king, but he did not accompany them on the venture. Instead, for reasons not stated, he delegated command to one or more subordinates. The fact that he did not lead the warband in person is remarkable and suggests that he regarded the venture as a minor event unworthy of his presence. Had it been a long-planned campaign of invasion and conquest he would surely have ridden at the head of his troops.[32] Or, if illness prevented his participation, he could have sent a son or another male relative. There is much debate about this king's name, with one school of thought identifying him in the poem as a shadowy figure called Mynyddog while another interprets *mynyddog* as an adjective pertaining to the *mynydd* or 'hill' of Edinburgh Castle Rock. In the battle of Catraeth the British warriors were heavily defeated, suffering heavy losses, but their bravery was commemorated in the *Gododdin* verses. A flavour of the latter can be gained from the following examples.

> Warriors went to Catraeth, embattled, with a cry,
> a host of horsemen in dark-blue armour, with shields,
> spear-shafts held aloft with sharp points,
> and shining mail-shirts and swords.[33]

> Amid scattered weapons, broken ranks, standing steadfast,
> with great destruction the champion overthrew the host of the men of
>   England.
> He cast lances in the forefront of battle in the spearfight,
> he laid men low and made women widows before his death,
> Graid son of Hoywgi formed a battle-pen against the spears.[34]

The *Gododdin* survives in a thirteenth-century Welsh manuscript, the *Book of Aneirin*, in two incomplete versions called by modern scholars A and B. The 42 verses of B contain archaic spellings, whereas the A text, which has 88 verses, is written in the style of the thirteenth century. Analysis of B shows it to be a copy of a much earlier text of the ninth or tenth century and thus brings it closer to the era of the battle. Although it is the older of the two versions, it was copied into the manuscript after A and by a different scribe. Both texts yield traces of older forms of the Welsh language and seem to represent two distinct paths of transmission deriving ultimately from a lost original of the sixth century or, more probably, of the seventh.[35] Whether this original poem, or collection of poems, ever existed in written form is unknown, but a period of oral preservation among North British bards is generally assumed. It was certainly known in Wales before the ninth century, perhaps before c.700, evidently in oral and written forms. At some point the process of transmission divided into two separate strands to eventually produce the A and B versions known today. Historians and archaeologists, as opposed to philologists and palaeographers, are accustomed to treat these two texts as a single work of literature. This is mainly for convenience and brevity and is the approach adopted here. The collection of verses is therefore cited in the following discussion as the *Gododdin* or as simply 'the poem' without further discussion of its possible origin as an anthology of separate works.

At the beginning of the thirteenth-century manuscript the scribe of the A text wrote in red ink: *Hwn yw e gododin aneirin ae cant*, 'This is the *Gododdin*. Aneirin sang it.' As we saw in the previous chapter, Aneirin appears in the *Historia Brittonum* alongside Taliesin and two other sixth-century poets. We will never know how much of the *Gododdin* should be attributed to him. He describes himself in the poem as a Votadinian, a contemporary of the slain warriors whose destruction he mourns, and – more controversially – as a survivor of the battle of Catraeth. In the two surviving versions the enemy is identified as English, appearing variously as the men of *Deor*, *Dewr* or *Deifr*, 'Deira', or of *Lloegyr*, 'England'. Bernicia, the English realm closest to Gododdin, appears in the A text as *Brynaich*. Its absence from the older B text seems curious, but we may note that B is the more incomplete of the two and might be a selective treatment of the original.[36] Moreover, given the possibility that Ida and his kin came originally from Deira, we need not assume that they would necessarily appear in the poem as 'Bernicians'. Some modern scholars believe that the references to English foes should be seen as later accretions after the poem's arrival in Wales.[37] The *Gododdin* is nevertheless consistent in describing the enemy as English and this theme might therefore have belonged to the original composition.

Aneirin is slightly more informative than Taliesin about the location of Catraeth, telling us that it lay on the frontier of the Gododdin kingdom. He adds that one objective of the British warriors was 'to redeem the land of Catraeth', a task which saw them 'defending their land' by advancing 'over their boundary'.[38] These references imply that Catraeth bordered on Votadinian lands at the time of the battle, that the English had conquered it, and that the British attempt to 'redeem' it was seen as an act of defence rather than aggression. Aneirin does not imply that Catraeth had recently belonged to Gododdin. The Votadinian warriors were sent not to reclaim it but to redeem it, to wrest it from an enemy who posed a grave threat along their border. At no point do we find any mention of Rheged, despite Taliesin's assertion that Catraeth lay within Urien's domains. This might indicate that Urien was already dead, or that he was ignored by Aneirin for some other reason, or that the surviving *Gododdin* verses represent an incomplete record of the British participants. Urien's absence is sometimes seen as evidence for dating the battle before (or after) his reign, but we know too little of sixth-century history to make such assumptions. It is even possible that he is not absent from the *Gododdin* at all, and that one verse refers to his warband's presence in the battle on the English side. The verse in question describes *meibyon Godebawg*, 'the descendants of Godebawg', as enemies of the Votadini and is usually seen as alluding to Urien's ancestor Coel Hen who bears the epithet *Godebawg*, 'Protector', in the North British pedigrees.[39]

Rheged's relationship with Gododdin at the time of the battle cannot be discerned, nor can the event be dated more precisely than the second half of the sixth century or the early years of the seventh. Surprisingly, no similar air of uncertainty surrounds the conventional identification of Catraeth as Catterick, despite its origin as a nineteenth-century guess. In describing the Votadinian warriors 'advancing over their boundary' and 'defending their land' Aneirin surely envisaged the battle being fought in a frontier zone between the Gododdin kingdom and its foes, whom he identifies as English. Gododdin's nearest English neighbour was Bernicia, south of which lay the longer-established realm of Deira. Catterick was an important site in the Deiran heartlands, a place selected by the Romans for a fort and civilian settlement. It lay at the junction of two major Roman roads, one of which followed a north-westerly course through the Pennines via the Stainmore Pass to provide a link between York and Carlisle. The other, known since medieval times as 'Dere Street', was the main north–south route running the full length of eastern Britain from London to the Firth of Forth. This road was the primary link between Deira and Bernicia, and also between Bernicia and Gododdin. Deira's precise limits are unknown, but it was broadly coterminous with the pre-1974 county of Yorkshire. If Deira's northern border reached as far as the Tees, and if the southernmost limit of Gododdin reached to the Tweed, then the distance between the two kingdoms was 90 miles. Since Catterick lies a further 10 miles south of the Tees, the Gododdin warband would have faced a journey of at least 100 miles to arrive there for a battle. Pre-modern military forces, whether on foot or horseback, typically travelled 20 or 25 miles per day, a rate of march which would have brought the Votadinian warriors to Catterick in four or five days. This seems less like an advance 'over their boundary' with the aim of 'defending their land' than a long-range invasion into the heart of a distant kingdom. Such an expedition would have required the British force to ignore the much closer menace of Bernicia, whose English-speaking elite was already flexing its military muscle under the rule of Ida's dynasty. The Bernician threat was sufficiently acute to occupy the attentions of Urien Rheged, Rhydderch Hael and other contemporary British kings but not – according to supporters of the Catterick hypothesis – the king of Gododdin. This important point, although rarely noted, drew the following remark from one commentator: 'It has never been fully explained why Urien should have concentrated his forces against Bernicia, while Gododdin ignored its neighbour and struck at the southern king-dom, based in Yorkshire.'[40]

Ignoring Bernicia while striking into the heart of Deira seems illogical not only politically but militarily. Aside from the logistical requirements of a 100-mile journey from Tweeddale to Catterick the Gododdin warriors would have had to take a considerable risk, as Kenneth Jackson recognised, 'for they would expose themselves to the whole line of the Bernician coastal settlement; particularly, at any rate, on reaching the Tyne at Corbridge'.[41] Indeed, if formerly British Berneich lay under the control of Ida's family, we should wonder how and why a Votadinian warband passed along the edge of this realm to attack a far more distant foe at Catterick. A theory that the power of Ida's kin was restricted to a strip of coastline around Bamburgh seemed at one time to answer this objection, but it has few supporters today. It contradicts the evidence for rapid and complete Anglicisation of Berneich during the sixth century and denies the embryonic English dynasty a substantial domain. The idea of an army from Edinburgh striking south at the Deirans while casually ignoring Bernicia thus raises several problems for the Catraeth = Catterick theory. Such objections are usually brushed aside by imag-ining the Gododdin force travelling not on the main north–south alignment of Dere Street but via an alternative route through Carlisle to approach Catterick from the Stainmore Pass, thus avoiding Bernicia by taking a wide detour. How this lengthy diversion equates to Aneirin's simple statement that the Votadinian warriors advanced 'over their boundary' is hard to explain when the inherent logistical difficulties are pointed out:

> The distance travelled was between a hundred and fifty and two hundred miles and there would have been many problems of organisation, particu-larly if both cavalry and infantry were involved . . . . How long the journey took can only be conjectured. Especially uncertain is how the Gododdin host coped with the question of supplies: did it live by plunder or did it receive support from any surviving inhabitants of Urien's former kingdom?[42]

A simple question arises: if both the western and eastern routes present prob-lems for the Catraeth = Catterick theory, is not the theory itself open to doubt? Adhering to the Catterick identification ignores the only geographical evidence supplied by Aneirin with regard to the battlefield, namely that the Gododdin warriors reached Catraeth by 'advancing over their boundary' in the hope of 'defending their land'. We are asked instead to picture a band of horsemen from Lothian seeking to protect their border by attacking faraway Catterick. Contrary to the views of some historians we cannot sustain this scenario by bolstering the warband with infantry regiments to turn it into a mighty invasion force. No additional troops are mentioned in the poem and there is no hint that they lurk in the background. In any case, a large mass of armed men marching down from Gododdin would surely have aroused the wrath of any realm through which they passed. Even a warband of 300, a respectable size for a raiding-party, would not have been allowed to pass unchallenged. Yet the Catterick theory asks us to imagine a docile, submissive Bernicia allowing the edge of her territory to be traversed in the very period when Ida's dynasty was engaged in aggressive warfare. The dynasty was neutralised between 617 and 633 when Edwin of Deira seized the Bernician lands and this period has been suggested as a possible window of opportunity for the Gododdin assault on Catraeth.[43] Although such an idea illustrates the broad chronology available for dating the battle, it nonetheless imagines a Bernician warrior-nobility acknowledging Edwin's overlordship while at the same time showing reluctance to fight on his behalf. Regardless of the fact that Edwin maintained a major royal centre at Yeavering in the heart of their territory, his Bernician clients would have sworn fealty to him as the price of retaining their estates and – willingly or unwillingly – would have given military service as part of the deal. All of the foregoing considerations suggest that the Catterick identification – which in any case originated as a guess based on 'sounds like' etymology – holds little credibility beyond a philological argument.[44] Away from the linguistic musings we see a range of logistical factors, including geographical clues in the poem itself, which point to an area much closer to the Votadinian heartlands. Catraeth might therefore be sought more objectively on the outer fringe of Lothian, perhaps in some district around lower Tweeddale at the interface between Bernicia and her British neighbours.

We must, however, pause to consider the place-name evidence which, we are told, weighs very heavily in Catterick's favour. It is because of this evidence that the Catterick identification is not only rarely questioned but frequently viewed as an incontrovertible fact. Almost all discussion of the battle of Catraeth advances from this 'factoid' with little acknowledgment of its theoretical basis. It rests on a detailed philological argument created to prove that modern English *Catterick* and Old Welsh *Catraeth* refer to the same place. Both names, it is argued, derive from variant forms of the Roman place-name *Cataracta* which the English of Bede's day knew as *Cetreht*. The origin of *Cataracta* is uncertain, but it ultimately derives from a native Brittonic term, perhaps *Caturacto*, 'battle rampart', whose spoken form sounded to Roman ears like Latin *catarracta*, 'cataract, waterfall'.[45] Philologists concede that *Catraeth* could not have evolved directly from

Caturacto, but, like *Cetreht*, may have descended from *Cataracto*, a name which in Late Roman times had become *Cataracta*.[46] There is no cataract or prominent waterfall at Catterick, the nearest being at Richmond 4 miles westward, but this did not deter the Romans from adapting an unfamiliar native name to a more familiar-sounding one in their own language when they established a settlement there. In the post-Roman period the name would have been known among speakers of Brittonic as *Cadarachta*, subsequently developing into *Cadracht* or *Catracht* and prompting the Old English form *Cetreht*.[47] The philological case for the Catraeth = Catterick equation hinges on the likelihood that Brittonic *Cadarachta* could have become Welsh *Catraeth*, and on the *possibility* that the latter name was formerly borne by Catterick. As Kenneth Jackson pointed out, in reference to a magisterial study of *Y Gododdin* by Sir Ifor Williams: 'Sir Ifor discusses at length whether the Catraeth of the poems can be Catterick, philologically speaking. There is no doubt that it can.' Jackson emphasised the point when he added: 'There is no doubt, therefore, that the traditional identification of Catraeth with Catterick is unobjectionable philologically.'[48] Neither of these assertions can be denied and there should be no doubt that Catraeth *could* be an Old Welsh form of the name we know today as *Catterick*. The philological argument does not, however, prove the geographical theory, namely that Catraeth and Catterick are definitely one and the same. It merely shows that, *philologically speaking*, their names might have the same origin. This is hardly remarkable, for many place-names in the British Isles share similarities in their modern or older forms and display similar etymologies. Moreover, the argument itself originated not to clarify geographical information provided by Taliesin or Aneirin but to offer linguistic support for a theory first aired by Thomas Stephens in 1853. The Catterick hypothesis is therefore circular in origin, a philological tail-chaser, proceeding from a linguistic guess to a historical guess and riding roughshod over any objections that lie between. It begins and ends with the unproven 'fact' of the Catraeth = Catterick equation rather than from a necessary consideration of other factors. It ignores, for instance, the literary evidence of the *Gododdin*, most notably a strong hint that the battle occurred near the Votadinian frontier. Even if we stretch this borderland to a hypothetical limit on the River Tees we cannot ignore the weightier opinion of archaeology. Material evidence indicates that the southern boundary of a Votadinian cultural identity lay on the Tweed in the late sixth century. A marked difference in material culture between areas north and south of the river is apparent as far back as the early fifth century, hinting at a political frontier along Tweeddale in Late Roman times.[49] There is no archaeological evidence for cultural unity between the native populations of these two areas, a point which suggests that the southern group were not in fact Votadinian. This might make it unlikely that the men of Gododdin could be regarded as 'defending their land' in any district south of the Tweed. Catterick, it may be noted, lies not only south of this river but also south of the Tyne and the Tees.

The philological argument is frequently reinforced by reminders of Catterick's 'strategic' importance in the context of Early Historic warfare. In particular, the location of the old Roman settlement at an important road junction has been seen as a key factor in its selection as a Votadinian target.[50] But would Catterick have seemed a useful objective for a warband of Britons from Lothian? What strategic purpose would have been served by launching a long-range assault on a place located deep inside Deiran territory? In answer to these questions supporters of the Catterick theory propose the idea of an attack at the interface between the English realms of Deira and Bernicia, on the grounds that 'the point of attacking them at Catterick would surely be the well-known principle of hitting such an alliance at the point of junction, where coherence is weakest'.[51] In the *Gododdin* the British warband is heavily outnumbered, overwhelmed and almost annihilated, thereby implying that the enemy's coherence at Catraeth was not very weak at all. The strategic argument in favour of Catterick is actually quite difficult to accept, not least because an outnumbered force striking at the heartland of its foes can hardly be said to employ any well-known principle of military tactics. Another school of thought places the battle against a backdrop of ethnic conflict:

> News had reached Dineiddyn that the English invaders, the Angles or Saxons of Northumbria, had pushed far inland and captured Catraeth, Richmond or Catterick, on the Roman road leading northwards. The road to the north was thus open to the enemy. Catraeth had to be recovered at all cost.[52]

We might wonder if news of the long-established Anglo-Saxon population at distant Catterick would have been more worrying to Votadinian ears than tidings of Bernician raids on the farmlands of Lothian. The 'road to the north' was open to the English not because the Deirans held Catterick but because the kingship of Bernicia had recently passed to Ida's family. At this point we should note a suggestion that the battle of Catraeth might have occurred not around c.600 – the date generally accepted by most commentators – but around c.540 before Ida's dynasty became a significant menace.[53] In this scenario the Votadinian warband was able to attack Deira because English Bernicia was not yet a major power. Although this neatly deals with the apparent absence of Bernicians from the older B text of the poem, it does not explain why a king of pre-English Berneich allowed a warband from Din Eidyn to ride past his lands. We have no reason to assume that British Berneich was subordinate to, or on friendly terms with, its northern neighbour. In any case, the conventional date of the battle seems a better fit with chronological clues given by the poet which point to the years around c.600. At that time a king of Gododdin would have been less concerned with the Deirans than with the much closer Bernicians. Deiran Catterick lay 150 miles away from Din Eidyn, a considerable distance in the context of Early Historic warfare. A week-long trek on foot or horseback to a faraway battlefield deep in hostile territory was no quick and easy venture. However, the perils and logistical problems are rarely noted by supporters of the Catterick theory, some of whom see the idea of a long and dangerous journey into the heart of Deira as consistent with themes of heroic sacrifice in the *Gododdin*. The most extreme form of this heroic interpretation sees the Catraeth expedition as a suicidal attempt by the Britons to dislodge the main concentration of Anglo-Saxons in Deira.[54] An eloquent picture of such selfless valour was painted by Sir Ifor Williams when he envisaged the king of Din Eidyn assembling a force of warriors, giving them a sumptuous feast, 'and then after mead, and in return for mead, he set them the hopeless task of riding through the enemy to Catraeth'.[55] Brian Hope-Taylor, an archaeologist whose excavations at Yeavering greatly advanced our understanding of early English settlement in the North, wondered why the Votadini would choose to attack the Deirans rather than the Bernicians around c.600. He suggested that 'acceptance of the Catraeth-Catterick equation at so late a date requires that the British expedition was mounted to make a desperately experimental raid beyond the Hadrianic line, designed to isolate Bernicia from Deira'.[56] With regard to Bernicia he added that the king of Gododdin 'would have done better to settle the petty little problem that lay on his own doorstep, at half the cost'.

Phrases like 'hopeless task' and 'desperately experimental' conform to the heroic ethos of the *Gododdin* and provide excuses for a suicidal mission but become unnecessary if we take the bold step of uncoupling Catraeth from Catterick. There is no reason why Catraeth should not be sought further north, in the present Anglo-Scottish borderlands, where a clash between the lords of Din Eidyn and their English neighbours might be reasonably expected. In any case, we should be wary of seeing the battle in purely ethnic terms, as a struggle between indigenous Britons on one side and immigrant Anglo-Saxons on the other. It was more likely to have been a contest between two competing elites whose leaders nurtured similar territorial ambitions. A closer look at the Taliesin poems and the triads shows Urien Rheged warring indiscriminately against Britons and Englishmen alike. He was slain by Britons, not by Englishmen, and the most famous battle of the Men of the North was fought among the Britons themselves in 573. Like Arfderydd and the campaigns of Urien, the battle of Catraeth was probably a frontier squabble or a contest for territory. Far from being an ethnic conflict fought between Celts and Saxons it should be seen as a normal response by Gododdin to a hostile neighbour. The Gododdin force apparently included Britons from other kingdoms,

Hadrian's Wall.

Birdoswald: the east gate of the Roman fort.

ABOVE AND OPPOSITE. The Yarrow Stone: a sixth-century monument commemorating Nudus and Dumnogenos, the sons of Liberalis.

Alt Clut, the Rock of Clyde, still dominates the landscape at the head of the firth.

Kirkmadrine in the Rhinns of Galloway: a place of Christian worship since Early Historic times.

Paisley Abbey: a modern carving, in wood, of the sixth-century Saint Mirin or Mirren.

The parish church at Luss on the shore of Loch Lomond. Here, according to tradition, Saint Kessog established a religious settlement in the sixth century.

The Stone of the Britons: *Clach nam Breatainn* on the western slopes of Glen Falloch.

Birdoswald Roman fort: markers showing the post-holes of an Early Historic timber hall built on the site of a Roman granary.

Paisley Abbey, built on the presumed site of an Early Christian basilica.

ABOVE AND OPPOSITE. Arfderydd and Caer Gwenddoleu: aerial views of the medieval motte at Liddel Strength. Was this the site of the battle of 573? Copyright © Cumbria County Council.

ABOVE AND OPPOSITE. The Arthurlie Cross: tenth- or eleventh-century craftsmanship from the kingdom of Strathclyde.

ABOVE AND OPPOSITE. Echoes of the Govan School in Clydesdale: the tenth-century Netherton Cross at Hamilton.

The expansion of Northumbrian power: the eighth-century Bewcastle Cross, 10 miles northeast of Carlisle.

Hogback gravestone at Luss, showing Scandinavian influence on the Govan sculptural tradition.

Alt Clut: a view of Dumbarton Rock from the south bank of the Clyde.

ABOVE. The church and village of Carham-on-Tweed. Near here was fought the 'great battle' of 1018.

RIGHT. The Giant's Grave, Penrith: a composite monument associated with the legendary giant Ewan Caesarius.

men who came to Din Eidyn because the king who resided there was a successful raider who shared his loot around. They did not come because he was mustering an anti-English army. The alleged non-Votadinian element in the warband carries no implication of a pan-British alliance. Among the 'British' heroes who fought at Catraeth some were possibly of English stock, or represented communities in which an English cultural identity was proudly displayed.

The Catraeth = Catterick theory exerts a huge and unwarranted influence over modern perceptions of sixth-century history. Although Catterick and Catraeth are not connected in any text before the mid-nineteenth century, they have become so inextricably linked that the 'battle of Catterick' is now an accepted term for the event described in the *Gododdin*. Doubts about the identification are surprisingly rare. Scepticism was voiced 30 years ago by Dr Hope-Taylor who would have placed Catraeth in the vale of Tweed had he not been convinced by the well-trodden philological argument.[57] Another dissenting voice was Matthew McDiarmid who regarded the Catterick theory as untenable for reasons similar to the ones given above. Dr McDiarmid rightly remarked that the identification origin-ated as nothing more than a philologist's guess and made the additional point, too often overlooked by historians, that there is no record of Catterick ever having been known as *Catraeth*.[58] Thus, although the eighth-century Northumbrian form *Cetreht* is philologically close to Welsh *Catraeth*, such similarity does not by itself *prove* the Catraeth = Catterick theory. The fragility of the identification was noted even by Kenneth Jackson when he suggested that, if Catterick was not the battle site, we should look for Catraeth 'somewhere further north, perhaps near the Roman Wall'.[59] If the battle was indeed fought in this region, perhaps between Tyne and Tweed, then the Votadinian warriors would have had no anxi-ety about the logistics of a long-range campaign, nor would their venture have seemed a desperately experimental or hopeless task. They would have ridden to the border to defend the territory of their king, travelling no great distance from the royal citadel at Din Eidyn. Likewise, when Urien Rheged surveyed his domain at Catraeth, he would have gazed across the northern heartlands of the *Gwŷr y Gogledd* rather than at a distant southern 'outpost'. By relocating Catraeth to Tweeddale or Lothian we might imagine Urien's kingdom as a compact, coherent realm rather than as the sprawling trans-Pennine empire so frequently assigned to him.

NORTHUMBRIA

After Urien

Urien Rheged was dead before the end of the sixth century, his demise at the instigation of Morcant ending the hegemony forged by his military achievements. With him died the networks of allegiance that had sustained his wealth and power. Any client rulers and subordinate kings to whom he had been overlord and patron were now freed to follow their own paths, either by pursuing independent ambitions or by seeking protection and patronage elsewhere. Welsh tradition indicates that Urien was succeeded by his sons, although we do not know which of these actually reigned or in what order they took the kingship. The famous Owain, presumably the heir-apparent of Rheged, either succeeded or predeceased Urien and is the only son identified by Taliesin. Long after his lifetime he was remoulded as a character of Arthurian legend and given a major role in tales such as 'The Dream of Rhonabwy'.[1] Rhun ab Urien, the only other son whose existence is not in doubt, stands at the centre of a particular controversy which will be addressed later in this chapter.

Siblings of Owain and Rhun appear in the triads and in poetry allegedly composed by Urien's kinsman Llywarch. How much of this material is historical and how much was devised in Wales are matters of debate. Llywarch's usual epithet is *Hen*, 'The Old', implying that he lived to an advanced age or, more likely, that he was adopted by the genealogists as an ancestor for later Welsh kings. None of the poems attributed to him are North British compositions of the sixth and seventh centuries: all were produced in Wales in the ninth century or later. They evidently incorporate some elements of genuine northern tradition and, at first glance, seem to fill gaps left by Taliesin, Aneirin and the *Historia Brittonum*. Problems arise when we try to distinguish the historical from the fictional, or when we attempt to reconstruct a reliable narrative from these poems. In this regard they are similar to the *Gododdin* and to Taliesin's Rheged poetry but without the archaic features indicative of sixth-century composition. Our understanding of the Llywarch poems owes a huge debt to Dr Jenny Rowland whose detailed analysis enabled them to be considered by historians alongside other North British material.[2] In the Llywarch poems we find mention of Pasgen and Elffin, two sons of Urien not named by Taliesin. In the triads we encounter Pasgen again, together with a fifth son Rhiwallawn and a daughter Morfudd. Any, all, or none of these could be genuine siblings of Owain and Rhun, but corroborative data is limited and unverifiable. Some appear in *Bonedd y Seint* and other ecclesiastical gene-alogies, but these texts are even less reliable than the northern pedigrees. Pasgen ab Urien appears in a genealogy of the Jesus College collection, but this traces the ancestry of a Welsh dynasty and is undoubtedly spurious. A triad praises Rhiwallawn's wealth and importance, describing him as 'broom-haired', but the historical context behind these snippets of information is unknown.[3] Another triad speaks of love between Morfudd and the *Gododdin* hero Cynon ap Clydno, but we cannot assume that this implies a political marriage between their families. Llywarch himself can be accepted as a historical figure and as a contemporary of Urien. The northern pedigrees make them first cousins through their fathers and this relationship is echoed in the Llywarch poems where Urien's death is a major theme. Taliesin's surviving verses ignore Llywarch, but, as they also ignore all except one of Urien's children, the omission is not an obstacle to Llywarch's historicity.

In the Llywarch poems we see Urien's sons being attacked by their father's contemporaries Morcant, Gwallawg and Dunod the Stout. If the tradition reflects real events, these conflicts may mark the decline of Rheged in the post-Urien years. Although an accurate picture of the kingdom's fate eludes us, some general obser-vations about the final decades of the sixth century can be made. First, it is clear that the English dynasty of Bernicia became the major power in the North before the century ended. According to Bede, the contest for supremacy in the years around 600 was a finely balanced struggle between Bernicians and Scots in which the Britons played little part. Secondly, the plethora of kingdoms implied by the poems and pedigrees of the *Gwŷr y Gogledd* seems to be a feature of the sixth century but not of the seventh. In the era of Urien and Arfderydd we encoun-ter numerous figures who appear as independent rulers capable of waging war in pursuit of their own interests. The brothers Gwrgi and Peredur are prime exam-ples, together with similarly obscure characters such as Pabo and Morcant. By the end of the sixth century the patchwork of petty realms is no longer evident in the sources. We are left to infer that the dynasties formerly represented by famous warlords such as Gwallawg and the sons of Eliffer did not survive. Their realms were presumably absorbed by other, more powerful ones whose kingships were less unstable and whose rulers had access to greater resources.

One notable survivor of the previous era was Rhydderch Hael, king of the Clyde Britons, who lived through the dawn of the seventh century to die a peace-ful death in its second decade. His survival may have owed less to good health

than to success in war and shrewd political maneouvering. Of particular significance here is his political relationship with Áedán mac Gabráin, a topic we have
already encountered in Chapter 2. Áedán's emergence in the 580s as a king of
great power and ambition gave his neighbours an incentive to seek his protection
and patronage. If Rhydderch ended the sixth century as Áedán's client or ally,
he might have gained some immunity from the endemic in-fighting among the
Britons. The downside of clientship, however, was an obligation to fight alongside
a powerful patron in pursuit of his interests. In Rhydderch's case an obligation
of military service may have been activated in 603 when Áedán marched from
Argyll to seek a showdown with Bernicia. The result was the first recorded battle
between Scots and Englishmen, an event in which the Bernicians were led by
Aethelfrith, a ruthless warrior-king whom the Britons called *Flexor*.

The Twister

Aethelfrith's father Aethelric, son of Ida, had ruled Bernicia from 568 to 572
before being replaced by his brother Theodoric against whom Urien had fought.
In the 580s the kingship passed to Hussa, a prince of a rival kindred, but Ida's
family returned to power when Aethelfrith became king in 592 or 593. By the
end of the century Aethelfrith had gained a fearsome reputation as one of the
great warlords of the age, the principal casualties of his aggression being native
communities west of his heartland. Bede, writing a hundred years after these
events, relished the carnage of the Bernician advance and saw Aethelfrith's paganism as no hindrance to an apt Biblical analogy:

> He ravaged the Britons more extensively than any other English ruler. He
> might indeed be compared with Saul who was once king of Israel, but with
> this exception, that Aethelfrith was ignorant of the divine religion. For
> no ruler or king had subjected more land to the English race or settled it,
> having first either driven out or conquered the natives.[4]

Bede's words paint a stark picture of ethnic conflict between indigenous and
immigrant groups. We should not feel tempted to accept it as accurate report-
ing. It contradicts not only modern views of Anglo-British relations in the North
but also the generally held belief, founded on archaeological evidence, that most
Bernicians had British ancestry.[5] Bede's contempt for the Britons is a major thread
running through the pages of the *Ecclesiastical History* and he made no attempt
to conceal it. But its origins were religious, not political, and it applied less to the
British kings and peasants menaced by Aethelfrith than to the priests of Wales
and Cornwall who had refused to evangelise the southern English kingdoms. This

distinction did not, however, deter Bede from gloating over the fate of North British communities trampled by the heathen Aethelfrith. God's vengeance upon the indigenous population was duly served by the swords and spears of Bernician warbands, as punishment for what Bede perceived as an unforgivable crime committed by the native clergy, 'that they never preached the Faith to the Saxons or Angles who inhabited Britain with them'.[6]

Behind this ecclesiastical grudge and beneath the rhetoric of ethnic feud we see one northern kingdom, under the dynamic leadership of an English-speaking elite, rising to prominence at the expense of weaker neighbours. The process had begun two generations earlier when the kingship of Berneich passed to a dynasty headed by Ida. Aethelfrith's military achievements at the end of the sixth century were a culmination of his grandfather's ambitions and a powerful springboard for his own. His campaigns were not driven by what the chroniclers of our own age grimly refer to as 'ethnic cleansing'. To Aethelfrith, who commanded what was essentially a mongrel army of 'Anglo-Saxons' composed partly of men of British ancestry, the mantle of ethnic crusader woven for him by Bede would surely have seemed a strange and unfamiliar garment.

What, then, did it mean to be 'Bernician' in the years around 600? To answer this question effectively we would need to know how deeply a sense of 'Englishness' had permeated through the population during the 50 years since the start of Ida's reign. Unfortunately, the corpus of archaeological clues pointing to cultural affiliation is not large enough to permit such an assessment to be made. Without a sizable sample of evidence we can do no more than offer a guess based on the results of limited excavation combined with other types of data. As noted in earlier chapters, the overall picture gives little hint of a mass colonisation by people of Germanic stock, either in Ida's time or later. On the other hand, the place-names of modern Northumberland – an area roughly corresponding to Bernicia – are overwhelmingly English with few Brittonic survivals. Of greater significance, perhaps, are the perceptions of Bede and his eighth-century contemporaries who regarded their forefathers in Aethelfrith's time as Englishmen. By the beginning of the seventh century, when any Bernicians with childhood memories of Ida's accession would have been the venerable elders of the community, Brittonic speech had ceased to play a part in important discourse south of the Lammermuir Hills. Like all displaced languages it may have lingered for a while as a *patois* among the Bernician peasantry before dying out altogether. Since linguistic affiliation is a major indicator of group identity we should have no hesitation in seeing the people of Aethelfrith's Bernicia as Englishmen and Englishwomen. This was their preferred ethnic affiliation, regardless of the British blood running in their veins.

Beyond the borders of his kingdom Aethelfrith was feared as a ruthless conqueror and pillager. To the Britons he was *Flexor*, 'The Twister', a name preserved in later Welsh tradition but presumably originating in earlier times. Why he was given this epithet – undoubtedly a pejorative nickname – is nowhere stated. We cannot ascribe it to the North rather than to Wales for both regions suffered the depredations of his armies. To the native populations of Gododdin, Calchfynydd and Tweeddale he was not so much a Germanic nemesis bringing doom to the Celts but rather an ambitious neighbour in the mould of Urien and Gwallawg. They had seen his like before and probably hoped that he might stumble and fall before his power grew too great. Aethelfrith did indeed meet a violent end, but not before his achievements had outshone those of all his peers. His greatest triumph in the North came in 603 when Áedán mac Gabráin, himself a warlord of boundless ambition, mounted a vigorous challenge. At that time Áedán stood at the pinnacle of his career, having spent almost 30 years warring and raiding in lands far from his Kintyre home.[7] In the 580s he had marched eastward across Druim Alban, the mountain mass separating Argyll from the fertile vales of Perthshire, to lay Pictish territories under his rule. South of the River Forth he had defeated the Maeatae, the Britons of Manau, in their Stirlingshire heartland, reducing them to tribute-paying clients. We have previously suggested that he may have received similar homage from Rhydderch Hael and could therefore demand military service from the Clyde Britons. At the dawn of the seventh century, with much of the North seemingly under his heel, Áedán's only serious rival was Aethelfrith.

The inevitable clash between these two mighty kings occurred at *Degsastan*, 'Degsa's Stone', a place regarded by Bede as *celeberrimo*, 'very famous'. The location is not identifiable today, despite a widely held belief that it lay near Dawston in Liddesdale. Like the Catraeth = Catterick hypothesis, the identification of Degsastan as Dawston originated as a philological guess based on 'sounds like' etymology. In Dawston's case the guess was first made in 1697 by the antiquary Edmund Gibson.[8] It has even less credibility than the Catterick idea and has no foundation beyond a very slight similarity between an ancient name and a modern 'soundalike'. But, whereas Catterick and Catraeth *could* be related philologically, no such argument can be advanced for Dawston and Degsastan. If the Bedan place-name had survived, it would now be something like *Daystone*. In the seventh and eighth centuries Degsa's Stone was worthy of the label *celeberrimo* and was presumably still visible in the landscape. It was either a monolith of natural origin – such as a large glacial boulder – or a standing-stone erected in prehistoric times. The name Dawston, by contrast, is borne today by no feature more notable than a stream and a stretch of moorland in a location so remote that any association with a great battle seems inconceivable. Degsastan, wherever it lay, would have been a place accessible with ease by the armies of Áedán and Aethelfrith. Bede implies that the site was *celeberrimo* not because of the battle but because of the monolith itself. Degsa's Stone was therefore an object of importance in its own right, a monument whose fame derived from some significant aspect of its shape, setting or history. It may have been a tall landmark, or a place of ancient ritual, or a feature associated with legendary heroes. Nothing in the vicinity of Dawston emerges as a likely candidate. We should look instead elsewhere, to some area less isolated and more accessible. The interface of Áedán's and Aethelfrith's ambitions seems a useful place to start, even if Bede offers no useful signposts. Bereft of his guidance we may tentatively suggest Lothian or Lanarkshire as possible zones of conflict. Such a geography would be consistent with an approach by Áedán through the lands of British clients on the Clyde or in Manau. He could have come from the north-west, arriving by ship via the Clyde estuary to march through Rhydderch Hael's domains, or down from the north through the lands of the Maeatae. How far south he ventured is an interesting question. Did he follow the Roman roads towards the Tweed Valley or did he wait for Aethelfrith's onset in a more northerly district? The mysterious Degsa's Stone might even still survive in the modern landscape, somewhere in the Anglo-Scottish border country, its ancient fame now long-forgotten.

The core elements of Áedán's army at Degsastan were Scots from Argyll, but contingents of Britons led by client-kings may have accompanied him. Irish traditions possibly alluding to this campaign assign royal warbands from northern Ireland to Áedán.[9] Aethelfrith undoubtedly had British kings under his sway at this time and their military service would have been demanded at Degsastan. Whatever the ethnic composition of the opposing forces the outcome was a decisive victory for the Bernician king. To Bede it was a triumph with long-lasting consequences: Áedán's army, described as 'immensely strong', was not only defeated but slaughtered. Áedán himself fled the field with a few survivors, never to mount another challenge against his Bernician rival. A hundred years later Bede was able to observe with pride that no king of the Scots 'has dared to make war upon the English nation to this day'. From a British viewpoint the short-term political consequences of Degsastan were almost certainly unpleasant. Aethelfrith was now the supreme power in the North, a mighty war-leader and predator whose position was unassailable. Those of his neighbours who had not been conquered in the years prior to the battle now faced stark choices: resist his ambitions and be defeated, or acknowledge his supremacy and pay tribute. Aethelfrith was not, however, content merely to acquire a temporary network of clients and sub-kings that would disintegrate on his death. He was a land-grabber accustomed to expelling the Britons and annexing their territories to his kingdom. This is implicit in Bede's use of *exterminare*, 'to drive out', in describing Aethelfrith's policy. We may imagine the native elites being displaced from their estates by an incoming Bernician aristocracy. The image is reinforced by a carefully chosen Biblical quote applied to Aethelfrith by Bede: 'Benjamin shall ravin like a wolf; in the morning he shall devour the prey and at night shall divide the spoil.'[10] Here, the prey were the British landholding families driven from their homes by English-speaking noblemen who became the main beneficiaries of Aethelfrith's success. At the lower levels of British society the peasants of confiscated estates remained *in situ*, bound to hereditary service as semi-free farmers, their labours now sustaining Bernician lords. By this process the English frontier expanded westward along the Tweed and northward across the Lammermuirs. Casualties of Aethelfrith's aggression included native realms along the eastern and central sectors of the Tweed Valley and on the southern fringe of Gododdin. The kingdom of Kelso presumably vanished soon after Degsastan, if not before, its ruling family – the heirs of Cadrod Calchfynydd – being ousted and replaced. Literary hints suggest that Rheged, wherever it lay, rode the storm to continue as a viable political entity, but its leadership surely reached a *rapprochement* with Bernicia. After 603, when Aethelfrith stood at the height of his power, the king of Rheged was probably among his tribute-paying clients. It is noteworthy that both Rheged and Gododdin survived the post-Degsastan era to outlast the fearsome *Flexor*. Perhaps their respective aristocracies were more useful to him as tribute-payers rather than as disinherited exiles?

Those Britons formerly under Áedán's hegemony would have transferred their allegiance and tribute-payments to his conqueror. Neither Rhydderch on the Clyde nor the Maeatae of Manau were capable of refusing Aethelfrith as their new patron. An extensive area bounded by the Ochil Hills to the north, the Clyde estuary to the west and the River Tees to the south may now have lain under his authority. Having neutralised the Scots and Britons, he turned his eye southward beyond the Tees to menace his English neighbours in Deira. What military actions or threats he used are unknown, but, within a year of Degsastan, he had toppled the Deiran royal dynasty and declared himself monarch of all the northern English. Bede called the unified realm *Northumbria*, 'the lands north of Humber', a name he may have invented himself.[11] In the early seventh century this concept of unity was meaningless, with no evidence that the Deirans and Bernicians saw themselves as one nation. In any case, the royal family of Deira although dispossessed was not destroyed. The heir-apparent Prince Edwin had survived and would continue to be a thorn in Aethelfrith's side. Edwin escaped into exile, fleeing for his life to seek refuge among the Britons of Gwynedd. There he stayed for some years, living as a guest at the court of King Cadfan while nurturing a desire to regain his inheritance.[12] He received similar hospitality from Cearl, a ruler of the Mercian people of the English Midlands, and received the hand of Cearl's daughter in marriage. Eventually, after much wandering, he found a more advantageous refuge with Raedwald, the powerful king of the East Angles, who saw in Edwin an opportunity to pursue his own ambitions. In the meantime, the hegemony of Aethelfrith continued to expand. The annexation of Deira diverted new revenues to his treasury and placed additional warbands at his disposal.

Aethelfrith's greatest victory over the Britons came in 615 when he marched across the Pennines to meet a Welsh army in battle at Chester.[13] His chief opponent was Selyf, king of Powys, who perished in the fray together with hundreds of British monks who had come from the monastery at Bangor-on-Dee to support their countrymen with prayer. As the most likely route of approach by the Bernician king lay through the Aire Gap near Leeds, it seems safe to assume that the British kingdom of Elmet lay firmly under his sway. One school of thought, now regarded as obsolete, saw the victory at Chester as part of a strategy to sever communication between the Britons of Wales and their countrymen in the North. This idea rested on a simplistic vision of ethnic conflict for which there is no warrant and on a failure to acknowledge the importance of sea-travel as a link between the two regions.[14] The Chester campaign was a substantial raid, a display of military power designed to extinguish a challenge to Aethelfrith's authority by a rival king. The likely challenger was Selyf who perhaps saw an opportunity to extend his own influence across the Cheshire lowlands. At some point his ambitions clashed with those of Aethelfrith and, as at Degsastan 12 years earlier, a decisive contest became inevitable. An alternative cause of the Chester campaign might have been Edwin of Deira to whom, according to a Welsh triad, King Cadfan of Gwynedd gave hospitality. It is possible that Cadfan's neighbours in Powys had offered similar refuge to the wandering Deiran exile, thereby inviting retribution from Bernicia.

Within a year of his triumph at Chester Aethelfrith was dead, giving up his life and his hard-won hegemony in a battle on the River Idle.[15] The scene of his demise was Bawtry, 5 miles south of Doncaster, where his hastily mustered army was vanquished by a much larger force led by the East Anglian king Raedwald. Victory over Aethelfrith allowed Raedwald to take his place as the dominant king south of the Forth–Clyde isthmus. The other beneficiary of Aethelfrith's fall was Edwin who, after living under Raedwald's protection, returned now to reclaim the Deiran kingship. He seized power in Bernicia too, apparently with ease, and turned the tables by chasing its royal family into exile. Thereafter he ruled the two Northumbrian kingdoms as a single realm, inheriting Aethelfrith's status as sole monarch of the northern English. As Northumbria's first Christian king, Edwin held an exalted status in Bede's eyes and received glowing praise in the *Ecclesiastical History*. Bede depicts him wielding authority over many lands: 'like no other English king before him he held under his sway the whole realm of Britain, not only English kingdoms but those ruled also by Britons'.[16] The northern part of this hegemony, comprising Bernicia and her neighbours, was unwittingly bequeathed by Aethelfrith; the southern part represented Mercian territory allocated to Edwin by his patron Raedwald or acquired after the latter's death in the early 620s. Bede mentions no campaigns by Edwin in the North. Instead, we are told of a major strike southward against the West Saxons, an invasion of Gwynedd and the expulsion of King Ceretic of Elmet. These actions extended Edwin's overlordship among the southern English and laid the Britons of North Wales and the South Pennines under tribute. The surviving British kingdoms of the North were seemingly left untouched. By then, of course, large areas of former native territory along the valleys of Tyne and Tweed already lay in the hands of a Bernician warrior-aristocracy installed by Aethelfrith. Beyond these conquered lands the Britons of Lothian, Clydesdale, Ayrshire and other areas continued to acknowledge their own kings. In the wake of Degsastan the rulers of Gododdin, Rheged and Alt Clut had undoubtedly sent regular tribute-payments to Bernicia, but we cannot be certain that they gave the same homage to Edwin. Bede's rhetoric on the extent of Edwin's hegemony, especially among the northern peoples, should not be accepted too literally in the absence of specific references to war and conquest.

Edwin, Neithon and Rhun

The sources shed little light on the North Britons during Edwin's reign. On the Clyde the reign of Rhydderch Hael ended with his death in the second decade of the seventh century. Thereafter the kingship of Alt Clut passed to a different family who held power in virtually unbroken succession for the next 200 years. They claimed descent from the Clyde forefather Dyfnwal Hen and considered Saint Patrick's adversary Coroticus as an ancestor. From this kindred came Neithon ap Guipno who seems to have been Rhydderch's immediate successor. Neithon appears in the main royal genealogy of Alt Clut as Dyfnwal Hen's grandson, which should place him in the generation before Rhydderch, so we must suspect that either the main Alt Clut pedigree or Rhydderch's sub-pedigree are corrupt at this point. That Neithon's adulthood spanned the early 600s seems certain from the rather more precise chronology of his grandson Owain who reigned in the 640s. The dynastic politics of the Clyde Britons in this period are too vague to offer any hint as to why Rhydderch was apparently not succeeded by his own son, but the transfer of royal authority to another family may have been amicable. Neithon did not seize power by slaying Rhydderch, for we know from the *Vita* of Saint Columba that the old king died peacefully in his bed. Perhaps Rhydderch had no surviving sons and was obliged to nominate an heir from among other descendants of Dyfnwal Hen?

Several theories currently surround Neithon ap Guipno, all of them based on speculation about possible political relationships between Britons and Picts. The focus of this speculation is a line of Irish poetry attributed to Adomnán, abbot of Iona, in which the Pictish king Brude – who died in 693 – is described as 'son of the king of Alt Clut'.[17] In the Pictish king-lists Brude's father is named as Beli who is therefore identifiable as Beli ap Neithon, a figure listed in the Clyde pedigree as the son of Neithon ap Guipno. Brude's ancestry is discussed further in the next chapter, but here we examine the dealings of his father and grandfather with the Picts. In particular, we need to consider how and why the dynasty of Alt Clut forged a strong link with a Pictish royal family. One possible explanation is that Neithon arranged a political marriage involving his son Beli and a Pictish princess, a union that produced Brude. An alternative scenario, favoured by some historians, sees Neithon as a king of great power who exercised direct rule over a part of the Pictish nation. The Irish annals note the death of Nechtan, son of Cano, in 621. This obscure figure – whom no other source mentions – has been equated not only with Neithon ap Guipno but also with Nechtan, grandson of Uerb, who appears in the Pictish king-lists. Out of this conflation of a trio of namesakes has arisen an imaginative scenario in which Neithon ap Guipno, king of the Clyde Britons, simultaneously ruled the Picts, his father's name becoming Cano in the Irish annals and his grandfather being remembered in Pictish tradition as Uerb.[18] The sources do not invite us to make this conflation and, if taken at face value, they merely show three separate individuals who happened to bear the same name. In its various forms this name was fairly common in the British Isles in Early Historic times and could easily have been borne by two or three seventh-century kings ruling different regions at roughly the same time. There is therefore no need to envisage Neithon ap Guipno as a mighty overlord of Britons and Picts. Setting aside the speculation, he emerges from the sources as Rhydderch Hael's likely successor, but little more can be said of him. His political relationship with Edwin is unknown, but the absence of any record of war between Northumbria and the Clyde Britons in this period suggests that some kind of accord was reached after Aethelfrith's demise, or that Edwin's well-documented southern ambitions left his northern neighbours in peace.

Beyond the northern frontier of Edwin's kingdom lay Gododdin whose kings are generally assumed to have paid tribute to Aethelfrith. At the time of Aethelfrith's death their borderlands must have been under intense pressure from Bernician expansion in Tweeddale and the Lammermuir Hills. By then, the risk of plundering raids by Votadinian warbands was sufficiently remote for Edwin to establish an undefended royal residence at Yeavering on the edge of the Cheviots.[19] This implies that Gododdin's scope for aggressive military action had been curtailed, either by mutual agreement with Edwin or by threats of war. If the Votadinian king at Din Eidyn had previously been a client of Aethelfrith, this subordinate relationship may have been continued by Edwin without the need for a new campaign but by menace alone, especially if Gododdin was smaller and weaker than it had been at the time of the battle of Catraeth.

Somewhere beyond the western limit of Aethelfrith's expanded Bernicia, the kingdom of Rheged survived under its own monarchy during Edwin's reign. According to the Welsh Annals and the *Historia Brittonum*, the Christian baptism of Edwin was performed by Rhun, son of Urien, a claim made in direct contradiction of Bede's account of the event.[20] Bede makes no mention of Rhun and is in no doubt that Edwin was baptised by Paulinus, a priest sent from Rome to preach among the English. On the other hand, Bede's silence need not deter us from seeing Rhun as a member of the clergy, for the idea entered Welsh tradition fairly early and might ultimately have a northern origin. We meet it not only in reference to Edwin's baptism but also in a curious item from the oldest known manuscript of the *Historia*, a version written c.900 and preserved at Chartres in France. At the beginning its author claimed to have used as a source *exberta filii urbagen de libro sancti germani*, 'excerpts made by Urien's son from the Book of Saint Germanus'.[21] This presumably refers to Rhun, the only son of Urien deemed worthy of mention in the *Historia Brittonum*. If the Chartres claim is true, we would have to assume that Rhun had spent some part of his life in holy orders, at a monastery where religious texts were studied and transcribed. Although the claim cannot be verified, its early date means that it cannot be completely ignored, even if the usual doubts and warnings about the *Historia Brittonum* are kept in mind. Nevertheless, Edwin's baptism is such a key moment in the *Ecclesiastical History* that Bede's account should be accepted without question. He knew the precise date of the ceremony – 12 April, Easter Sunday of the year 627 – and knew that it had been performed at York in the newly built church of Saint Peter.[22] His detailed testimony contrasts sharply with the vague report in the *Historia Brittonum*: 'Edwin was baptised the following Easter and twelve thousand men were baptised with him. If anyone wants to know who baptised them Rhun, son of Urien, baptised them . . . .' These words were written in Wales in the early ninth century, a hundred years after Bede's death and two hundred years after Edwin's baptism. Bede was much closer in time and place to the event. Moreover, he was a contemporary of Edwin's granddaughter Aelfflaed, abbess of the Northumbrian monastery at Whitby until her death in 714. That he gave his readers a true and accurate report of Edwin's baptism cannot be doubted, but can the Welsh version be reconciled to it?

A remarkable amount of effort has been expended on this question and several ingenious solutions have been proposed. One theory imagines Rhun and Paulinus undertaking the baptism together, as a joint initiative. This might seem unlikely, given the conflict between the 'Celtic' and 'Roman' baptismal rites that arose later in the century.[23] Whether or not this conflict had arisen as early as the 620s is unknown. Another theory sees Edwin receiving not one baptism but two, the first being performed by Rhun under the auspices of the 'Celtic Church' whose outmoded rites were despised by Bede.[24] Edwin's induction into Christianity, supposedly undertaken during his period of exile, was then corrected by a second baptism performed at York in accordance with the more modern practices of the Roman clergy to which Paulinus belonged. The unlikelihood of this scenario was demonstrated by Caitlin Corning in her comprehensive review of the conflicting traditions. Dr Corning pointed out that the disagreements between Celtic and Roman customs were not sufficient to require re-baptism. Crucially, she drew attention to papal prohibitions against second baptism and added that Paulinus would not have performed such an unorthodox ritual.[25] Corning's own theory envisaged Rhun not as a priest but as king of Rheged and secular sponsor of Edwin's conversion. She suggested that Rhun was present at the York ceremony to witness the Northumbrian king's baptism by Paulinus. This theory certainly has merit and requires no rejection of the conventional image of Rhun as a priest: he might have retired from secular life to take holy orders, a path pursued by several Early Historic kings. The idea requires us to imagine an otherwise undocumented friendship between the royal houses of Rheged and Deira. When we turn to the sources, we do indeed find a 'special relationship' involving Urien's family and Northumbrian royalty, but the latter were not Edwin's kin. The relationship in question linked Rheged and Bernicia rather than Rheged and Deira. Before looking at how this connection arose, we return to the year 617 when Edwin seized power in the wake of Aethelfrith's fall.

After Aethelfrith's defeat and death on the banks of the River Idle, his children fled into exile in fear of Edwin. Leaving Bernicia, they sought sanctuary among the northern Celtic realms, dispersing here and there to receive protection and hospitality. Eanfrith, the eldest child, was welcomed by the king of the Picts and nurtured as a fosterling. Oswald, the second son, found refuge in Kintyre among the Scots of Cenél nGabráin.[26] The old warlord Áedán mac Gabráin, Aethelfrith's adversary at Degsastan, had died in 608, but his son Eochaid Buide received the adolescent Oswald and the younger Bernician royals. Among this group of refugees was Oswiu, a child of barely five years who was third-in-line behind his two elder brothers. According to Bede, all of Aethelfrith's children were baptised into the Christian faith during their exile, by priests of the Columban Church, and thus became adherents of 'Celtic' Christianity. They spent nearly 17 years in exile, not daring to return home while Edwin remained in power. Finally, in 633, messengers came North bringing news of Edwin's fall in a great battle south of the Humber. Eanfrith, the crown prince of Bernicia, took leave of his Pictish hosts and embarked on the long homeward journey. Things had changed, however, and no warm and friendly welcome awaited him in his ancestral lands.

Cadwallon

Edwin was slain in October 633, at Hatfield on the borders of Nottinghamshire, Yorkshire and Lincolnshire, facing a combined force of Welsh and Mercian warbands.[27] The leader of the victorious army was Cadwallon, a British king, whom the *Historia Brittonum* identifies as the ruler of Gwynedd. The identification has recently been challenged by a suggestion that Edwin's slayer may have been Cadwallon ap Guitcon, an obscure North British figure who appears in the Harleian pedigrees.[28] The idea of a northern Cadwallon has not found wide acceptance among historians, most of whom continue to follow the *Historia Brittonum* on this point. It is worth noting that Edwin and the Welsh Cadwallon had a connection dating back to the years of Aethelfrith's ascendancy, when the Deiran prince received hospitality at the court of Cadwallon's father King Cadfan. In the battle of 633 Cadwallon's ally was Penda, an ambitious Mercian king whose stubborn adherence to paganism allowed Bede to compare him unfavourably with religious converts such as Edwin. The *Ecclesiastical History* portrays these two allies – a ruthless Christian Briton and his heathen English henchman – as far removed from the ideal of kingship personified by the pious Edwin. Bede does not explain why Cadwallon and Penda mounted an attack on Deira's southern frontier but their campaign was no hit-and-run raid. After destroying Edwin and his army, they went on a rampage, marching across the River Don into the Deiran heartlands before pushing north towards the royal residence at York. Paulinus, by then bishop of the kingdom, fled south to Kent with Edwin's wife and children, never to return. The shattered Deiran aristocracy rallied to Edwin's cousin Osric, but he, too, was killed by Cadwallon. Further north, the Bernician kingship was claimed by the returning Eanfrith, Aethelfrith's eldest son, but his reign was brief and ignominious. He was no great captain in the mould of his father and had little prospect of resisting an assault by the marauding Welsh and Mercians. After renouncing the Christian baptism bestowed by his Pictish foster-kin he embraced the old gods, perhaps in the hope of currying favour with the still-pagan Bernician elite. He then arranged a meeting with Cadwallon. The ensuing peace negotiations ended abruptly when Eanfrith and 12 noblemen who accompanied him were slaughtered. With both Northumbrian realms now leaderless, the Welsh king and his Mercian ally unleashed a wave of indiscriminate violence.[29] The extent of their savagery may have been exaggerated by Bede, but there can be no doubt that the inhabitants of Deira and Bernicia endured many months of misery. Cadwallon's campaign has often been viewed in ethnic terms as a deliberate attempt to extinguish the English presence in the North, but such an interpretation might be taking Bede's rhetoric about 'Celts versus Saxons' too literally or too far. The real objectives of the campaign are more likely to have involved consumption of agricultural resources, acquisition of loot and the subjugation of local aristocracies. Folk of English, British and hybrid stock would have shared similarly gruesome fates on the points of Welsh and Mercian swords. The only ethnic aspect, if one needs to be sought, is that a Briton held sway over Bernicia and Deira for the first time in a hundred years or more. But there was to be no revival of native rule, nor were the English-speaking elite of Northumbria destined to pay long-term homage to a Welsh overlord. Nor is there any reason to think that the Britons of the North welcomed Cadwallon as a national hero or made alliance with him. To the kings of Rheged, Gododdin and Alt Clut he was simply one more hungry predator posing a serious threat to their lands.

The end of Cadwallon's occupation of Northumbria came in 634, a year after his victory at Hatfield. He fell in battle at a place known to Bede as *Denisesburn*, 'the stream of the Denise', now the Rowley Water running south of Hexham.[30] His opponent was Oswald, second son of Aethelfrith, returning from exile to reclaim the Bernician throne. Having received baptism during his adolescence at the court of Cenél nGabráin, Oswald conformed to Bede's template of Christian kingship and was duly praised in the *Ecclesiastical History*. Bede contrasted Oswald's piety with the psychotic savagery of Cadwallon and the paganism of Penda. In concentrating on the religious aspects of Oswald's career Bede gave scant information about the great victory at Denisesburn. We learn that a wooden cross was erected prior to the battle and that a church was later built on the spot. On other matters, such as the identity of the troops under Oswald's command, we gain little insight. Bede implies that they were Christians, but some were surely heathen Bernicians rallying to their prince. A small number were baptised English nobles who had accompanied Aethelfrith's family into exile, while a contingent of Scots may also have been present to bolster the numbers. Such musings are mere speculation and all we really know from Bede is that the fearsome Welsh warlord was slain. Cadwallon's surviving allies and clients fled back to their own lands, Penda of Mercia being the most prominent among them. Whether any North British kings took part in the battle is unknown, but they would not necessarily have marched under Cadwallon's banner. Indeed, the sources hint that Oswald negotiated some kind of agreement or alliance with Rheged around this time, its terms being sealed by a political marriage involving his younger brother Oswiu.

Rieinmelth

In a list of Bernician kings the *Historia Brittonum* says of Oswiu that he had two wives: Rieinmelth and Eanflaed.[31] The latter was Edwin's daughter and did not become Oswiu's wife until sometime after 642 when he succeeded Oswald as king. Bede is silent about Rieinmelth and may have been unaware of her existence, but he mentions Eanflaed several times and clearly held her in high regard. She was an English queen of impeccable ancestry and religious devotion who, in later life, played a role in Northumbrian ecclesiastical affairs as abbess of Whitby. In contrast, Rieinmelth was a Briton and therefore in all likelihood a follower of the 'Celtic' Christianity so despised by Bede. For this reason alone he may have felt justified in omitting her from his narrative. It might be partly because of Bede's omission that the author of the *Historia Brittonum* made a point of mentioning Rieinmelth in the Bernician king-list. There she is identified as the daughter of Royth and grand-daughter of Rhun. The latter, although not identified by a patronym, was almost certainly the son of Urien Rheged and the alleged baptiser of Edwin. The prominence given to Urien in a subsequent section of the *Historia*, together with the Chartres manuscript's mention of Rhun ab Urien as a source of information, leave us in little doubt that Royth was Urien's grandson. Rieinmelth was therefore a princess of Rheged. Although ignored by Bede, her existence is confirmed by her inclusion in a ninth-century list of Northumbrian queens and abbesses compiled either at Lindisfarne or Wearmouth-Jarrow.[32] Her name begins the list, Anglicised as *Raegnmaeld*, with Eanflaed appearing next. The marriage between Oswiu and Rieinmelth cannot be precisely dated, but it preceded the union with Eanflaed in c.643 and probably occurred in the 630s. Oswiu's eldest son Alchfrith was presumably Rieinmelth's child and a young man of weapon-bearing age in 655 when he fought in a battle against the Mercians. A date around 635 for Alchfrith's birth seems plausible and this would be consistent with his parents marrying in 634, the year of Oswald's accession as king. An earlier date for the marriage cannot be ruled out, but the political situation would then have been more difficult. It is hard to imagine the exiled Oswiu travelling to Rheged or to any other region near the Bernician border while Cadwallon remained dominant, or while Edwin still lived, although the notion of Rieinmelth's father sending her north to wed an exiled Bernician prince in the land of the Scots is a faint possibility. The most likely political context for the marriage is the beginning of Oswald's reign, at a time when the forging of useful relationships with Bernicia's neighbours would have gone some way to repair the damage wreaked by Cadwallon. Here, the word 'useful' has the specific meaning of 'beneficial to Oswald' and carries no implication of friendship or mutual advantage. The union between Oswiu and Rieinmelth is best viewed as the ritual or symbolic aspect of an alliance between kingdoms.[33] The oaths of fealty between husband and wife would have mirrored a formal agreement between Bernicia and Rheged. This may indeed be the correct context and, if so, would provide remarkable evidence for the continuing high status of Urien's family in the generation of his great-grandchildren. Other contexts are possible. Of these, the least credible still attracts a surprisingly large measure of support. It sees Royth offering not only his daughter's hand but also his entire kingdom as a wedding gift or dowry, thereby allowing Rheged to be subsumed into Bernicia.[34] This kind of passive diplomacy, involving the blood-less surrender of land and people, would have been most unlikely in an age when aggressive warrior-kingship was the norm.[35] Even if Royth had no surviving sons and hoped to preserve his dynasty by joining it to Oswald's, he would have faced violent opposition from factions within Rheged, especially from other male descendants of Urien who had legitimate claims on the kingship. A more real-istic scenario for unequal or unfriendly relations between Rheged and Bernicia sets the marriage alongside an oath of loyalty sworn by Royth to Oswald. It can be assumed that the destruction of Cadwallon would have persuaded Oswald's neighbours to acknowledge him as their new overlord and patron. He had already proved himself a mighty war-leader at Denisesburn by vanquishing the most dangerous predator of the day. His close friendship with the Scots gave him powerful allies who, we may suppose, were willing to intervene on his behalf in a northern crisis – as long as it served their own interests to do so. British kings such as Royth were thus faced with the same choices that had faced their fathers during the supremacy of Aethelfrith: resist Bernicia, and risk a devastating mili-tary response; or pay homage to the new English sovereign of the North. We must also allow the possibility that Oswiu's marriage to a princess of Rheged repre-sented not an amicable agreement between kings but the subordination of one king to another. Oswald may even have demanded Royth's daughter as a token of fealty, with Rieinmelth going to Bernicia as a tribute-payment in human form to symbolise her father's subservience. Finally, we should also envisage a scenario whereby Rheged was not merely placed under tribute but conquered and tram-pled, its ruling house suffering exile or destruction. Into the vacuum Oswald may then have installed his brother as a Bernician sub-king, legitimising the change of monarchy by marrying Oswiu to a princess of the defeated dynasty.

By the middle of the seventh century Bernician expansion had reached the southern shore of the Firth of Forth. This was not merely a hegemony by English kings over tribute-paying neighbours but direct rule resulting from territorial conquest. The main winners in this process were those members of the Bernician aristocracy whose military service was rewarded with grants of confiscated land in Lothian. Other beneficiaries included high-ranking priests and nuns appointed as abbots and abbesses to the new English gentry and to the conquered natives. The losers were the secular and religious elites of Gododdin, most of whom would have retained a diminished status or none at all. To examine how the conquest might have been achieved we need to look at Oswald's dealings with the Britons in the early years of his reign.

Whatever political circumstances lay behind the marriage between Oswiu and Rieinmelth we can be sure that it negated a possible threat posed by Rheged. Any immediate danger of King Royth's warbands harming Bernician interests was thus removed, at least temporarily. Rheged was presumably one of the unnamed territories alluded to by Bede when he described Oswald holding under his sway 'all the peoples and kingdoms of Britain'.[36] Other British rulers still capable of independent action no doubt sought treaties with Bernicia. Of the surviving native realms at this time we know of only three: Rheged, Alt Clut and Gododdin. It is unlikely that these were the only ones in a broad belt of territory stretching west from Upper Tweeddale, but the names of the others are lost. The royal genealogy of Alt Clut suggests that the Clyde Britons were ruled in the 630s by either Beli ap Neithon or his son Owain, both of whom are confirmed as kings in other sources. Gododdin's genealogical data has not been preserved so we cannot even hazard a guess as to who held the kingship at Din Eidyn in 634. Whoever it was, they and their dynasty soon had to deal with a Bernician invasion.

The Fall of Gododdin

Bede had scant regard for the Britons and, unsurprisingly, his writings shed little light on the fortunes of Gododdin. He never mentions the kingdom by name, despite its undoubted significance in the evolution of Bernicia. Rather more surprising, given the veneration accorded to the *Gododdin* verses by later Welsh poets, is the apparent absence of any record of Anglo-Votadinian conflict in the *Historia Brittonum*. The omission is unlikely to be an oversight by the author and suggests that the Votadinian kingdom lay outside his literary interests. Earlier in this chapter we noted that the English annexation of Lothian began under Aethelfrith's leadership in the final decade of the sixth century. It was a slow process involving the gradual erosion of Gododdin territory by a combination of raid and colonisation. By the mid-630s Bernician settlements were thriving in the river valleys on the northern side of Tweeddale at places such as *Hruringaham* where the Northumbrian saint Cuthbert spent his childhood. This unidentified village seemingly lay in Lauderdale, close to the hills where the young Cuthbert tended a flock of sheep, and was therefore no more than a day's ride from Din Eidyn. English rule over Lothian was sufficiently secure by c.680 to allow a Bernician bishopric to be established at Abercorn on the Firth of Forth, but the warfare that achieved this stability must have been fought many years before. The Irish annals suggest that a key event in this process, perhaps the defining moment in the conquest of Gododdin, occurred during Oswald's reign. Turning to the Annals of Ulster we find an entry for the year 640: *bellum glend mureson et obses[s]io etin*, 'the battle of Glen Mureson and the siege of Etin'. Similar information is given by the Annals of Tigernach, although in a slightly different form and in a mixture of Latin and Gaelic: *cath glinne mairison in quo muindter domnaill bricc do teichedh et obses[s]io etain*, 'the battle of Glen Mairison in which Domnall Brecc's men fled, and the siege of Etain'.[37] The glen or valley of Mureson or Mairison defies identification, but Domnall Brecc was a seventh-century king of the Scots and a grandson of Áedán mac Gabráin. His battle in 640 and the *obsessio* in the same year were probably not connected: the annalists commonly inserted *et* between events that were otherwise unrelated. As for *Etin* or *Etain*, historians generally agree that this was Din Eidyn, the great fortress of Gododdin at Edinburgh, although the identification is by no means certain.[38] The names *Etin* and *Etain* in the annals are the expected Old Irish forms of *Eidyn*, as Kenneth Jackson demonstrated in a detailed philological study 50 years ago.[39] In the same paper Jackson proposed that the *obsessio* or 'siege' of 640 was mounted by Oswald as part of a campaign to conquer Gododdin. Siege warfare in Early Historic Britain was not an exercise in military technology as it had been in Roman times: it did not, for instance, involve large pieces of equipment such as catapults and wheeled towers. There is some evidence that fire was used as a weapon, but otherwise the typical *obsessio* of this period probably involved the attackers trying to starve the defenders into submission.[40] If Oswald's Bernicians laid siege to Din Eidyn, they most likely surrounded the impregnable Castle Rock in the hope of forcing the inhabitants to capitulate before a relief force could arrive. The result of the siege is unknown, but it may have been, as Jackson suggested, a profound disaster for the Gododdin elite. If Bernician warbands were roaming below the ramparts of the royal citadel, one implication is that the Lothian heartlands had already been despoiled. One or more major defeats of Gododdin can be envisaged in the months preceding the siege, each loss further reducing the kingdom's capacity to offer effective resistance. When the *obsessio* at Edinburgh commenced, there might not have been much resistance left. In the aftermath, assuming that the fortress capitulated, Oswald may have spared the occupants, but the terms of the surrender would have been onerous, especially if the war had been precipitated by a Votadinian revolt against his overlordship. The king of Gododdin would have been deposed and a pro-Bernician puppet installed in his place, or Oswald might have placed the entire kingdom under his own direct rule. Much of this is speculation based on inferences from small amounts of data, but it offers a plausible narrative for the demise of British rule in Lothian. Even if some vestige of native authority survived the *obsessio*, the Votadinian kingdom was surely on the brink of collapse in the aftermath. Proximity to Bernicia had always placed Gododdin on the front line, making it a prime target for encroachment and aggression. Aethelfrith's military ambitions undoubtedly accelerated the decline, but the *coup de grâce* was surely delivered by Oswald. Even if the usual interpretation of *obsessio Etin* is incorrect, and the annal for 640 refers not to Edinburgh but to a different place altogether, we may nonetheless assign the demise of Gododdin to Oswald's reign.

The kingdom was annexed to Bernicia by a conquest so thorough that Lothian remained in English hands for 300 years. Not even Oswald's death on a faraway battlefield beyond his southern border could restore the fortunes of Gododdin. The old kingdom faded into obscurity until even its name was forgotten in the North.

Oswald perished in August 642 while fighting the Mercians somewhere in the English Midlands at the unlocated battlefield of *Maserfelth*, the architect of his downfall being Cadwallon's former henchman Penda.[41] Territories formerly under Oswald's sway were able to reclaim their independence and exploit the situation to their own advantage. Rheged, Alt Clut and perhaps other North British kingdoms may have fallen into this category, but it is unlikely that Gododdin was in any sense a functioning entity by then. The Votadinian elite had already been conquered and dispossessed and their ancient house of kings was no more.

VICTORS AND VANQUISHED

Oswiu and the Britons

Penda's victory at Maserfelth in August 642 left him in a dominant position. All lands south of the Forth–Clyde isthmus now lay exposed to his ambitions. As king of the Mercians he ruled a kingdom whose central location gave him ample scope to launch aggressive raids in any direction. South and east he was able to menace his English neighbours: the East Angles, the West Saxons, the men of Kent and others. In the west he secured the allegiance of several Welsh kings who were thus obliged to march under his war-banner. In the Midlands he absorbed a number of small, English-ruled territories into the expanding Mercian realm. Northward across the Humber he set about the task of dismantling Oswald's hegemony.

The united realm of Northumbria, a fragile entity whose cohesion in the first half of the seventh century was somewhat exaggerated by Bede, separated into its constituent parts in the wake of Maserfelth. Deira, the southern portion, reverted to independence under the leadership of Oswine, a kinsman of Edwin. Bernicia passed to Oswiu, Oswald's younger brother, whose wife was Rieinmelth of Rheged. Rieinmelth was no doubt still alive in August 642, when her husband obtained the kingship. At the moment of Oswiu's accession the fortunes of her family back home in Rheged may have risen sharply, reaching the kind of elevated status not seen since Urien's time. In a period when king and queen maintained separate entourages Rieinmelth would have been in a position to offer opportunities for advancement to those in Rheged who held her favour. Her father King Royth or his successor may have benefited from her patronage, perhaps in the form of gifts from the Bernician royal treasury at Bamburgh. All such benefits would have depended on the political context prevailing at the time of her betrothal to Oswiu, and on whether or not this union was forged in friendship or coercion. It is difficult to imagine any advantage accruing to Rheged in August 642 if the marriage itself had been a component of Royth's subservience to Oswald.

Any benefits to Rieinmelth's family ended when she died or was set aside, an event which certainly occurred in the first two years of Oswiu's reign. The divorced or widowed king soon found a new wife in the youthful form of Eanflaed, a Deiran princess and daughter of Edwin, who was then in her late teens. She had spent the

years since her father's death as an exile in Kent, but, in 643 or 644, Oswiu sent
a Bernician priest to bring her back to the North to be his bride.[1] The reason for
Queen Rieinmelth's disappearance is unknown, but, if it was not due to death, we
can consider the possibility that she was repudiated and replaced. Oswiu's preda-
tory ambitions towards Deira, well-attested by Bede, might have prompted him
to curry favour with the aristocracy there. What better way to endear himself to
the Deirans than by marrying the daughter of their late king Edwin? The removal
of Rieinmelth, whether by untimely death or royal policy, opened the way for a
union of the northern English dynasties.

Oswiu's dealings with his neighbours were necessarily limited in the early part
of his reign, when he ruled in the shadow of Penda while Bernicia still reeled from
the disaster at Maserfelth. In an entry for 643 the Irish annalists noted *bellum ossu
contra britones*, 'Oswiu's battle against the Britons'.[2] Given the northern interests
of the Iona annals from which this information originally came, the *Britones* here
should be identified as the warband of a North British kingdom. If Rieinmelth
was alive at this time, and still queen of Bernicia, the neutrality of her homeland
may have been maintained. If she was dead, or had been set aside by Oswiu, the
Britones of 643 might have been a warband of Rheged renewing old hostilities.[3]
They may equally have come from elsewhere, even if Oswiu's list of potential
foes at this time was restricted by the new distribution of power after Maserfelth.
The kings of North Wales, for example, were Penda's allies and therefore under
his protection. They are unlikely to have been the *Britones* who fought Oswiu.[4]
Rebellious remnants of the shattered Gododdin elite are possible candidates, but
any North British community still capable of fielding a warband could feasibly be
considered. We might even look further west to the Clyde, to the stronghold of Alt
Clut, where an energetic warrior-king was putting his own ambitions to the test.

'Freckled Donald'

At the time of Oswald's death in 642 his former foster-kin among the Scots were
headed by Domnall Brecc, 'Freckled Donald', a king whose military ventures had
hitherto yielded mixed fortunes. Both his father Eochaid Buide and grandfather Áedán mac Gabráin had been ambitious and illustrious warlords. Domnall
appears to have inherited their ambition but not their tactical skills. Entries in
the Irish annals suggest that his military career was characterised by ill-judged
alliances, misdirected energies and woeful defeats. He was, nevertheless, a prolific
belligerent on both sides of the Irish Sea, even before he became king of Cenél
nGabráin. His first recorded battle took place at Cend Delgthen in Ireland in
624 where he fought on the winning side as an ally of the Uí Néill king Conall
mac Suibhne.[5] At that time his father Eochaid still held the kingship, wielding

authority not only over the Kintyre domains of Cenél nGabráin but across a broader swath of Argyll. Eochaid, like Áedán, ruled as overking of the Scots and no doubt expected his son to achieve the same status. After the victory at Cend Delgthen, however, Domnall's military career began to roll steadily downhill.

Eochaid died in 629, but the kingship bypassed Domnall and came instead to Connad Cerr, a prince of the neighbouring kindred of Cenél Comgaill whose territory encompassed the Cowal peninsula and the Isle of Bute. Connad may have succeeded Eochaid through an alternating system of succession agreed between their families in times past, or he may simply have seized Kintyre by force. He perished in battle at Fid Eoin in Ireland, in the year 631, after becoming embroiled in a complex web of Irish dynastic conflict. His successor was Domnall Brecc who, for a few years at least, kept a safe distance from Irish affairs and sought instead to carve a military reputation in Britain. Among Domnall's first targets were his fellow Scots, perhaps those of Cenél Loairn whose kingdom lay north of Kintyre in the part of Argyll still known as Lorn.[6] In 636, in the district of Calathros between Lorn and Kintyre, a defeat for the Cenél nGabráin army left Domnall nursing an injured pride. Three years later he crossed the Irish Sea to participate in an inter-dynastic war which culminated in the great battle of Mag Rath, now Moira in County Down.[7] There he fought on the losing side in a disastrous defeat that effectively ended Cenél nGabráin ambitions in Ireland. The following year saw him suffer another bruising encounter, this time at the unidentified *Glinne Mairison* or *Glend Mureson*, where the rout of his army was noted by the annalists. This battle's location in a 'glen' suggests a Highland setting in a mountain pass, but tells us little about the opposing side who might have been Picts, Britons or Scots. By 640 Domnall's military failures had cancelled out many of the gains made by his forebears. On both sides of the Irish Sea the power of Cenél nGabráin was waning and his own martial reputation lay in tatters. Yet his desire for glory urged him onward to a final roll of the dice.

South and east of Domnall's kingdom his former foster-brother Oswald held sway until August 642 as overlord of many lands. Domnall may have felt compelled to acknowledge Oswald's supremacy by becoming a client and tribute-payer, especially after the reduction of his own status in the wake of Mag Rath and Glend Mureson. The Britons were under similar pressure, those not already in thrall to Bernicia finding additional incentives to capitulate after the collapse of Gododdin. A list of Oswald's British clients in c.640 probably included Domnall's neighbours on the Clyde and the Maeatae of Manau. If, as seems likely, a siege of Din Eidyn in that year dealt a fatal blow to the Votadinian kingdom, we may envisage a period of political uncertainty in the ensuing months, a time of shifting allegiances in the borderlands around the Firth of Forth. Whether this amounted to a power vacuum, as some historians believe, is hard to deduce but the person best placed to exploit the situation was Oswald. Only when the Mercians cut him down in August 642 did new opportunities arise in the volatile frontier zone of the Forth–Clyde isthmus.

Oswald's death heralded a contest between rival powers, the chief prize being overlordship of Manau and domination of the Maeatae. Whoever won the contest would gain control of the important crossings of the River Forth together with revenues from the farmlands of Stirlingshire. Regional politics theoretically heralded a five-way fight between Alt Clut, Bernicia, Cenél nGabráin, the Maeatae themselves and perhaps also the Picts. In reality only three key players entered the fray: Owain ap Beli, king of the Clyde Britons, Domnall Brecc of Kintyre and the anonymous ruler of the Maeatae. Oswald's fall had left Bernicia paralysed and the Picts evidently chose not to get involved. The role played by the Maeatae is unknown, but their king is unlikely to have remained on the sidelines in any contest for mastery of his lands. His predecessors had formerly acknowledged the Cenél nGabráin overlordship imposed by Domnall's grandfather Áedán. This probably continued under Eochaid Buide, but almost certainly passed to Oswald when Lothian fell to Bernicia in c.640. The redistribution of power after Maserfelth gave Domnall an opportunity to reimpose his family's dominance in Manau, although he cannot have expected either the Maeatae or their fellow Britons on the Clyde to let an army of Scots march unchallenged to the Forth estuary. Oswald's demise similarly stirred the ambitions of Owain ap Beli who responded by mustering the warbands of Alt Clut. The temporary neutering of Bernicia and the impotency of Gododdin gave Owain free rein to extend his domains eastward into Lothian and northward towards Manau. In the latter area he probably hoped to place the Maeatae under tribute before their erstwhile clientship to Cenél nGabráin could be restored. There is little reason to imagine him welcoming refugees from the Votadinian nobility into his realm, or feeling empathy with the deposed leadership of Din Eidyn. On the contrary, Gododdin's decline was unlikely to have caused much grief on the Clyde.

Penda slew Oswald at Maserfelth in the summer of 642, but it was a further 16 months before Domnall Brecc led his army on the long march to Manau. In undertaking this venture he clearly had specific objectives, not least the thwarting of Alt Clut ambitions in the region. An additional incentive for his campaign may have been a growing friendship between his Cenél Comgaill rivals in Cowal and the dynasty of Owain ap Beli. The late Elizabeth Rennie suggested that Cenél Comgaill and the kings of Alt Clut may have shared an ancient, well-defined border running southward from Tyndrum through the Cowal peninsula and the Firth of Clyde.[8] It is inherently feasible – and consistent with hints in the sources – that the two neighbours reached a political accord in the seventh century.[9] If such a relationship did indeed exist in the 640s, Domnall Brecc may have hoped to undermine it with a vigorous challenge to Owain. The long journey from Argyll to the Forth was not, however, an easy or simple undertaking. It involved an arduous trek through a network of Highland glens and mountain passes. It was best travelled in summer or autumn, but something prompted Domnall to attempt the journey in December, several months after the end of the campaigning season. The timing seems strange, especially in the highlands of northern Britain where adverse weather conditions pose a major problem even for modern travellers. Winter campaigning in the seventh century raised an additional set of logistical challenges, the most obvious being the non-availability of agricultural produce for provisions. Surpluses of grain were already stored away for subsistence consumption by civilian communities, leaving little left as rations for an army. Domnall's winter march looks almost like a rash decision triggered by a sense of urgency. Perhaps rumours of a sudden move by Owain ap Beli had reached Cenél nGabráin ears? The king of Alt Clut may have deliberately waited until late autumn before advancing towards Manau, thereby challenging Domnall to hazard the wearisome trudge from Kintyre under the threat of heavy snow. The preliminary sequence of events is unknown, but Owain perhaps cowed the Maeatae into submission before sealing his lordship over them in a formal ceremony. We might imagine such a ritual taking place at a totemic site such as Giudi, the great citadel on Stirling Castle Rock, or beside the sacred Stone of Manau on the northern shore of the firth. Alternatively, Owain may have simply sent raiding-parties to plunder and terrorise the Maeatae until their leaders sued for peace with a tribute-payment. Whatever the circumstances the stage was set in December 643 for a decisive clash with Domnall Brecc.

The Battle of Strathcarron

Domnall would surely have preferred to spend the winter months in the comfort of his firelit hall while leisurely planning a summer campaign in the East. Instead, he found himself having to muster an army in the final weeks of the year. He and his warriors faced a 90-mile trek, shortened daylight hours and the ever-present menace of adverse weather. Such a venture required not only boldness but considerable organisational skills. It might seem remarkable, given Domnall's catalogue of failed endeavours, that he was not dissuaded by doubters among his advisers and that the warrior-nobility of Kintyre honoured their oaths of fealty to him. The fact that he could plan, launch and complete a winter march through the mountains indicates that his authority over the Cenél nGabráin elite remained strong. Nor was he a stranger to campaigns far from home, having led a warband to Cend Delgthen in the Irish midlands nearly 20 years earlier. His grandfather Áedán had campaigned successfully in the East on more than one occasion and had managed to feed an army on the long marches far from home. The resource-networks that

had sustained Áedán's wars in Stirlingshire and Perthshire must have been similarly available to Domnall, otherwise he would not have been able to mount an
assault on Manau. How these networks functioned is a matter for speculation as
few clues are offered by the sources. Early medieval writers rarely concerned themselves with the technical aspects of war unless a specific literary purpose could be
served, hence their scant references to military logistics. We are left to wonder
how Domnall's army was supplied with essential provisions: food for the soldiers
and fodder for the horses. Did man and beast alike consume winter reserves from
the estates of subordinate lords along the route of march? This would have caused
deprivation and resentment among donor communities and is hard to accept as
an effective logistical model. It implies coercion rather than overlordship, subservience rather than clientship, and food stocks plundered rather than rendered. If
this was how Domnall provisioned his troops in December 643, we may envisage
him entering Manau as a hostile invader and marauder. Perhaps his hegemony and
client-networks at that time reached no further eastward than the present-day
border between Argyll and Stirlingshire?[10]

Domnall's march to the Forth involved a journey of four or five days. It no
doubt began at a muster-point within his core territory, at a site of ceremonial
significance where the warbands of Cenél nGabráin were accustomed to assemble
when their king summoned them to war. Contingents from other kindreds, such
as Cenél Comgaill and Cenél Loairn, may have marched to the muster behind
noblemen who still regarded the luckless Domnall as their liege-lord. It would be
a mistake, however, to think of the expeditionary force as a roll-call of the Scots,
for only those parts of Argyll under Domnall's sovereignty would have felt an
obligation to attend. The location of the muster-point can only be guessed at, but
a site somewhere in the ancient ritual landscape of the Kilmartin Valley, close to
the iconic fortress of Dunadd, seems a strong possibility.

The primary route from Dalriada to Manau remains unchanged since
Domnall's time. It still provides the quickest, least perilous overland link
between the Hebridean coastlands of Argyll and the Forth estuary at Stirling.
The key objective for travellers, then and now, has always been the great hub of
Highland routeways near Crianlarich. On a hillside a few miles south of this
point stands *Clach nam Breatainn*, 'The Stone of the Britons', and, in the trough
of Glen Falloch below, the main route to Alt Clut. But the Rock of Clyde was
not Domnall's objective. Continuing east he led his army onward through Glen
Dochart and Strathyre to the Pass of Leny. From there he had a choice of routes
into Manau, either by crossing the River Forth at the ancient fords of Frew or
by continuing south-east to Stirling. The latter option was probably more prefer-
able in December, a month when the trackless mosses of the Forth Valley would
have been particularly treacherous. At Stirling the decaying remnants of a Roman

highway still marked the best course for an army on campaign. Also at Stirling stood the towering stronghold of Giudi, the royal citadel of the Maeatae. Under its shadow the Roman road ran down from the old ford at Cornton and thence towards Lothian. Seven miles south of Giudi, in the vale of the River Carron, the warriors of Kintyre found the Clyde Britons waiting for them.

Owain ap Beli had a far easier journey to the battlefield. For him, the task of leading an army to Strathcarron presented few logistical problems in terms of distance and supply. His route lay along the Military Way, the old Roman road that in earlier times had served the forts of the Antonine Wall.[11] Although the lands traversed by this ancient highway were in British hands, it cannot be assumed that their lords willingly aligned themselves with Owain. His army would have set out from a muster-point in the heartland of Alt Clut, a plausible setting being the north bank of the Clyde at its junction with the Kelvin, opposite the ancient church of Govan. From here the Military Way followed the Antonine Wall on its southern side through what are now the northern suburbs of Glasgow. In the seventh century the old road was still a prominent feature in the landscape, its surface falling into decay but not yet destroyed by subsidence and vegetation. Its original breadth of 16 to 18 feet was no doubt much reduced, but its structural integrity and sure alignment offered Owain a straight route pointing directly at the Carron. Few traces survive today, but the line is preserved by Thorn Road and Roman Road in Bearsden and thereafter by visible traces in the countryside beyond.[12] Along this highway the soldiers of Alt Clut would have marched via Kirkintilloch and Twechar to Croy, and thence to the Roman fort at Castlecary, always with the turf ramparts of the Antonine Wall on their left. At some point the march would have turned north to cross the Wall, perhaps at Castlecary itself or some other fort further east, before fording the Bonny Water to approach the Carron Valley from the south.

The general location of the ensuing battle is found in the Irish annals:

domnall brecc in bello sraith cairuin in fine anni in decembri interfectus est ab
hoan rege brittonum; annis xv regnavit.
Domnall Brecc was slain in the battle of Strathcarron at the end of the year,
in December, by Owain the king of the Britons; he reigned fifteen years.[13]

There is no doubt that the river named by the annalists is the Stirlingshire Carron.[14] This rises in the Campsie Fells before taking an eastward course down to the lowlands at the head of the Forth estuary. It is not a particularly long river: the distance from source to mouth is a mere 20 miles, although numerous meanders make the actual length slightly greater. The battle of 643 took place somewhere along this course, in an area identifiable to contemporary observers as a *strath*. This Gaelic topographical term is fairly specific and describes a broad valley floor rather than the narrow *glinne* or glen of a river's upper course. It allows us to dismiss the higher reaches of the Carron from our search for the scene of the fighting. It is hard to believe, in any case, that a major battle was fought on the slopes of Campsie Moor near the sources of the river or even lower down in the trough now submerged beneath the modern reservoir. In fact, even without the designation *strath*, we could probably exclude any point between the moorland and the town of Denny from our search. East of the reservoir as far as the outskirts of Denny, the river twists and turns in the rocky gorge of the Carron Glen. Today the only crossings along the Glen's entire 4-mile length are footbridges laid across the ravine. Neither the Scots coming from the north nor the Britons marching up from the south would have been able to ford this part of the river. Our search for the battlefield thus moves further east to where the valley broadens into a recognisable *strath* in an area now bounded by the urban centres of Denny, Larbert, Falkirk and Bonnybridge. More specifically we might consider a river-crossing somewhere in this zone to be a likely focus for a major contest of the Early Historic period. The sources suggest that many important battles occurred at fords, such places not only having strategic value in terms of communication but also – especially in frontier regions – holding ritual significance as natural boundaries between kingdoms.[15] An example is Aethelfrith's fatal clash with the East Angles on the River Idle which probably marked the southern boundary of Deira in the seventh century. In 643, either Owain or Domnall had to cross the Carron to begin the battle. Today the river can be traversed at several points, but in early medieval times the only crossings were at Carronfoorde on the site of the present-day Carron Bridge and at Larbert where a Roman road ran down from Stirling to meet another coming up from the south. The Stirling road reached Larbert from the north-west via Plean and Torwood and was possibly used by Domnall on the final stage of his march from Argyll. It crossed the river 200 metres west of the present railway viaduct, presumably via the Roman bridge marked on old maps or, if the bridge had fallen by 643, via a stony ford formed by its ruins.[16] Domnall's alternative approach lay south-west of Stirling towards Canglour and then over the hills to Carronfoorde via Loch Coulter, although this would have brought him to the western end of the Carron Glen and thence to the narrow upper section of the *strath*. In tactical and logistical terms the Larbert crossing seems a more realistic objective for both armies to aim for, especially in winter. Whether the Scots or Britons were first across the river is immaterial as both leaders were presumably claiming lordship over the surrounding region. Given the former presence of Áedán mac Gabráin in Manau and his dominance of the Maeatae, his grandson may have felt the stronger claim and may have crossed the river to signal the start of hostilities.

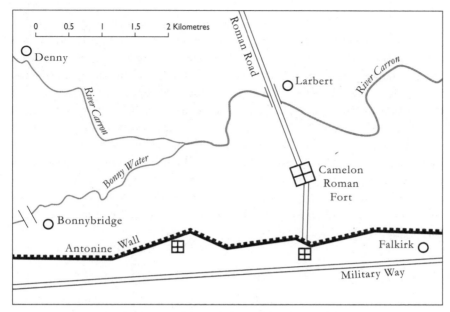

Strathcarron: geographical context of the battle of 643.

We do not know how the battle of Strathcarron was fought, how long the fighting lasted, or how many combatants were involved. We can nevertheless make a few tentative observations. First, neither of the two armies would have seemed large by modern standards. This was an era when a few hundred men constituted a viable campaigning force and it is reasonable to suppose that neither Alt Clut nor Cenél nGabráin mustered more than a thousand warriors apiece.[17] How long the ferocious carnage of close-quarter combat went on is difficult to estimate, but a duration of two or three hours would not be an unrealistic guess. When the mêlée finally ended the result was not in doubt: Domnall Brecc lay dead and Owain had the victory. The triumph of the Britons was later celebrated in heroic poetry, of which a lone fragment survives:

> I saw an array that came from Kintyre
> who brought themselves as a sacrifice to a holocaust.
> I saw a second one who had come down from their settlement,
> who had been roused by the grandson of Neithon.
> I saw mighty men who came with the dawn,
> and it was Domnall Brecc's head that the ravens gnawed.[18]

This stanza eventually found its way into the *Gododdin* to be preserved among verses commemorating the Votadinian warband at Catraeth. It is a solitary survivor of what must once have been a large corpus of poetry composed at Alt

Clut. How, when and why it was grafted onto the *Gododdin* are questions that have been debated for many years. No consensus has yet been reached beyond a general acceptance that this verse – sometimes referred to as the 'Strathcarron Stanza' – may be an authentic literary relic of the Clyde kingdom. Among the various theories is a belief that it was composed at Alt Clut as an integral part of the *Gododdin* before the latter arrived in Wales in the eighth century.[19] This view should be compared with others which see the stanza as a piece of poetry grafted onto the *Gododdin*, either by a scribe at Alt Clut or by a Welshman who had little knowledge of the historical context.[20] A more radical or minimalist view considers the possibility of the stanza being pseudo-northern verse composed in Wales.[21] The detailed philological studies behind these theories lie outside the scope of this book, but the debate can be followed in literature cited in the Bibliography.

Owain's Victory

Strathcarron was a great triumph for Owain ap Beli. It broke the military strength of one of the northern powers and removed a belligerent individual from the political arena. Owain's claim to overlordship in Manau was duly confirmed and we can assume that the Maeatae accepted him as their patron, their own king becoming a docile client of Alt Clut. Elsewhere, the old Gododdin aristocracy of West Lothian and any Bernician settlers among them had little choice but to acknowledge the supremacy of Owain. Din Eidyn and its environs probably remained in thrall to Oswiu, but he was in no position to prevent a drift of outlying territories in Lothian towards Owain's new hegemony. Despite Bede's silence on the destruction of Domnall Brecc it is certain that news of the event would have added to Oswiu's woes. After December 643, Bernicia's western frontier lay in dire peril of invasion by the resurgent Clyde Britons. The prospect of Bamburgh, Lindisfarne and other core areas being plundered by the Men of the North was now back on the agenda for Ida's descendants. In the wake of Maserfelth, Oswiu's position had depended primarily on the behaviour of Penda, but he had also now to consider the new threat from Alt Clut. He was caught between the ambitions of two powerful warlords and could do little except wait for one of them to make a move. By early 644 an uneasy stalemate may have descended on the old conflict-zone of Tweeddale, with Owain and Oswiu reaching some kind of truce while sharing in the slow dismemberment of Gododdin.

The fate of Cenél nGabráin in the aftermath of Strathcarron is unclear. The Irish cleric Cumméne, who held the abbacy of Iona from 657 to 669, wrote a Life of Saint Columba which antedated Adomnán's by several decades. Cumméne's book might have been written before he became abbot, perhaps at the request of Ségéne who held the post from 637 to 652.[22] The Life itself is lost but an extract has been preserved in the oldest surviving copy of Adomnán's *Vita*. According to this extract, Columba had long ago issued a warning to Áedán mac Gabráin, prophesying that if Áedán's descendants attacked the saint's Irish kinsmen, they would lose their position as over-kings of the Scots. Cumméne duly observed that this prophecy was fulfilled in his own time, as a consequence of Domnall Brecc's participation in the battle of Mag Rath. 'From that day to this,' Cumméne added, 'the family of Áedán is held in subjection by strangers, a fact which brings sighs of sorrow to the breast'.[23] The identity of these 'strangers' is a matter of debate. One theory sees them as a rival kindred of Scots who replaced Cenél nGabráin in the overkingship of Dalriada following Domnall's demise at Strathcarron.[24] Another sees them as Bernicians, either before Oswald's death in 642 or after the beginning of Oswiu's ascendancy in 655. In the latter year Oswiu finally defeated Penda to make Bernicia the dominant power in Britain, a position maintained until his son Ecgfrith's death in 685. Against the first of these scenarios we could argue that Cumméne's use of the term *extranei*, 'strangers' or 'foreigners', implies that the subjection of Cenél nGabráin came from a foreign power outside Argyll and not from a rival group within. The second theory requires that Cumméne wrote his book after 655, when Oswiu's domination of the northern Celtic realms was a collateral benefit of his victory over Penda. However, it is hard to see how the defeat at Mag Rath in 639 would seem to Cumméne the catalyst for a supposed Northumbrian dominance of Cenél nGabráin by Oswiu 18 years later. A third and simpler explanation sees the *extranei* as the Britons of Alt Clut under their king Owain ap Beli.[25] It should be remembered that the battle of Strathcarron was a clash between two ambitious rivals in a region outside their respective heartlands. At stake was the question of who would be the new overlord of Manau. In the aftermath of such a contest the victor would have been in a position to demand homage and tribute from the vanquished. Thus, the subjection observed by Cumméne might represent the temporary neutering of Cenél nGabráin as a major northern power after December 643. A regular flow of tribute from Kintyre to Alt Clut may then be envisaged in the remaining years of Owain's reign.

Oswiu, Penda and Atbret Iudeu

Owain's great victory severely limited Oswiu's options on the northern and western frontiers of his kingdom. He still ruled Bernicia, but had no realistic hope of emulating Oswald's expansionist policy while both Owain and Penda were alive. To the south Deira lay under the kingship of Oswine, a kinsman of Edwin, whom Oswiu resented bitterly, and beyond lurked the ever-present menace of Mercia. During this period Penda launched a series of devastating raids on Bernicia and, on one occasion, set fire to the royal stronghold at Bamburgh. These attacks were intended to beat Oswiu into submission and to remind him of his obligations as a contributor to the Mercian treasury. Defaulting on tribute-payments was likely to provoke an aggressive response and this was probably the chief cause of Penda's retribution. The raids imply that Oswiu had no intention of becoming a passive, well-behaved vassal of the man who had slain his brother at Maserfelth.

By c.650, however, Oswiu was ready to pursue his own destiny. He had spent the previous eight years rebuilding Bernicia's strength and now felt a desire to test it. In 651, he challenged Oswine to battle, but the Deiran king lost his nerve and disbanded his forces, an act of hesitation which ultimately cost him his life when he was murdered by Oswiu's assassins. In his place Oswiu installed Oethelwald, a son of Oswald, perhaps with Penda's permission or acquiescence, but Oethelwald nurtured his own ambitions and ultimately refused to support his uncle. In 653, a political marriage between Penda's son Peada and Oswiu's daughter Alchflaed was negotiated through the efforts of Alchflaed's brother Alchfrith.[26] The latter's wife was Cyneburh, a daughter of Penda, and both he and Alchflaed were probably the children of Rieinmelth of Rheged. These inter-dynastic links imply a thawing of relations between Bernicia and Mercia, but, in a seventh-century context, friendship between royal families was not a necessary component of intermarriage. Mutually hostile kingdoms often forged marital ties while continuing to engage in warfare with one another.[27]

In 655, the simmering enmity between Penda and Oswiu reached a climax. The Mercian king invaded Bernicia to ravage and plunder the whole kingdom. Oswiu tried to buy him off by offering a huge payment of tribute or, as Bede describes it, 'an incalculable and incredible store of royal treasures and gifts, as the price of peace'.[28] The offer was dismissed by Penda who resolved instead to destroy Oswiu in battle. The two sides eventually clashed not in Bernicia but further south near the margins of Deira, on the unidentified River Winwaed in the vicinity of Leeds. There, in what had formerly been the British realm of Elmet, the Mercians were vanquished and Penda was slain with the majority of his allies. A slightly different version of this sequence of events is given by the *Historia Brittonum* in its notes on Oswiu's reign. Here, the battlefield at Winwaed is referred to by its British name:

And he killed Penda at the Field of Gai, and now was the slaughter at the Field of Gai, and the kings of the Britons who had gone forth with King Penda in his campaign to the city called Iudeu were slain. Then Oswiu delivered all the riches that he had in the city into the hand of Penda, and Penda distributed them to the kings of the Britons, that is the Distribution of Iudeu.[29]

Reconciling the Welsh account with Bede's is impossible: either Penda refused the offer of payment or he accepted it. One account is clearly mistaken, and not necessarily through accidental error on the writer's part. If the error was deliberate, our initial suspicion falls on the author of the *Historia Brittonum* who was a less reliable chronicler than Bede. But how would a ninth-century Welshman gain from altering the truth of a fairly obscure event whose focus was primarily English? Bede, on the other hand, had good reason to show Penda refusing Oswiu's payment. The Mercian king's rejection allowed Bede to describe the Bernician royal treasury being offered instead to God via Oswiu's promise to build 12 monasteries if he emerged victorious. The offer, its rejection, its presentation to God alongside Oswiu's sacred vow, the triumph of Christian over pagan at Winwaed, and finally the founding of new English monasteries – each of these elements was essential to Bede's narrative. He wanted to make an important point about Christian kingship – namely that it was better to surrender the wealth of a kingdom to God than to an aggressive enemy – but the impact of his message would have been lost if the narrative had showed Penda accepting the payment. We therefore have good reason to suspect Bede of tampering with the truth about what really happened in 655. On this occasion we may cautiously accept the *Historia Brittonum* as the more correct source.

How, then, are we to interpret the Distribution of Iudeu? The central event – Oswiu's offer of tribute – is associated in both accounts with the battle of Winwaed, but when and where did the offer and the 'distribution' take place? On the one hand, we find Bede describing a geographical context associated with the southern frontier of Deira near Leeds. On the other, we find the *Historia Brittonum* referring to *Iudeu*, a place usually identified as Giudi, the fortress of Manau at Stirling. Bede gives no hint that a substantial gap of time and distance lay between the offer of tribute and the victory at Winwaed. His narrative suggests rather that the one followed the other in a single sequence leading to a dramatic conclusion. There appears to be no pause in the sequence for a trek by the two kings from faraway Stirling to the southern border of Deira, a journey of 230 miles which would have taken a fortnight to complete. We might also wonder how or why Oswiu would gather an 'incredible and incalculable' amount of royal wealth at a place so far away from the core of his kingdom. Some historians think that he conquered Manau sometime before 655 in an otherwise unrecorded campaign which mirrored the triumph of Owain ap Beli at Strathcarron 13 years earlier. Even if he had – although it seems an unlikely occurrence in a period when Bernicia was reeling under Mercian raids – the notion of Stirling being chosen as a ceremo-nial venue for an act of homage to a southern English king stretches the bounds of plausibility. Why would Stirling seem to Penda a suitable site for receiving the submission of a vassal? Without the reference to Iudeu we might imagine Penda demanding 'the price of peace' at a site within his own or Oswiu's realm, perhaps at a place traditionally associated with Mercian or Northumbrian royal rituals. Could such a location, rather than Stirling, be the correct geographical context envisaged by the author of the *Historia Brittonum*? The Iudeu of 655 might not therefore be Giudi but a different place with a similar-sounding name. In later times, long after the descendants of Ida had faded into memory, a centre of power called *Iudanburg* existed somewhere in eastern Mercia or southern Northumbria. Here, in 952, the troublesome Archbishop Wulfstan of York was imprisoned by a West Saxon overking.[30] If the Distribution of Iudeu and the battle of Winwaed were events closely connected in time and space, they might perhaps be sought more realistically in southern Deira or north-east Mercia rather than at Stirling. The Iudeu of 655 might then be equated with the unidentified *Iudanburg* where Wulfstan was incarcerated three centuries later. Against this alternative theory we should note a small detail which may weigh heavily in Stirling's favour. In the Latin text of the passage quoted above did the author of the *Historia Brittonum*, or a later scribe, intend to write *in manu Pendae*, 'into the hand of Penda', or *in manau Pendae*, 'in Manau, to Penda'? The latter spelling actually occurs in the Harleian manuscript of the *Historia*, the one regarded as the most authoritative, and would confirm the identification of Iudeu as Stirling.[31] If *manau* is the correct reading, it presumably originated as a gloss by a scribe who believed that the distribution of riches did indeed occur at Giudi on the Firth of Forth. However, we might then ask why a ninth-century Welshman would feel compelled to add a minor geographical note about seventh-century northern Britain. From whom would he have acquired such information? Further debate on Iudeu lies outside the scope of this book and is best left to scholars involved in textual analysis of the *Historia Brittonum*. In the meantime our focus returns to the great battle between Penda and Oswiu.

At Winwaed the previously invincible Mercians were completely routed. Their king lay slain on the field, together with many of his English and Welsh subor-dinates. The 'kings of the Britons' who had benefited from a share of the riches at Iudeu died alongside him or fled in the ensuing rout. Their identities are largely unknown, but most, if not all, hailed from Wales rather than from the North. Only one is known by name: Cadfael of Gwynedd, later nicknamed *Catguommed*, 'Battle-dodger', because he sneaked home on the eve of battle.[32] It is often assumed that some northerners were present at Winwaed, but this stems partly from the conventional view of Oswiu's offer of tribute being made at Stirling.

There is in fact no reason to imagine Penda's authority encompassing large tracts of the North. His political ambitions lay primarily among the southern English kingdoms. Bernicia and Deira came within range of his aggression not because he harboured northerly ambitions but because their kings frequently interfered with his plans in the South and Midlands. Given his southern focus it is unlikely that his hegemony encompassed any of the northern Celtic realms. It has been suggested that Owain ap Beli perished at Winwaed fighting alongside Penda, but there is no warrant for this. It is far more likely that the victor of Strathcarron died in the North, either on a military campaign against rebellious vassals or at home in one of his royal residences on the Clyde.

After Winwaed

Owain's death is not recorded in the sources, nor is it known who succeeded him. In the genealogy of Alt Clut he has a son Elffin, but the latter need not have held the kingship. The Irish annals note the death in 657 of Guriat, king of Alt Clut, a mysterious figure whose name is absent from the North British pedigrees.[33] Where such discrepancies occur the Irish annals should normally be regarded as superior to the Welsh genealogical material. Although ignored in the pedigrees, Guriat's reign can therefore be accepted as historical. He was probably a younger brother of Owain ap Beli and may have been king at the time of the battle of Winwaed. If so, he had the unenviable task of dealing with Oswiu in the immediate aftermath of Penda's fall. This was a period of renewed Bernician expansion, with Deira being re-absorbed into a unified Northumbria and receiving Oswiu's son Alchfrith, most likely a great-great-grandson of Urien Rheged, as its puppet-king. The Mercians were subjugated to Oswiu and acknowledged his authority until a successful revolt in 658 restored their independence. On the northern marches after 655 Oswiu's hegemony reached across the Firth of Forth to encompass, in Bede's words, 'the greater part of the Pictish race'.[34] Even if this is an exaggeration, it does suggest that some portion of the Picts, presumably those nearest to Bernicia in Fife and Strathearn, were placed under tribute. Whether this domination was achieved by warfare, or merely by threats, it necessarily required the lands in between to be subjugated. The Britons of Manau, formerly in vassalage to Owain ap Beli, now came under Oswiu's heel, their leaders exchanging a Clyde overlord for a Bernician one. Pictish homage to Oswiu suggests proximity of his warbands to Perthshire and a real rather than an imagined menace. This might mean that Manau had been ravaged as far as the Pictish border and that its southern half, the old district of Manau Gododdin between the rivers Carron and Avon, had been annexed as a Northumbrian province. It was around this time that Rheged probably lost its independence. Rieinmelth, Oswiu's first wife, had been a princess of Urien's kindred, but this was not enough to save her homeland from annexation. There can be little doubt that Rheged along with other surviving North British realms had fallen under the domination of Owain ap Beli after 643. By then its royal house would already have held a much-reduced territory which would have been easy prey to a resurgent Bernicia 12 years later. Rheged was surely annexed by Oswiu between his triumph at Winwaed and his death in 670. The kingdom's disappearance was part of a steady erosion of British rule in the North, a process less concerned with temporary hegemony than with permanent conquest and ruthless dispossession. Since Aethelfrith's time the Bernician expansion had been characterised by the expulsion of native elites and their replacement by an English-speaking aristocracy. Along the Tweed Valley and throughout Lothian this was the new landholding pattern and it presumably enveloped Rheged during Oswiu's reign. As a Christian ruler he possessed an additional weapon of control in the form of English priests whose spiritual allegiance to God went hand-in-hand with loyalty to their king. By placing a Bernician clergy on conquered lands, in monasteries founded with royal grants, Oswiu effectively set up a network of outposts to consolidate the outer provinces of his realm.[35] By the end of his lifetime there were few, if any, areas left under sovereign British rule east of a line drawn between the River Clyde and the River Annan. Clues offered by archaeology and place-names hint that the area represented today by Renfrewshire, Ayrshire and Galloway still lay outside Bernician control at the time of Oswiu's death. However, with parts of Dumfriesshire already falling to English encroachment, the shorelands of the Solway Firth were vulnerable to raiding or colonisation and Clydesdale was similarly threatened. A likely casualty of Oswiu's conquests was the kingdom formerly ruled by Gwenddoleu with its probable focus at the junction of Liddesdale and Eskdale a few miles north of Carlisle. This obscure realm may have continued to function long after the battle of Arfderydd in 573. Indeed, there are no objective grounds for assuming that it existed only in the late sixth century, or that Gwenddoleu's relations were so demoralised that not a single male kinsman remained to claim the vacant kingship. Remnants of his family may still have been ruling from the presumed ancestral seat at *Caer Gwenddoleu* when Oswiu's warbands dispossessed them.

The last known act of defiance by a descendant of Urien against Ida's dynasty came when Alchfrith rebelled against his father.[36] Bede does not say why Rieinmelth's son turned renegade but we can assume that he was either slain or exiled in the aftermath. Nothing more is heard of him. As sub-king of Deira and husband of Penda's daughter he had perhaps grown too close to the Mercians and may have taken sides with them against Oswiu. Alternatively he may have felt threatened by his half-brothers Ecgfrith and Aelfwine, his father's sons by the marriage to Eanflaed. Rivalry and strife between a king and his family were by no means uncommon but Alchfrith's revolt marked an ignominious end for a man who had hitherto been a loyal heir. His sister Alchflaed was seemingly not embroiled in these troubles but she, too, may have regarded Eanflaed's offspring as rivals.[37] She herself was no stranger to treachery, having been implicated in the murder of her Mercian husband Peada in 656, less than a year after his appointment by Oswiu as a puppet king.[38]

Alchfrith had played a major role in one of the most important religious events of the Early Historic period. In 664 an ecclesiastical synod was summoned at the Northumbrian monastery of Whitby, its purpose being to debate the respective merits of the 'Roman' and 'Celtic' customs employed at that time in the churches of Oswiu's kingdom.[39] The key issue was the question of how the date of Easter Sunday should be calculated, this being a major bone of contention for both sides. Churches of the Roman tradition used a method of calculation current across contemporary Western Europe. This was regarded by the papacy as not only the correct method but also the only one permissible. The Celtic churches, including those founded in Northumbria by Irish priests invited from Iona during Oswald's reign, used an older method regarded by Rome as obsolete. To some of the more zealous elements among the Roman faction in Northumbria the Celtic Easter seemed almost heretical, despite the fact that Iona and all other churches in the Celtic-speaking areas of the British Isles acknowledged papal authority. A related issue discussed at the Whitby synod was the form of tonsure worn by the Celtic clergy, a style which differed markedly from the Crown of Saint Peter employed by priests of the Roman tradition.[40] Both matters were debated at Whitby in the presence of King Oswiu himself and, in spite of a stern defence on the part of Iona's representatives, the result was a defeat for the Celtic side. Oswiu decreed that all Northumbrian churches, including the great monastery on Lindisfarne, should henceforth conform to Roman usage. Those priests who wished to retain the old customs were obliged to leave the kingdom and return to Iona.

As far as is known, there were no Britons at the synod. If any British priests still ministered in Northumbria at this time, they were subject to English or Irish bishops who were in turn under Oswiu's secular jurisdiction. Beyond Northumbria's western border, the kingdom of Alt Clut still had its own churches and its own clergy. Other outposts of North British Christianity may have similarly survived in unconquered lands. Like Iona and her satellite churches among the Picts, these British enclaves practised the Celtic customs. So, too, did those of other British regions such as Wales and Cornwall. Not until the following century did these churches fall into conformity with the rest of Western Christendom.

Ecgfrith

Oswiu died in 670. With Alchfrith gone the overkingship of the northern English passed to Ecgfrith, Oswiu's son by his second wife Eanflaed. Ecgfrith maintained his father's expansionist policy and was even more aggressive in his dealings with Northumbria's neighbours. From his time onward the realm was more-or-less permanently unified, although at first a token kingship was maintained in Deira for his younger brother Aelfwine. West of the Pennines Ecgfrith unleashed military campaigns to conquer large tracts of territory at the expense of the Britons.[41] In an area represented today by the counties of Lancashire and Cumbria his warbands uprooted the native nobility and destroyed whatever minor kingdoms still remained there. During his reign the Northumbrian expansion moved westward along the northern shore of the Solway Firth from consolidated gains in the fertile farmlands around Carlisle. By then the erstwhile Roman city lay under the authority of an English *praepositus* or 'reeve' appointed by the king.[42] There also a convent of Bernician nuns was established, perhaps replacing an earlier religious community of Britons, but the character of any secular occupation at this time is unknown.[43] Further south, Ecgfrith inherited his father's long-running feud with Mercia, this eventually escalating into a personal vendetta after his brother Aelfwine was slain in battle in 679. The latter encounter resulted in a net loss of Northumbrian territory south of the Humber and left Ecgfrith nursing a grievance that he plainly intended to avenge. In the meantime he switched his attentions westward and, in 684, despatched an army across the Irish Sea to plunder the Uí Néill kingdom of Brega in Meath.[44] The reasons behind this assault are unknown, but it involved a destruction of Irish churches that brought condemnation from every corner of the British Isles. Bede, who was 11 or 12 years old at the time, later looked back on the raid as a deed of profound wickedness.[45] In the following year Ecgfrith marched north to impose his authority on the Picts. The apparent ease with which he was able to lead an army through Stirlingshire suggests that the Britons of Manau were his vassals. Their leaders would have been obliged by oaths to supplement his force with their own warbands, or, as a minimum obligation, to render food and other provisions to his troops. Similar terms of clientship had presumably been rejected by their Pictish neighbours in defiance of Ecgfrith's demands. He had previously launched punitive raids against the Picts after their leaders defaulted on tribute-payments, but the campaign of 685 was a major strike into the Perthshire heartlands. Its objective was simple: to beat the defaulters into submission. The paramount Pictish king at the time was Brude, son of Beli, whose military prowess had already been proved in campaigns against northern Picts in Aberdeenshire and Orkney. Brude's father had also sired Owain, king of Alt Clut and victor of Strathcarron, but the two sons were unlikely to have been full brothers. Owain's mother was probably a Briton of the Clyde, but Beli had evidently taken a Pictish princess as wife or lover and it was through this lady that Brude's kingship was acceptable to the Picts. Brude was therefore a man of mixed blood, although the presumed ethnic boundary along the River Forth may have seemed less defined to contemporary Pictish or British eyes than it seems to ours today. The two sons of Beli need never have met, for their childhood years were most likely spent far apart with their respective maternal families. Nor, indeed, should their shared paternal ancestry be seen as evidence for friendship between Alt Clut and the Picts throughout their lifetimes. The relationship between Beli and a female Pict should be seen in the context of matrilinear succession, a system designed to prohibit father-to-son inheritance of kingship. There is a long-running debate among historians about the extent to which this system was used by the Picts, or even if it was used at all, but the discussions lie outside the parameters of this book.[46] The stance adopted here is that, to a greater or lesser degree, matrilinear inheritance was employed by the Picts as a preferred method of selecting a royal heir. Pictish matriliny, as it is sometimes called, seems to have incorporated the related custom of exogamy whereby princesses were married or otherwise matched to males outside their kin-group or even beyond the frontier. The offspring of these unions were raised within the mother's family, with male children being groomed as potential kings. If these customs lie behind Beli's relationship with a Pictish princess, it is not unlikely that Brude never met his father, still less his half-brother Owain.

The *Historia Brittonum* calls Brude the *fratruelis*, 'cousin', of Ecgfrith and here again the kinship may be due to Pictish matriliny.[47] The fathers of both men are identifiable and so is Ecgfrith's mother, but other close relatives are either unknown or have no likely bearing on the alleged cousinhood. We are thus left to construct elaborate genealogical structures, each held together by guesswork, in the hope of identifying how these two men were related. It is an interesting exercise, but ultimately a fruitless one and, in any case, the kinship plainly had little relevance when the *fratrueles* went to war in 685. Their armies met at *Dún Nechtáin*, traditionally identified as Dunnichen near Forfar, where the Northumbrians were trapped and slaughtered.[48] Ecgfrith was slain, but his body was allegedly borne with honour from the field and conveyed to Iona, the mother-church of the Picts and Scots, for burial alongside a distinguished array of kings and abbots.

Brude's victory at *Dún Nechtáin* ended a long period of Bernician supremacy over the northern realms. Forty years later Bede looked back on the battle with a sigh of regret, his words acknowledging that it marked a turning-point in the history of Northumbria. 'From this time,' he wrote, 'the hopes and strength of the English kingdom began to ebb and fall away'.[49] He observed that the Picts liberated those parts of their territory that had lain under Northumbrian rule since the reign of Oswiu. In the wake of *Dún Nechtáin* they swept down from Perthshire to attack the estates of English noblemen in Fife and Manau. The monastery at Abercorn on the Lothian shore of the Firth of Forth was abandoned by its Northumbrian bishop who fled southward in terror. Bede went on to describe Abercorn as being 'in English territory but close to the firth' and gave no indication that it was actually assailed by the marauding Picts, nor that its brethren followed their bishop in flight. His narrative implies rather that the Northumbrian gains in Lothian remained intact. In other words, the English withdrawal halted at the old northern border of Gododdin on the River Avon, and neither Abercorn nor its environs were completely abandoned. In the West the Scots were released from the shadow of Northumbrian overlordship, but unlike the Picts they had no lost territories to reclaim. Bede wrote also that Brude's victory allowed 'some part of the British nation' to regain full independence. These were North Britons rather than Welshmen and their leaders may be identified as former client-kings of Oswiu and Ecgfrith. In the absence of any hint that the Northumbrian conquests in Lothian, Tweeddale, or around the headwaters of Solway unravelled after *Dún Nechtáin* neither Rheged nor any other native realm previously annexed to English territory should be included within Bede's description. There was to be no reprieve for the land of Urien's kin, no revival of independence. Rheged, like Gododdin, had been fully absorbed by Bernicia before the death of Oswiu in 670. When Bede wrote of 'some part' of the Britons regaining their independence in 685, he surely meant those whose territories had not already been conquered and annexed. Although the rulers of these lands had rendered tribute to Bernicia for 30 years, they had never been ousted from their seats of power, nor had they lost their capacity to pursue military ventures for their own ends. Thus, in 677, while Ecgfrith was overlord of the North, the Britons defeated the Scots in battle.[50] The losing army was led by Ferchar *Fota*, 'The Tall', a vigorous leader of the Cenél Loairn kindred and a bitter rival of Cenél nGabráin. Ferchar's kingdom may have shared a frontier with lands ruled by Britons in the district marked today by the communication hub around Crianlarich and Tyndrum, a plausible setting for a clash of ambitions. The broader geography points to his adversaries hailing from the Clyde or, less probably, from some western district of Manau within raiding distance of his core domains in Lorn. The clash occurred at *Tirinn*, a place no longer identifiable, but sufficiently removed from Ecgfrith's interests to be unworthy of his participation. Despite an apparent similarity of names, the battlefield need not be sought on the island of Tiree, although this unlikely location has been suggested.[51]

After his death, Ecgfrith was succeeded by his alleged half-brother Aldfrith, a man who claimed to be Oswiu's son but whose shadowy origins lay in Ireland.

He was raised there by his mother's kin, a royal family of the northern Uí Néill. Whether or not he really was a son of Oswiu is immaterial, for his claim was accepted by the Bernician elite. He was primarily a cleric and religious scholar rather than a war-leader and this pious reputation earned him a generally favourable portrait in Bede's narrative. His first task as king was to maintain the cohesion of Northumbria in the wake of *Dún Nechtáin*. 'He ably restored the shattered state of the kingdom,' wrote Bede, 'although within narrower bounds.'[52] Aldfrith rejected the aggressive expansionism of his predecessors in favour of a less ambitious policy which included generally peaceable relations with the northern peoples. It may even have been at the instigation of the Picts and Scots, supported by the Irish and the Clyde Britons, that he succeeded Ecgfrith. In the early years of his reign he perhaps ruled as a vassal or client of Brude, exchanging homage to the Pictish king for guarantees of peace along the border. The sources suggest that peace was indeed assured, at least until Brude's death in 692.

FRIENDS AND FOES

Beli ab Elffin

The Northumbrian expansion in the seventh century changed the political landscape of northern Britain. South of the Forth–Clyde isthmus the old tribal groupings of the Iron Age and the patchwork of later kingdoms had been replaced by a new distribution of power. By c.700 only the western part of this region still belonged to the Britons, the central and eastern portions having been thoroughly conquered by the English. Or, to describe the situation slightly differently, the native elites of Lothian and of the Tweed Valley had been ousted by a new aristocracy who spoke a different language. A hundred years of aggressive warfare by English-speaking kings may have sharpened a sense of 'Britishness' among some of their foes, but there were still enough 'Englishmen' of mixed blood to blur the ethnic boundaries drawn so starkly by Bede.

King Aldfrith, whose rule of a unified Northumbria spanned the transition from the seventh century to the eighth, had no pretensions to emulate his forebears. During his 20-year reign the unconquered Britons beyond his western border were apparently left in peace, although on both sides there was undoubtedly watchfulness. Of the North British realms still surviving in this period, only Alt Clut is mentioned in the sources. The proximity of the Clyde kingdom to Argyll kept it within Iona's sphere of interest and ensured that the deaths of its kings and other significant events continued to be noted by the annalists. With no other British kingdoms having survived the Bernician advance – or none of any notable size or significance – Alt Clut emerges as the last refuge of the Men of the North. Thus, whenever the Iona annalists referred to 'Britons' in northern contexts after c.670, they invariably meant those of the Clyde.

In 693, the annalists noted the passing of 'Domnall, king of the Britons'.[1] This was Dyfnwal ab Owain, son of the victor of Strathcarron and a man of considerable age at the time of his death. There is no hint that he died in battle. He was succeeded by his nephew, Beli ab Elffin, whose ambitions seem to have been directed mainly at Ireland. Twelve years before Beli's accession a force of unidentified Britons had defeated and slain an Irish king in Antrim, the part of Ireland nearest to the Firth of Clyde.[2] They probably came from Alt Clut.[3] Whatever factors led them to campaign in Irish territory arose again in 697 when another British warband fought at Muirthemne, in County Louth, in alliance with an Ulster king against his southern Uí Néill enemies. The same alliance was presumably still in place in 702 when the southern Uí Néill king Irgalach of Brega perished in a battle with Britons near Dublin. In the following year a shift of policy or allegiance led to a battle in Ulster and a defeat for the Britons at the hands of their former allies. No great success seems to have been achieved by these interventions in Irish affairs and in 709 the Britons endured another defeat while fighting on the side of King Cellach of Leinster. In the campaigns of 697 to 709, the prime mover on the British side can be seen as Beli ab Elffin who, we may assume, shared a common political purpose with his Irish allies. Although the arrangement eventually broke down it may have originated as an equal partnership based on friendly relations rather than on obligations of clientship. It should be noted that two alternative interpretations of the data have been advanced. The less implausible of these uses Welsh genealogical material to make a case for the British warbands emanating not from Alt Clut but from the Isle of Man.[4] The other alternative sees the Britons as mercenaries fighting in Ireland as swords-for-hire. According to this scenario the warriors were exiles from Rheged who, after the Bernician takeover of their lands, migrated across the Irish Sea to seek new patrons and new battles.[5] This is extremely speculative and is not supported by even the slightest hint in the sources. Nothing in the form of the annal entries suggests that the Britons who fought in Ireland were refugees, or that they served any interests other than those of their own king. The annalists give no hint of a connection between these warbands and a recently conquered kingdom such as Rheged. Our only geographical clue is the term 'Britons', which in this period of Irish annal-writing usually means the people of the Clyde. The monks on Iona who composed these entries had minimal contact with British communities elsewhere.

Beli ab Elffin was king at Dumbarton Rock when the Northumbrians again clashed with the Picts. This happened in 698 and, although perhaps no more than a border skirmish in north-west Lothian, it resulted in the slaying of a high-ranking Bernician noble.[6] King Aldfrith's passive attitude towards war suggests that the Picts were the aggressors on this occasion. Under their new monarch Brude, a namesake of Ecgfrith's destroyer, they may have raided deep into Manau, taking plunder from the Maeatae Britons before threatening the Northumbrian frontier. Unlike his father and half-brother, the cautious Aldfrith did not respond in kind by launching a punitive strike across the Forth. No more battles involving his forces are recorded for the rest of his reign which came to an end with his death in 705. In the previous year, an army from

Dalriada was slaughtered in *Glenn Lemnae*, possibly Glen Falloch at the head of Loch Lomond.[7] The kindred to which these Scots belonged is not known, but, if the battle occurred on the northern frontier of Alt Clut, the victor can again be cautiously identified as Beli ab Elffin. Seven years later, in 711, a battle between Scots and Britons took place at *Lorg Eclet* where the Scots had the mastery. Although the annalists who noted this event gave no further information about the circumstances, we can assume that the Britons were warriors from the Clyde fighting for their king. *Lorg Eclet* might therefore lie in the borderland between Beli's realm and the eastern fringe of Argyll. Beyond these broad assumptions no specific context can be defined for the battle because neither its location nor the identity of the Dalriadan leader is retrievable from the data supplied. At that time the most powerful figure among the Scots was Selbach, king of Cenél Loairn, who thus emerges as a likely candidate.[8] Another victory of unspecified Scots over Britons occurred in 717 at a stone known as *Minuirc*.[9] Here again the battle-site is unlocated although it probably lay near a prominent boundary-marker. *Clach nam Breatainn*, the 'Stone of the Britons', above Glen Falloch, is a possible candidate, but any prominent monolith on the frontier could also be considered. It has been suggested that *Minuirc* might incorporate a Brittonic word meaning 'roebuck', perhaps in the sense of a leaping deer, a description which fits the dramatic shape of *Clach nam Breatainn* well enough.[10]

Further east, in the same year as *Lorg Eclet*, the Picts and Northumbrians clashed again along their turbulent interface in Stirlingshire, their armies meeting on *campus Manonn*, 'the plain of Manau', between the River Avon and the River Carron.[11] Here the English side was victorious and a Pictish leader was slain. Osred, son of Aldfrith, was king of Northumbria at this time, but he was barely 14 years old, having succeeded his father as a child of eight. This youthful monarch was killed five years later, beyond his southern border, presumably in battle with the Mercians. His death brought a hiatus in the line of succession which diverted briefly to a different family before his brother Osric regained the kingship. Osric ruled for 11 years, but, when he died in 729, the dynasty founded by Aethelfrith finally came to an end. During Osric's reign a major religious change occurred among the Scots and Picts, both peoples abandoning the 'Celtic' method of calculating the date of Easter Sunday in favour of the 'Roman' alternative. In the previous chapter we discussed the Easter controversy and also the Synod of Whitby which heralded the adoption of Roman customs in the churches of Northumbria. Fifty years after the Synod, in the second decade of the eighth century, Northumbrian clergymen helped their Pictish counterparts to abandon the Celtic tradition.[12] This was undertaken in conjunction with a formal treaty between the two peoples, a peace-pact designed to put an end to their differences in the Forth borderlands. A further defeat of the Celtic Easter in the North came in 716 when the monks of Iona conformed to the Roman custom at the prompting of Ecgbert their Bernician-born bishop. Although no record survives of the date when the North British churches adopted the change, they did not immediately follow their neighbours into conformity, nor had they done so by 731 when Bede noted their continuing adherence to 'their incorrect Easter and their evil customs'.[13] At this time the only British priests in conformity with Rome were those of Cornwall who had been persuaded by the West Saxon abbot Aldhelm. The North British clergy on the Clyde and in other western enclaves may have clung to their old ecclesiastical ways until 768 when their compatriots in Wales finally embraced reform.[14]

Eadberht and Óengus

The early part of the eighth century brought peace to the Anglo-Pictish conflict zone in Manau. This was the ancestral domain of the Maeatae, the Britons of Stirlingshire, whose fortress at Giudi still dominated the surrounding lands. Whether this people still answered to their own kings after c.700 or were ruled instead by frontier lords of Pictish or Bernician origin no chronicle relates. Their lands may have been so ravaged by the shifting tides of war that any older structures of authority had long since collapsed to leave a scattering of petty fiefs and small lordships. South-west of this region, beyond the broad swath of Clydesdale and Ayrshire, another group of Britons was being pushed aside and dispossessed. These were the inhabitants of Galloway who were now subjected to a new wave of English encroachment. The final conquest of the northern Solway shorelands should probably be associated with the 11-year reign of Osric (718–29) rather than with that of his brother, the boy-king Osred, or with the passive reign of their father Aldfrith. This is the period when a confident Northumbrian elite commissioned the great carved crosses at Bewcastle, north-east of Carlisle, and at Ruthwell in Dumfriesshire. Further west the distribution of early English place-names indicates a takeover of British estates by Northumbrian lords. At places such as Arsbotl and Cruggleton, for instance, English noblemen established centres of power from where they held sway over the surrounding districts.[15] By 731 their hold on Galloway was sufficiently secure to warrant the establishment of an English bishopric at Whithorn, the first incumbent being Bede's friend Pehthelm. Beyond the enclaves of Northumbrian power the Britons remained relatively untouched by English influence and, unlike their fellows in Lothian and Tweeddale, they retained their cultural identity. The conquest nevertheless provided the springboard for a new phase of expansion in the 740s when King Eadberht campaigned in Ayrshire. Eadberht was the last of the great Northumbrian warrior-kings, a man cast in the mould of Aethelfrith's sons although of a different lineage. He harassed the Britons as fiercely as any of his seventh-century predecessors had done. By 750 he had conquered the plain of Kyle, wresting it from unidentified native rulers who may have been vassals of Alt Clut.[16] A likely stronghold of the Kyle Britons was Dundonald, 4 miles south-east of Irvine, where an Early Historic fort seems to have preceded the later castle.[17]

At the same time the Clyde kingdom itself was facing aggression from the Picts under their fierce king Óengus, son of Fergus. Óengus had recently emerged from a long war with the Scots of Cenél Loairn which had left them subjugated to his overlordship. It is a reasonable assumption that their Cenél nGabráin neighbours in Kintyre were similarly compelled to acknowledge his authority. By 741, when the last of his Dalriadan opponents was defeated, his martial reputation had made him the most powerful warlord in the North. The annalists briefly noted a battle between Picts and Britons in 744 without naming the site or the protagonists. There can be little that this was a clash between Óengus and his Alt Clut counterpart Teudubr ap Beli in which the Pictish king was the aggressor.[18] Perhaps the Britons invited an attack by Óengus after rejecting the type of subjection recently imposed upon the Scots? Whatever the cause and outcome of the battle, it was followed six years later by a far more significant encounter on the northern frontier of Teudubr's kingdom. Here the Britons achieved a major victory which claimed the life of Talorcan, brother of Óengus. Notices of the event appeared in the Irish and Welsh annals, reflecting its importance in Ionan and British tradition. In the *Annales Cambriae* the site of the battle was given as *Mocetauc*, a place identifiable as Mugdock, between Milngavie and Strathblane.[19] The broader topographical setting is a gap between the Campsie Fells and Kilpatrick Hills above the northern bank of the Clyde, a likely point of access for Pictish warbands coming down from Perthshire. Mugdock sits astride a primary communication route marked today by the A81 road between Glasgow and Aberfoyle, its strategic importance in earlier times confirmed by the presence of a fourteenth-century castle. In 750, it may have been a border district of Alt Clut and thus an appropriate place for Teudubr to make a stand against Pictish raiders. Whatever the circumstances underlying the battle, its result was a severe blow to the power of Óengus. When the Iona annalists reported that his overlordship began to ebb after 750, they surely meant that *Mocetauc* had dented his aura of invincibility. Tensions among the Picts themselves erupted in open war and, in 752, a battle between rival factions was fought in the Perthshire heartlands. How Óengus fared in this period of upheaval is unknown, but, by 756, his position had stabilised and he was ready to launch a new campaign against Alt Clut.

Teudubr, the victor of Mugdock, had in the meantime bequeathed the kingship to his son Dyfnwal. The latter now faced an onslaught from a combined force of Picts and Northumbrians led jointly by Óengus and Eadberht. Never before had these two peoples marched side by side to war, nor would such an unprecedented coalition be repeated. Indeed, the two allied kings had recently been enemies on the battlefield. Their coming together in 756 might have involved nothing more than an agreement to share the spoils of a joint raid on the Britons. Alternatively, they may have regarded Dyfnwal as a stubborn adversary whom neither of them wished to challenge alone. They invaded Clydesdale in strength, advancing as far as the royal citadel at Dumbarton Rock.[20] Facing what was probably a very large Anglo-Pictish army encamped at the foot of his stronghold, Dyfnwal capitulated and sued for peace. On the first day of August he offered homage to the allies, almost certainly in a public ceremony under the gaze of his assembled nobles. The venue was likely to have been a place of special significance for his dynasty and two locations immediately arise as strong candidates: Alt Clut itself or Govan further upstream. Govan was a centre of early Christianity with a church and cemetery both possibly dating back to the fifth or sixth century.[21] That this was indeed the place of Dyfnwal's formal surrender seems especially likely when we consider what happened next. Óengus and Eadberht remained on the Clyde, no doubt to gather a tribute-payment of cattle rendered by the Britons. They then dissolved the united army and began their respective journeys back to their own lands. On 10 August, at a point between *Ouania* and *Niwanbirig*, the Northumbrians were ambushed and almost annihilated. The identity of the attackers is unknown, but suspicion falls immediately on Óengus who, in an act of treachery, may have sought to neutralise a future threat posed by his English ally. Or, he may have simply coveted Eadberht's share of the loot. Another possibility is that the Northumbrian army was attacked by vengeful Britons, although this seems less likely given Dyfnwal's recent defeat and oath of submission. Finally, we should consider the possibility that a rival Northumbrian faction may have been responsible.[22] A convincing argument for the identification of *Ouania* as Govan is now generally accepted.[23] *Niwanbirig*, however, remains a mystery. The name is of English origin and would appear today as Newburgh, Newborough, or Newbury. In the North our search for modern equivalents finds two places called Newburgh: one in Fife, the other in Northumberland. The Fife example was not on Eadberht's homeward march and can be disregarded. Its Northumberland namesake lies near Hexham, deep in the heart of Eadberht's realm, a setting which seems to rule out an ambush by Picts or Britons. A recent suggestion that the ambush might have taken place in Mercia, near Newborough in Staffordshire, takes us even further away from events on the Clyde.[24] Such a journey could have been achieved if Eadberht left Govan on 1 August, immediately after taking Dyfnwal's submission, but equally he might have remained on the Clyde for a week or more. It is possible, of course, that the *Niwanbirig* of 756 has not survived as a place-name in any recognisable modern form. It probably lay on one of the principal routes leading south or east from the Firth of Clyde, perhaps in Lanarkshire or somewhere along the line of the Antonine Wall. Its English name might be a much later formation, or could even be artificial, originating as a translation or back-formation of an original British name that has itself been lost.

It has been suggested that the famous battle scene carved on an eighth-century Pictish stone at Aberlemno in Perthshire celebrates a victory over the Clyde Britons.[25] This monument is traditionally associated with the great clash between Brude and Ecgfrith at *Dún Nechtáin* in 685, but the date of the sculpture and the possibility that a symbol carved at the top represents the name Óengus allow alternative interpretations.[26] If the stone commemorates a Pictish victory won by Óengus, then the vanquished soldiers in the battle scene represent one of the two peoples under his hegemony – the Scots in 741 or the Britons in 756 – although this leaves us with the problem of identifying the defeated leader whom we see as a corpse being devoured by a raven. As far as is known, Dyfnwal ap Teudubr did not die at Pictish hands so he is presumably not this figure.

The death of Dyfnwal in 760 was followed a year later by the passing of the mighty Óengus himself. Eadberht of Northumbria resigned the kingship in 758 to pursue a religious life and died ten years later. After 761, with Óengus dead and Eadberht in monastic retirement, the subjection of Alt Clut would have ended. It hardly needs stating that this assumption is based on an informed guess rather than on hints provided by the sources. Indeed, the history of the North Britons now enters a long period of uncertainty for which almost no information exists. Our primary guide for the second half of the eighth century is once again the Harleian genealogy of the Clyde kings, but the names listed there can no longer be cross-checked against the annals. After Dyfnwal's death the annals make no further reference to any member of the dynasty for more than a hundred years. Only one North British event of the period 760 to 800 is recorded by the annalists: the burning of Alt Clut in early January 780.[27] Responsibility for this act of destruction – if it was not mere accident – should lie with internal strife or with an external power. As far as external foes are concerned, no obvious candidates emerge. The greatest king of the period was Offa of Mercia, but there is no hint that he claimed overlordship in the North or that he invaded Clydesdale. He perhaps held the Northumbrians under his sway, but his primary interests lay along his southern and western borders. The Scots had recently regained their warlike reputation under the Cenél nGabráin king Áed Find who, in 768, led them to victory against the Picts, but Áed died two years before the burning of Alt Clut and was therefore not responsible for the deed. His brother and successor Fergus, of whom little is known, is a possible culprit. Another is the obscure Pictish king Alpín who died in 780, or his successor Dubthalorc, 'Black Talorc'. One curious aspect of the burning is its occurrence in early January, in the middle of winter, when an attacking force would have met logistical problems similar to those faced by Domnall Brecc on his journey to the Carron in December 643. The chronology of the Harleian pedigree suggests that the king of Alt Clut in 780 was Owain ap Dyfnwal, a grandson of Teudubr.[28] Since the destruction by fire of such an iconic royal site has ritual connotations of defeat and loss of status, we may assume that Owain – if he survived the destruction – was forced to become the vassal of whoever ordered the burning. It is tempting to see this subjection being reinforced, or reimposed, some years later by the powerful Pictish king Constantine (ruled 789–820) whose reign included a long phase of overlordship in Dalriada. Constantine's gains at the expense of the Scots echoed the achievements of his illustrious predecessor Óengus who was perhaps an older kinsman.[29] Like Óengus, and perhaps in imitation of him, Constantine might also have sought to dominate Alt Clut.

Away from the Firth of Clyde, enclaves of Britons continued to survive in lands held by the Northumbrian kings. In Ayrshire and in the lands around the Solway Firth the English still controlled territories conquered by their forefathers, but the cohesion of their sprawling realm was beginning to weaken. At Whithorn, in 791, a new bishop named Badwulf was appointed, but he may have been the last incumbent and nothing certain is known of him after 803. A cleric called Heathored who was active in the 830s is sometimes regarded as Badwulf's successor, but his association with Whithorn is doubtful and the bishopric was probably already defunct in his time. With rival claimants competing for the Northumbrian kingship, there is no record of further expansion westward and, apparently, no attempt to retain the gains of earlier times. In this period some English lordships around the Solway may have drifted out of royal control as the grip of the kings lessened. The place-name evidence points to an English-speaking elite remaining *in situ* until the tenth century, but its members were increasingly forced to share power with a resurgent British aristocracy. If parts of the Solway coast were slipping away from Northumbrian rule, then so too were districts further north, such as Kyle, which had been conquered by Eadberht in the 740s. Some British communities in Ayrshire and Galloway may have fully extricated themselves from the English yoke by c.800, their elites rejecting the old kingships of the past to form a more fragmented pattern of authority. By then, of course, a new and challenging element had appeared in the seaways around Britain and Ireland.

The Vikings

Scandinavian raiders or 'Vikings' had probably been sailing to the British Isles
for many years before they came to the attention of the annalists and chroniclers.
Towards the end of the eighth century the frequency and ferocity of their attacks
increased. They began to select high-profile targets and, in 793, the Northumbrian
monastery on Lindisfarne was plundered and devastated. The first Viking raid on
Iona occurred two years later and, by the end of the century, coastal settlements
on both sides of the Irish Sea were enduring sporadic assaults. Iona was plundered
again in 802 and 806. By then, with the Hebridean seaways rapidly becoming
unsafe, the Columban community had already resolved to transfer its headquarters to a new site at Kells in Ireland.

This first phase of raiding was undertaken chiefly by Norwegians, otherwise
known as Northmen or Norsemen. Why these adventurers left their homes to
engage in piracy in faraway lands is a question beyond the scope of this book, but,
in general terms, the so-called Viking Age had its roots in social and economic
contexts within Scandinavia itself.[30] At first the main objective of the raids
was plunder in the form of portable loot such as livestock, treasure and human
captives, but, inevitably, some of the raiders decided to make permanent settlements. Colonies were established, some serving as pirate bases, others sustaining
communities of farmers and fishermen. By the 830s the Norsemen were settling
on the east coast of Ireland and along the west coast of northern Britain. Place-
name evidence suggests that Galloway began to be colonised at this time, a process
at least partly achieved by violent land seizures in which local Britons were among
the victims. The Northumbrian withdrawal from Whithorn and other sites
around the Solway was likewise undoubtedly hastened by an increasing Viking
presence in the Firth.

Although there is no record of warfare between Norseman and North Briton
in this period, the kings of Alt Clut would not have allowed longships to roam
freely in the Firth of Clyde. Skirmishes, broken treaties and threats to territorial interests presumably occurred. The neighbouring Scots certainly came under
attack, as did the Picts further east. In 839, these two peoples stood side by side
against a Viking army in a great battle. The allied forces were led by the Pictish
king Eoganán and his Cenél nGabráin counterpart Áed, son of Boanta, both of
whom perished in the fighting. Victory went to the Vikings and, in the chaotic
aftermath of the battle, rival claimants rose up to compete for the vacant kingships. Cenél nGabráin power was eventually seized by Cináed mac Ailpín, a
controversial figure whom some historians prefer to see as a Pict rather than as a
Scot.[31] Within a few years Cináed claimed the Pictish kingship and enforced his
candidacy by force. The sources give a confused account of the course of events,

but, sometime before 850, Cináed emerged as ruler of Picts and Scots alike. His authority spanned a wide domain between the North Sea and the Hebridean islands and, in bringing the peoples of east and west together under one monarch, he laid the foundations for a unified kingdom of Scotland.

The Vikings, meanwhile, had not been idle. One group of Norsemen settled at Dublin to establish a dynasty of pirate-kings. Other warlords founded small lordships of their own in the Hebrides or in the far northern isles of Orkney and Shetland. Before the middle of the ninth century, a second wave of raiders burst upon the shores of Britain and Ireland. These newcomers came not from Norway but from Denmark and had no great fondness for the Norsemen. In 851, a fleet of marauding Danes plundered the Norse fortress at Dublin and, in the following year, Danish and Norwegian Vikings fought a savage battle in northern Ireland. Across the sea in mainland Britain a Danish army ravaged the Perthshire domains of Cináed mac Ailpín, but his rule over the Scots and Picts remained intact. During his reign he faced aggression from the Clyde Britons whose warbands attacked his southern frontier at Dunblane[31] One cause of this strife may have been the status of the volatile border region of Manau, formerly the land of the Maeatae and a crucible of conflict in past centuries. If this was the case, then at some point Cináed must have gained the upper hand in this area for, according to the *Scottish Chronicle*, he raided Northumbria six times and plundered as far south as the River Tweed. Racked by internal troubles and menaced by Viking armies, the Northumbrian kingdom was already teetering on the brink of collapse. Cináed's raids exploited the crisis by attacking his southern neighbour at a time when her capacity to defend her lands was weakest. He died in 858, in his palace at Forteviot beside the River Earn, nine years before two of Northumbria's last kings were captured and slain by Vikings.

The collapse of the northern English kingdom would not have been mourned by the Britons, but it was an ominous event and its repercussions were felt in many lands. The old enemy of the *Gwŷr y Gogledd* lay broken and leaderless, a territory ripe for exploitation by ambitious Scandinavian warlords. In 876, a Viking force seized control of York to establish a new realm between Humber and Tees. Thus began the Anglo-Scandinavian kingdom of Northumbria, a land corresponding roughly to the pre-1974 county of Yorkshire. Its kings maintained close links with other Viking groups and could rely on support from allies and kinsmen in many parts of the British Isles. From his citadel on Dumbarton Rock the Clyde king Arthgal ap Dyfnwal watched the situation closely, wondering where the new masters of York would strike next. His own doom was imminent, yet the architects of his ruin came not from the South but from the West, from Ireland. In 870, a fleet of longships entered the Firth of Clyde and sailed upstream to assail the towering bulk of Alt Clut.[33] These Vikings were led by Olaf and Ivar, kings of the Dublin Norse, and their venture may have been no mere foray for loot. Their objectives perhaps included neutralising the Britons as a maritime power in the western seaways.[34] The targeting of Alt Clut is clear testimony to the continuing power of the old kingdom for, as has recently been remarked, no other campaign by Olaf and Ivar involved such a concentrated assault on one site.[35] Ordering their troops to surround the ancient fortress, they placed it under siege, cutting off food supplies to the occupants. Outwardly the great Rock was impregnable and unassailable, but its strength brought little comfort to King Arthgal and his entourage. They were trapped inside and had only two bitter choices: surrender, and face slavery – or worse; or endure the siege and hope for some twist of fortune that might lure the Vikings away. They chose the latter option and endured four months of attrition before the well on the summit ran dry.[36] Without water they could not survive and were forced to capitulate. The response of the besiegers was brutal: Olaf and Ivar unleashed an orgy of plunder and destruction. A huge number of Britons were taken captive from the citadel and its hinterland, among them King Arthgal himself. All were herded onto the waiting longships and, after languishing in misery for many months, they were eventually brought to Dublin to be sold as slaves.[37] With these unfortunates went numerous other prisoners – Picts, Scots and Northumbrians – captured by Olaf and Ivar in earlier raids. The fates of all but one of the captives are unrecorded, but the general picture can no doubt be imagined: ninth-century Dublin was one of the premier slave-markets of Europe. The only prisoner whose specific fate is known is Arthgal, the deposed king of Alt Clut. For two years he was kept alive, perhaps as a hostage at Dublin, before his Norse captors murdered him in cold blood. According to the annalists, his slaying was undertaken at the request of Constantine, a son of Cináed mac Ailpín and ruler of the Scots and Picts.[38]

Rhun ab Arthgal

The defeat of the ancient Clyde kingdom and the captivity of its monarch removed a potential competitor from Constantine's political strategy, but he seemingly wanted to finish the job by destroying Arthgal. The fact that he could demand the murder presupposes a treaty or alliance with the Dublin Norse or, at the very least, some mutually agreed policy regarding the Britons. Olaf and Ivar had kept Arthgal alive for their own reasons, perhaps hoping to restore him to the Clyde as their puppet, but the inducement or reward offered by Constantine persuaded them to change their minds. An additional factor in these events was a dynastic marriage between Arthgal's son Rhun and a daughter of Cináed. As a son of this union was old enough to be a candidate for kingship in the late 870s, the marriage must have occurred long before the Viking siege of Dumbarton. It could feasibly have taken place before Cináed's death in 858, but probably not later than the accession of his son Constantine in c.862. Rhun ab Arthgal became king on the Clyde after his father's murder in 872, probably as a subordinate of his brother-in-law Constantine. Some historians propose that the subordination outlived the deaths of Rhun and Constantine to become a permanent feature of political relationships between the two kingdoms. This scenario imagines a total collapse of British rule on the Clyde after the catastrophe of 870 leading to the imposition of a new line of mac Ailpín kings.[39] Much of this thinking derives from the fourteenth-century chronicler John of Fordoun who stated that the post-870 Clyde monarchs were Gaelic princes, the heirs-in-waiting of the kingship of the Scots. Fordoun had in mind a system of succession whereby the ruling king's designated heir was appointed to oversee a subordinate realm. The old kingdom of the Clyde was thus depicted by Fordoun as little more than a mac Ailpín fief, a training-ground for princes of the Picto-Scottish kingdom. Recently, however, this picture has been questioned on the grounds that it finds no support in the earliest sources.[40] It seems, in fact, to be applicable to succession systems current in Fordoun's own period rather than to the dynastic policies of earlier times. As we shall see in this chapter and in the next, there is no evidence that the Clyde Britons were in thrall to mac Ailpín kings after 870 and every indication that their native dynasty regained its independence.

Constantine mac Cináeda was killed in 876 in a battle with Vikings at Inverdovat in Fife. Rhun ab Arthgal died around the same time or perhaps a year earlier. Even if both kings departed in the same year, they need not have perished together, in the same battle, for Rhun may already have shaken off his brother-in-law's overlordship. Hostility between the two is suggested by a reference in the obscure *Berchan's Prophecy* where, in addition to three battles against Vikings, Constantine is said to have fought 'a fourth battle, the battle of Luaire, against the king of the Britons of green mantles'.[41] We can assume that the *Prophecy* is here referring to Rhun ab Arthgal, king of the Clyde. The battle of Luaire may have been Rhun's showdown with Constantine after rejecting mac Ailpín authority and attempting to restore British independence. In the *Prophecy* the three battles fought by Constantine against Vikings are credited as victories whereas the result of his encounter with the Britons is left unstated. The battle of Luaire might have been a victory for Rhun. Even if it was not, it would have marked an important milestone in the revival of his kingdom. That such a revival took place is clear from the literary sources, which continue to refer to a British dynasty on the Clyde, and from archaeological evidence for the creation of a new centre of power. The old citadel at Dumbarton Rock was not wholly abandoned, but its importance now dwindled in favour of a site further upstream near the inflow of the River Kelvin. Here, at Govan on the south bank of the Clyde, a pre-existing ceremonial venue became the primary seat of royal authority.[42] The key features were an ancient church and cemetery, a princely estate across the Clyde at Partick and an artificial mound, known in later times as the Doomster Hill. It is to this latter feature that Govan probably owes its name, if Brittonic *go-ban*, 'little hill', is accepted as the most likely derivation.[43] Unfortunately, the mound was lost to industrial development in the nineteenth century, but old illustrations show it to have been a substantial structure with a distinctive stepped shape.[44] It may ultimately have been of prehistoric origin and could have served the ancient Damnonii as a site of public ritual long before the first Christian presence at Govan. Archaeological investigation has revealed traces of a pathway linking the Doomster Hill to the church and it is tempting to wonder if all three features were utilised when Dyfnwal ap Teudubr submitted to Óengus and Eadberht in 756.

Rhun ab Arthgal is the last king named in the Harleian genealogy of Alt Clut. This means that he occupies the most significant position in the document. The long list of patronyms extending back through the centuries is therefore an affirmation of his ancestry. Such documents were usually produced to illustrate the bloodlines of candidates for kingship and were obviously useful in times of uncertainty when issues of legitimacy and right-to-rule became crucial. A genealogist on the Clyde perhaps compiled the pedigree for Rhun around the time of his appointment as king, or at the time of his marriage to a mac Ailpín princess. Alternatively, the document may have been created to affirm the ancestry of his heir in response to a challenge from rival claimants. An additional point is the literary context in which the pedigree is preserved and, in particular, the possibility of a kinship link between Rhun and Owain ap Hywel, a tenth-century king of Deheubarth in Wales, whose pedigree stands at the head of the Harleian collection. Perhaps one of Owain's female forebears in the previous century was a princess of Alt Clut? Leaving the various genealogical questions aside, our attention turns back to the fortunes of Rhun's kingdom in the years after his death. The key figure in the ensuing sequence of events was his son Eochaid who, as a man of mixed blood, was both heir-apparent of the Clyde Britons and a grandson of Cináed mac Ailpín.

The Govan School

Before examining Eochaid's career it is worthwhile to consider what kind of kingdom he inherited from his father. In this context the various relationships between Britons, Scots and Norsemen in the years after 870 become especially relevant. At the outset an important general point needs to be made, or rather reiterated, namely that the idea of the Clyde kingdom being absorbed by the larger mac Ailpín realm appears to be a later invention. Having made this observation, there is no reason to doubt that in the immediate aftermath of the Viking siege the British kingdom experienced a period of upheaval, having lost Arthgal its king and a portion of its aristocracy. We have already envisaged a temporary overlordship being imposed on the Britons by Constantine mac Cináeda who, with the help of his Norse friends in Dublin, was in a position to dominate the dispirited remnant of the Clyde elite. The beginning of the reign of Rhun ab Arthgal, whom we have tentatively identified as Constantine's vassal, probably marked a low point in the long history of the dynasty. To this period, roughly spanning the years 870 to 878, can be assigned various inroads made by Norse and Gaelic cultural influences, a process seen most clearly in a remarkable collection of sculptured stones from the lands around the Firth of Clyde. A number of common stylistic features allow us to identify these stones as the products of a 'school' of craftsmen active from the late ninth century to the early twelfth.[45] The period of greatest output was the tenth century when the best surviving works of these craftsmen were produced. A concentration of monuments at Govan, especially in the environs of the old parish church, suggests that this was the key stoneworking centre from where the distinctive style emanated. Similar monuments in settings further afield, from Loch Lomond to Ayrshire, are regarded by archaeologists and art historians as products of the same 'school'. In addition to the premier workshop at Govan there were probably other centres, each developing its own variant style from a shared portfolio of designs and techniques.[46] Several types of monument are represented: crosses, cross-slabs, sarcophagi and hogback tombstones. Some survive only as fragments while others are complete. The finest of the surviving monuments is a sarcophagus adorned with interlace patterns and carved figures, one of which is a horseman hunting a stag.[47] In art-historical terms the school's stonework reflects a blend of influences – British, Pictish, Irish, English and Scandinavian – from which the Govan craftsmen selected particular elements to create a distinctive style of their own. The Scandinavian aspect, most vividly illustrated by the hogbacks, has given rise to a suggestion that a Norse elite seized positions of power on the Clyde in the wake of the siege of Alt Clut. Some proponents of this theory take it one stage further by envisaging the growth of a hybrid British-Scandinavian aristocracy in the ensuing decades. This is an interesting hypothesis, but not the only one available, nor is it the most plausible explanation of the sculptural evidence. A simpler alternative sees no large-scale infiltration of Viking noblemen into the society of the Clyde Britons, but instead regards the Norse artistic elements – like the Irish and English designs – as selective borrowings adapted by enterprising native craftsmen. It is worth noting that much of the stonework exhibits distinctly 'British' features reminiscent of contemporary sculpture in Wales.[48] The presence of Scandinavian designs might have no direct connection with the aftermath of the Norse siege and may have arrived on the

Clyde with friendly Hebridean Vikings rather than with a belligerent group from Dublin. Many of the Hebridean Norse were *Gall Gáidhil*, 'foreign Gaels', of mixed parentage, the offspring of intermarriage between Scandinavian settlers and native Scots. Communities of these Gall Gáidhil seem to have been established in northern Ayrshire and in other districts close to the Firth of Clyde.[49] Their contact with neighbouring Britons, via trade and other forms of communication, might explain the Norse influence on the Govan craftsmen. That this influence was a short-lived trend rather than a statement of imported Scandinavian ethnicity seems to be implied by its dwindling presence in the sculpture as the tenth century progressed. The notion of a significant Norse immigration into the Clyde in the period 870–900, in the form of an elite takeover, is therefore unsupported by the stylistic development of the Govan School. A related theory, in which the alleged Norse takeover was accompanied by a simultaneous influx of Scots, is similarly at odds with the essentially British character of the monuments. Some limited penetration of the native aristocracy by mac Ailpín henchmen is perhaps to be expected during Constantine's presumed suzerainty over Rhun ab Arthgal in the 870s, but the idea of a major colonisation by Scots followed by permanent subjugation of the Britons is inconsistent with the sculptural evidence. We may envisage instead that the Govan craftsmen borrowed freely from the artistic styles of neighbouring artisans to enhance an indigenous British stonecarving tradition.

Eochaid and Giric

As noted above, Rhun ab Arthgal married a daughter of Cináed mac Ailpín. Their son Eochaid may have succeeded to the Clyde kingship after Rhun's death in the late 870s, perhaps in 876 when Constantine mac Cináeda, the probable overlord of the North Britons, died in combat with Viking raiders. Constantine's death heralded a period of strife and uncertainty in which the unified kingship of Scots and Picts was fiercely contested between rival factions. The upheavals began after the accession of Áed mac Cináeda, Constantine's brother, a king whose one-year reign ended when he was slain in battle by his *socii*, 'associates', in Strathallan on the Perthshire–Stirlingshire border.[50] His slayer was apparently Giric, a mysterious but significant figure whose connection to the mac Ailpín royal line is difficult to assess. Giric's father was the otherwise unknown Dungal, who may have been a member of the extended mac Ailpín family, although the possibility that there was no kinship at all cannot be ruled out. The sources are somewhat confused on what happened next, but it would appear that Eochaid ap Rhun claimed the mac Ailpín kingship by virtue of his being a grandson of Cináed. In this role he is variously accorded a reign of 11, 12 or 13 years, during which time he also presumably ruled the Clyde Britons. According to one tradition, reflected in Scottish king-lists compiled much later, the immediate successor of Áed mac Cináeda was not Eochaid but Giric. The two conflicting traditions are reconciled in the *Scottish Chronicle* where Giric is called Eochaid's *alumnus*, 'foster-father', and *ordinator*, 'governor', a scenario which might hint at Eochaid being a child under Giric's guardianship. *Berchan's Prophecy* offers an alternative solution to the contradictory data by having Giric appear during Eochaid's reign to take the mac Ailpín kingship for himself. Unsurprisingly, there is no consensus of opinion among modern historians on the question of who ruled the Scots and Picts after Áed's demise. A popular compromise envisages Giric and Eochaid ruling jointly, with the former in a position of dominance as Áed's successor while the latter ruled only on the Clyde.[51] Another scenario sees Giric as a 'king-maker' who replaced Áed with his own foster-son Eochaid.[52] Turning to the name of Giric's father Dungal, the most famous bearer of this name was an eighth-century king of Cenél Loairn whose family had competed with Cenél nGabráin for the overlordship of Argyll. This earlier connotation of the name has prompted a suggestion that Giric and his father were Lorn princes engaged in a later phase of rivalry with Cenél nGabráin, the dynasty from which the mac Ailpíns claimed descent.[53] A minimalist interpretation of the data dismisses Eochaid from the debate by attributing his alleged kingship of Scots and Picts to scribal error.[54] Removing Eochaid does indeed simplify the situation by leaving Giric as Áed's successor, but requires rejection of the statement in *Berchan's Prophecy* that 'a Briton from the Clyde is placed over the Gaels'. Controversial though the *Prophecy* undoubtedly is, we cannot so easily disregard this veiled reference to Eochaid when other texts also support the idea that he ruled the Scots and Picts as well as the Britons. From the *Prophecy* we glean an additional piece of information, namely that Eochaid's mother was 'the woman from Dún Guaire', a place usually identified as the Bernician royal fortress at Bamburgh. The name *Dún Guaire* is seen as a Gaelic rendering of *Din Guayroi*, the original Brittonic name of Bamburgh, chiefly because of an old Irish reference to *Dún nGuaire i Saxonaib*, 'Dún Guaire in England'.[55] There was, however, a Dún Guaire in Ireland and other places so named perhaps existed elsewhere in the Gaelic-speaking regions. Since Eochaid's mother was a daughter of Cináed mac Ailpín and a princess of Cenél nGabráin, and thus most probably Kintyre-born, her Dún Guaire might be more logically sought in Argyll rather than in Northumbria. For her to be 'the woman from Bamburgh' we would need to construct an elaborate scenario in which she spent a significant amount of time in Northumbria, perhaps as the wife of an English nobleman, before being betrothed to Eochaid's father Rhun. This seems an unnecessarily complicated tale for a mac Ailpín princess, even in an age of inter-dynastic marriage. A far simpler context can be proposed for her: as Cináed's daughter her true place of origin, and the true location of Dún Guaire, may have lain in the Cenél nGabráin heartlands.

Whatever the precise nature of the relationship between Eochaid and Giric, both were toppled from power in 889. Eochaid's achievements went unsung, but *Berchan's Prophecy* portrays Giric as a warlike king who conquered English territory and whose subordinate clients included Britons and Scandinavians.[56] There is a hint that Giric's power passed briefly to his brother, but, within a short time, the main mac Ailpín line was restored in the person of Domnall, son of Constantine mac Cináeda. Domnall's accession coincided with an important change in the way contemporary annalists and chroniclers referred to his kingdom. In the annals his predecessors are usually given the title *rex Pictorum*, 'king of the Picts', but he is the first to be called *rí Alban*, 'king of Alba'. The change of terminology is highly significant and reflects the forging of a new political identity for the various peoples under mac Ailpín rule.[57] Henceforth, these folk would be encouraged by their masters to think of themselves not as separate ethnic groups but as *fir Alban*, 'the men of Alba'. The name is of Irish origin and was originally coined to denote the whole island of Britain. It was selected as an appropriate name for the newly unified realm in the North. Eventually, the inhabitants of Alba, even those of Pictish ancestry, were to become a nation of Gaelic-speaking 'Scots'. By the end of the ninth century, under the strong rule of the mac Ailpín dynasty, the early stages of this process were already bringing the various groups together as one people. Around the same time another terminological shift appears in the sources when references to Alt Clut suddenly disappear. This is the period when Govan rose to prominence as a new centre of power, and when its craftsmen began to produce impressive monuments commissioned by high-status Britons. The sculptural tradition represented by the Govan School begins at the end of the ninth century, its birth coinciding with the decreasing importance of Dumbarton Rock. Relocation to a less vulnerable site further inland made sound strategic sense in an era when the Firth of Clyde was navigable by Viking longships. After c.900, the annals and chronicles no longer mention Alt Clut, but refer instead to *Strat Clut*, 'Strathclyde', a name acknowledging the migration of the elite to the comparative safety of Lower Clydesdale.

Around this time, according to one curious tale, a section of the North British aristocracy who 'refused to unite with the English' migrated to Wales. The source is usually cited as *Brut y Tywysogyon* or 'Lay of the Princes', a thirteenth-century chronicle based partly on the Welsh Annals. According to this tale, King Anarawd of Gwynedd allowed refugees from the Clyde to settle on his lands in exchange for military aid against hostile English neighbours.[58] The required help was duly given by these latter-day Men of the North and the English were defeated.

Historians often quote this story in the context of social and political change on the Clyde in the late ninth century, the exiles being seen as staunch adherents of 'Britishness' who either resented Scandinavian and Gaelic influences or who wished to escape subjugation by the Scots.[59] The entire tale, as Alex Woolf has recently reminded us, is a sixteenth-century fiction.[60] Its origin can be traced not to *Brut y Tywysogyon* but to a much later English translation of a similar chronicle. The idea of a ninth-century migration from Strathclyde to Gwynedd is a red herring with no historical value.

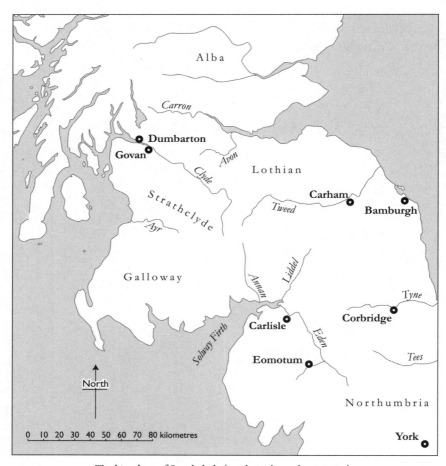

The kingdom of Strathclyde (tenth to eleventh centuries).

STRATHCLYDE

There is no mention of Eochaid ap Rhun after his expulsion from power in c.889. Contrary to a scenario promoted by medieval Scottish writers such as John of Fordoun, and still current in some quarters today, Eochaid's successors in the Strathclyde kingship were not mac Ailpín princes awaiting their turn on the throne of Alba but members of the ancient dynasty of Alt Clut. It is clear from the sources that they were men of British stock who continued to bestow Brittonic names on their offspring.[1] Their participation in the key events of the tenth century confirms their status as major players on the northern political scene. Any doubts that this was the case are dispelled by a consideration of Eochaid himself, a king whose rule over the Scots and Picts – regardless of possible deference to Giric – was a remarkable achievement for a Briton. His career not only contradicts the formerly widespread image of the post-870 Clyde kingdom as a playground for the mac Ailpíns, but implies that, if only for a brief time, the reverse may have been true. As Benjamin Hudson has remarked, the case of Eochaid surely demonstrates that within ten years of the Viking raid on Dumbarton 'the men of Strathclyde were strong enough to intrude one of their own into the kingship of Cenél nGabráin'.[2]

Whether Eochaid died before or after Giric is not known, nor is there any record of who succeeded him as king of the Britons. The Harleian pedigree of Alt Clut ends with his father Rhun and without its guidance we begin to lose sight of the dynasty's subsequent generations. Our attention switches back to the annals and chronicles where sporadic mentions of Strathclyde enable us to reconstruct, more or less, the kingdom's history in the tenth century and beyond. After Eochaid there are no useful references until the *Scottish Chronicle* mentions the death of Dyfnwal, 'king of the Britons', during the very long reign in Alba of Constantine, Áed's son, another of Cináed's grandsons. Although no patronym is given for Dyfnwal, he was probably a member of the old royal family of Dumbarton. The date of his death is unknown, but he was dead by c.930, after which time the sources refer to other kings ruling on the Clyde. In so far as a rough chronological context can be devised for Dyfnwal he appears to be a figure of the first quarter of the tenth century, in which case his father or grandfather might be Eochaid ap Rhun.[3] Alternatively, the succession could have passed through a nephew or brother of Eochaid to a different branch of the royal family represented by Dyfnwal. Meanwhile, in Alba, Constantine mac Áeda became a prime mover in the complex web of military alliances and shifting allegiances that characterised tenth-century politics. His interests and ambitions extended southward to bring him into contact with the kingdoms of southern and midland England. Thus, although his primary focus lay in the North, the political circumstances of the time drew him into a tangled net of relationships involving all the peoples of the British Isles. At the centre of this net stood the powerful English kingdom of Wessex, the realm of the West Saxons, ruled by the heirs of Alfred the Great. As the tenth century progressed, the West Saxon kings began to change forever the political map of Britain by redrawing boundaries and allegiances in line with their own ambitions. In so doing, they laid the foundations for what was soon to become a unified England. Their primary contacts included the Scandinavian rulers of Dublin, York and elsewhere, together with various Welsh and Irish kings. Constantine of Alba, himself a monarch of considerable power and ambition, was not the kind of man to stand on the sidelines. He became deeply embroiled in the political fray on many occasions. With their mac Ailpín neighbours taking part in these great events, it was inevitable that the Strathclyde Britons would also get involved.

Constantine's kingdom stretched from Kintyre in the west to the North Sea coast of eastern Perthshire, and from Stirlingshire in the south to the Grampian Mountains. North of the Grampians lay a separate realm of Scots and Picts ruled by Gaelic-speaking kings who claimed descent from the Cenél Loairn of Argyll, and further north in Caithness a group of Norse colonies were ruled by their own earls. South-east of Alba lay Lothian, still nominally a Northumbrian province but under increasing pressure from the Scots. West of Lothian the Strathclyde Britons still held sway over their ancient lands. The distribution of the sculptural style exemplified by the Govan School indicates that the artistic and religious patronage – and thus the secular authority – of the tenth-century Clyde kings encompassed an area at least as large as the core territory of ancient Alt Clut. Sculptural evidence in Ayrshire shows not only the south-western expansion of the Govan style but also that of its patrons into a region formerly menaced by Northumbrian warbands. There was little prospect of those warbands returning, for Northumbria in the early 900s was not the land-hungry realm of former times. The outer provinces of its former hegemony had already been lost and the majority of its kings were now Scandinavian rather than English. A rump of English power still remained in the old Bernician heartlands north of the Tees, but districts further west were being coveted by opportunist neighbours. Among the latter were the Strathclyde Britons who, having emerged bruised but intact from the first century of Viking aggression, now began to turn the tables on their ancient foe.

The Barochan Cross, a striking monument of the Strathclyde Britons, now
stands in Paisley Abbey. Drawing reproduced from J.R. Allen & J. Anderson,
The Early Christian Monuments of Scotland (Edinburgh, 1903).

Cumbrians

Northumbria entered the tenth century as a divided land. Bernicia, the northern part, lay under the rule of English lords whose base lay at Bamburgh. Much of Lothian, including what had once been the Gododdin fortress at Edinburgh, still answered to their authority. Deira, Northumbria's southern province, had been conquered by Vikings in the 860s and was now the core of a Scandinavian kingdom ruled from York. Across the Pennines a long swath of coastline from the Mersey to the Solway supported a scatter of Norse settlements. North of the Solway in Galloway and Dumfriesshire the surviving English lordships coexisted with Scandinavian and British neighbours. It was during the early 900s that the eastern end of this region, including the lands around Carlisle, reverted to the Britons. No contemporary source tells how this *reconquista* was achieved, but the place-name data for Dumfriesshire and the former county of Cumberland provide the evidence. This is revealed most clearly where names of English origin, coined during three centuries of Bernician rule, were encountered by incoming Brittonic-speakers.[4] The result in each case was a variant of the English name or a hybrid formed by prefixing a Brittonic element to an English one. Examples include Carlatton, a rendering into Brittonic speech of Anglo-Norse *Carlatun*, 'village of the churls', and Carhullan, the *caer* or fortified residence of an Englishman called Holand.[5] Behind some of these changes lay a transfer of land-ownership from Englishman to Briton and, by inference, the expulsion of Northumbrian aristocrats from their estates. That the incoming Britons were able to alter the names of human settlements and topographical features identifies them as members of a powerful elite capable of seizing and holding territory by force. In other words, the reconquest was achieved not by a mass immigration of peasants but by a takeover at the upper levels of society. At that time, the only group of North Britons with the military muscle to achieve such a takeover was the aristocracy of Strathclyde. Hardened by a grim struggle for survival in the previous century, the Clyde Britons now ruthlessly exploited Northumbria's decline. By the 920s their authority reached as far south as the River Eamont whose course in later times marked the county boundary between Cumberland and Westmorland.[6] To this remarkable expansion Cumberland owes its name, as does its post-1974 successor Cumbria. Both names mean 'land of the Britons' and contain Old English *Cumber* which in turn derived from a word used by the Britons of themselves.[7] The ancestral term was Brittonic *Combrogi*, 'fellow countrymen', which also produced *Cymry*, 'The Welsh', and *Cymru*, 'Wales'. As we shall see in this chapter, contemporary English writers of the tenth and eleventh centuries often called the Strathclyde Britons *Cumbrenses*, 'Cumbrians', for in those days the term did not have the restricted geographical meaning it has today.

Wessex and the North

Alfred the Great thwarted the ambitions of Viking warlords in southern and midland England. At his death in 900 the Danes held East Anglia, much of Northumbria and the eastern part of Mercia – regions known collectively as the Danelaw – but Wessex, western Mercia and the southernmost English king-doms remained unconquered. Alfred's son, Edward the Elder, succeeded to the West Saxon kingship and was the acknowledged overlord of non-Scandinavian England. Edward resolved to continue his father's policy of driving back the Danish armies and recovering lost English territories. Beyond the Mersey and Humber the chief landward menace came from the Viking kingdom of York, while in the seaways the Dublin Norse and the Gall Gáidhil posed a continuing threat. Edward's military forces could not deal with these northern and western perils while campaigning elsewhere so he wisely sought allies and clients among the Celtic peoples. In his anti-Scandinavian ventures he was assisted by his sister Aethelflaed and her husband Aethelred, who jointly ruled western Mercia under West Saxon overlordship. After Aethelred's death in 911, Aethelflaed became sole ruler and was known thereafter as *Myrcna hlaefdige*, 'The Lady of the Mercians'.[8] She continued to harass the Danes and supported the campaigns of her brother Edward, assisting him in building a line of fortresses across central England from the Thames to the Dee. Taking an active role in war, she led her Mercian soldiers on many successful forays, mostly in the Danelaw but also against the Welsh. In 917, she greatly enhanced her reputation by capturing the Danish stronghold of Derby. Her anti-Viking policies were not, however, confined to the frontiers of Mercia. She was acutely aware of the threat posed by Norse coastal settlements in Lancashire and Cheshire and across the Solway Firth in Galloway. Her anxieties about the situation in these northern regions were not alleviated by the arrival in Anglo-Scandinavian York of the Dublin warlord Ragnall, an ambitious and powerful figure whose grandfather Ivar had led the great raid on Dumbarton in 870. In response to the growing uncertainty Aethelflaed forged a military alliance with the Scots and Strathclyde Britons.

English sources say little of Aethelflaed's dealings with the North, perhaps to avoid any dilution of her brother's achievements. The only record of her alliance with the northern powers is a brief account preserved in the *Fragmentary Annals of Ireland*, a source of probable eleventh-century origin preserved in a seven-teenth-century manuscript.[9] According to these annals, 'the Scots and Britons fell upon the towns of the Scandinavians, destroyed and pillaged them', a reference perhaps to raids on frontier settlements of the York kingdom. Ragnall retaliated by attacking Strathclyde, but was unable to subdue it and withdrew after taking plunder.[10] These raids and counter-raids occurred either before or after a battle between Ragnall and the Scots on the banks of the Tyne at Corbridge in 918. Although the Britons are not mentioned among the participants, we may assume that they were present as allies of Aethelflaed. The location makes it rather less likely that the Lady of the Mercians herself took part, or that she sent a contingent of her own warriors so far north. English troops did fight alongside the Scots and Britons, but they were men of Northumbrian stock led by Ealdred, son of Eadwulf of Bamburgh, whom Ragnall had ousted from the kingship of York. In the end the battle was indecisive, but it left Ragnall still *in situ* as king of Northumbria.[11] In June of the same year, Aethelflaed died in her palace at Tamworth, having played a key role in rallying the northern Celtic kings to join Wessex and Mercia in an anti-Scandinavian coalition. Her brother Edward maintained the impetus of her diplomacy and, two years after her death, he is said to have secured Ragnall's formal submission. The ceremony occurred soon after Edward built a fortress at Bakewell in northern Mercia and may have taken place there. Aethelflaed's former allies were also present alongside Ragnall, but whether he or they actually paid homage to Edward is debatable.[12] The starting-point for any discussion of the event is the entry for 920 in the *Anglo-Saxon Chronicle*, which says of Edward:

> He was chosen as father and lord by the king of the Scots and all the Scottish people, by Ragnall, and Eadwulf's sons, and all who dwell in Northumbria, English, Danes, Norse and others, and the king of the Strathclyde Welsh (*Straecledwealas*), and the Strathclyde Welsh themselves.

Here the *Chronicle* may be showing West Saxon bias by exaggerating Edward's dominance over the northern peoples. It seems unlikely, for instance, that he had defeated or subdued Ragnall at this time, still less the Scots and Britons further north. A more realistic interpretation of the event of 920 may be that it sealed a non-aggression pact whereby the northern Celtic kings would refrain from attacking Ragnall as long as the latter refrained from stirring the Danelaw against Edward.[13] Ealdred of Bamburgh returned to his coastal stronghold and relinquished his claim on the York kingship. The king of Scots at this time was Constantine mac Áeda, by then entering the third decade of his long reign. He had been Aethelflaed's partner in the recent Northumbrian wars and had led his army against Ragnall at Corbridge. His Strathclyde counterpart is not identified in the sources but may have been the Dyfnwal who appears at the beginning of this chapter. Nothing in the various chronicles and annals suggests that the Clyde Britons were under Constantine's heel or that their king was a lesser partner in the alliance with Aethelflaed. Nevertheless, the mac Ailpíns were very powerful neighbours whose military resources were undoubtedly greater than those available to the Strathclyde dynasty. The relationship between the two realms during

Constantine's reign might therefore have been unequal in some measure, even if it fell short of formal subjugation. Some form of homage seems possible, perhaps couched in terms of mutual obligations of which Alba was the main beneficiary. On the other hand, Strathclyde's membership of Aethelflaed's alliance implies that she and her brother Edward regarded the North Britons as independent of the Scots and capable of making their own political decisions.

Athelstan

Edward the Elder died in 924. His son Athelstan succeeded him as king of the West Saxons and as overlord of what was gradually becoming 'England', the kingdom of the English. The new monarch soon displayed the energy and ambition of his forefathers and, in 927, he received the submission of a group of Welsh and northern rulers at a ceremony beside the River Eamont near Penrith.[14] Constantine mac Áeda was present, together with the Bernician lord Ealdred of Bamburgh, two Welsh kings and, according to the twelfth-century chronicler William of Malmesbury, a king of Strathclyde called Owain. Whether the latter was indeed present we cannot be sure. In one version of the *Anglo-Saxon Chronicle* 'Owain, king of the people of Gwent' is listed among the participants, but modern historians generally regard this as a garbled reference to Owain of Strathclyde.[15] Meetings of this kind, involving several powerful figures, required an appropriately symbolic location such as a frontier between an overlord and one or more clients. The spread of Brittonic place-names into the lands south of Carlisle at this time makes the River Eamont the likely southern limit of a newly enlarged Strathclyde.[16] Eamont probably marked the interface between Athelstan's England and the Celtic North. The actual site of the ceremony is not pinpointed by the sources and we are left to wonder where it lay. The ancient crossing-place at Eamont Bridge south of Penrith, the Northumbrian monastery at Dacre and the Roman fort at Brougham are all possible alternatives. Brougham has the advantage of being closer to the confluence of Eamont and Lowther from which the Old English name *Eomotum*, 'river junction', arose.[17] On the other hand Penrith bears a name similar to Welsh *pen rhyd* which, as well as denoting 'ford-end', can also convey the meaning 'chief ford'. If the latter is the true meaning behind the place-name, it implies that the ford on the Eamont held special status in the eyes of local Britons.

If Owain represented the Clyde Britons at Eamont in 927, he had probably not long succeeded Dyfnwal. The latter's death is listed by the *Scottish Chronicle* as one of several events occurring during Constantine's reign in Alba.[18] Dyfnwal's passing is immediately followed by that of the Irish ruler Domnall mac Áeda, king of Ailech, who died in 915. Because Domnall's kingdom is given in the

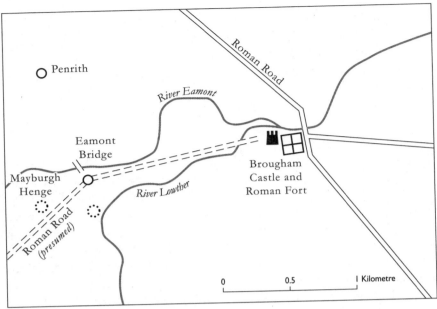

Eomotum: geographical context of the meeting of kings in 927.

form *Elig* it was long unrecognised by modern historians and misunderstood as an abbreviation for Latin *eligitur*, 'was elected'. This led to the information on Domnall being seen not as a note of his death but as a reference to his 'election' as Dyfnwal's successor. From it sprang a widespread belief that Constantine mac Áeda had a brother called Domnall who was elected to the Strathclyde kingship after Dyfnwal's death. With the true reading of *elig* as *Ailech* now revealed we can dismiss any notion that the Britons received a mac Ailpín prince as their king.[19] Dyfnwal's actual successor was Owain, who was probably his son.

Whatever the terms of Constantine's submission to Athelstan on the Eamont in 927 they were eventually disregarded and, in 934, the West Saxon king marched north to enforce his supremacy. An English fleet harried the east coast as far north as Aberdeenshire or even further towards Caithness, while an army invaded Perthshire from the south. A reference to Edinburgh lying along the land-route suggests a march by Athelstan's forces through the domains of Anglo-Scandinavian clients in Northumbria. Constantine mac Áeda was defeated and his territories ravaged. It is hard to imagine Strathclyde avoiding a similar fate, either during Athelstan's northward march or on his triumphant homeward journey. If so, then the English king secured the submission not only of the Scots but also of the Britons. His superiority in the North was certainly restored, thereby giving substance to the grandiose description proclaimed on his coinage: *rex totius Britanniae*, 'king of all Britain'. During the next couple of years both Constantine and Owain were obliged to attend his court as obedient vassals. Charters confirming land-grants to Athelstan's English henchmen show the two northern kings in attendance, their names heading lists of witnesses. These grants took place in southern England, in Athelstan's core territory, and were regarded as important demonstrations of royal authority. Vassal-rulers visiting their overlord's court were expected to witness royal charters, as were various noblemen and bishops of his realm. The order of names on the witness-lists reflects the status of each witness and it is worthy of note, as Alex Woolf has recently pointed out, that Owain is listed second only to Constantine and above the kings of Wales.[20] Any notion that the Strathclyde Britons were minor players in the tenth-century political arena can thus be discarded. In the short term, both Constantine and Owain had little choice but to fulfil their oaths to Athelstan by visiting his court and witnessing land-grants. In the longer term both intended to break free of their obligations. Athelstan's ambition to dominate the whole of Britain, and the possibility that he might achieve it, meant that he had to be stopped at some point. Eventually, the two northern kings joined other Celtic and Scandinavian powers to form a combined front against him. Setting aside their own differences the allies began to devise a strategy for his downfall.

The Battle of Brunanburh

A tenth-century poem, the *Armes Prydein* or 'Prophecy of Britain', was composed in Wales as a rallying-call for the coalition. The poet does not mention Athelstan by name, referring to him only as the 'Great King'. It was not, however, from Wales that the most vigorous challenge eventually came but from the North and from across the Irish Sea. The campaign to thwart Athelstan's ambitions commenced in late summer or early autumn of 937 with an attack on Northumbria by coalition warbands. These were led by Olaf Guthfrithsson of Dublin, Constantine of Alba and Owain of Strathclyde. Olaf's Vikings were supplemented by others from York, but his main force sailed over from Ireland to unite with the Scots and Britons as they marched south from their own lands. The landing-place of the Dublin fleet has not been located, but it lay on the western coast of Britain and was not, as the twelfth-century chronicler John of Worcester erroneously believed, in the Humber. The ensuing battle was one of the most famous events of the Viking Age and was widely reported by contemporary observers. To the Irish annalists it was chiefly a conflict between English and Norse interests:

> A great battle, lamentable and terrible, was savagely fought between Saxons and Northmen, and in it fell many thousands which have not been counted,

of the Northmen. But their king Olaf escaped with a few. And on the other side a multitude of Saxons fell, but Athelstan the king of the Saxons obtained a great victory.[21]

A much briefer notice appears in the Welsh Annals as *bellum brune*, 'the battle of Brune'. The most detailed information comes from West Saxon sources, the earliest of which are a celebratory poem in Old English embedded in the *Anglo-Saxon Chronicle* and the writings of the tenth-century chronicler Aethelweard. Additional data comes from twelfth-century English texts such as the chronicles of John of Worcester and William of Malmesbury and the *Historia Regum Anglorum* attributed to Symeon of Durham. From the various references we learn that the battle was fought at a place called *Brunanburh* or *Brunnanwerc*, both names possibly meaning 'Bruna's fort', and that an alternative name was *Weondune* which seems to mean 'Hill of the Swelling'. The question of where the battlefield actually lay has narrowed in recent years to focus on three locations: Bromborough on the Wirral peninsula, Burnswark in Dumfriesshire and Brinsworth in South Yorkshire. The latter's candidacy requires accepting the Humber as Olaf's route of approach, a scenario incompatible with the Norse fleet's identification as a Dublin force.[22] On geographical grounds Bromborough's western setting makes it a realistic suggestion and it has a place-name that *could* have evolved from an original Old English *Brunanburh*.[23] However, the low-lying Wirral has no plausible candidates for Weondune, 'Hill of the Swelling', nor is there an obvious *burh* or *werc* or similar fortification in the vicinity. These objections do not apply to Burnswark which satisfies the required topography far better.[24] A somewhat larger obstacle for supporters of the Bromborough theory is the matter of military logistics, a topic all too frequently ignored in studies of early medieval battles. How, for instance, would the Scots and Strathclyde Britons have travelled to a site on the Mersey estuary? One solution envisages the northern Celtic armies arriving by sea, either in their own vessels or as passengers in Olaf's longships. This is not a necessary deduction from the Old English poem which, while describing the Norsemen fleeing to their ships after the battle, observes that Constantine of Alba simply 'went in flight north into his own land', presumably on foot. The traditional route for mac Ailpín raids on English territory lay not via the seaways but overland through Stirlingshire and Lothian along well-trodden highways. There is little need to imagine Constantine abandoning this tradition in favour of a sea voyage, even if his rendezvous with Olaf took place near the Mersey. The same doubts about sea transportation apply also to the Strathclyde Britons, whose only known naval ventures are a series of short voyages to Ireland in the seventh and eighth centuries. A voyage to the Wirral was an entirely different prospect. Neither they nor the Scots were great seapowers in the era of Brunanburh, nor indeed were any non-Scandinavian people in the waters around the British Isles.[25] Any suggestion that the northern Celtic armies were transported by Olaf's fleet requires us to imagine space being made available on his longships or surplus craft being loaned to his allies, neither of which seems a plausible scenario. A more realistic solution is to envisage Constantine and Owain leading their forces to Brunanburh by overland marches from their respective kingdoms. Whether this was a long march to the Wirral or a shorter march to Burnswark is an unanswerable question.

Regardless of where the 'great battle' was fought, it had profound consequences for all involved. Athelstan's victory reaffirmed his status as overlord of Britain and strengthened his position as king of all the English. Constantine of Alba, by then a grey-haired veteran nearing the end of his reign, presumably submitted to Athelstan and renewed his oath of fealty. He seems to have remained a subordinate of the West Saxon kings until his retirement to a monastery in c.943. Olaf of Dublin died in 941 while raiding English lands in Lothian. Athelstan himself died in 939. It is not known if Owain of Strathclyde survived the slaughter of 937, but it may be assumed that he or his successor – his son Dyfnwal – also acknowledged Athelstan as lord. Even if Owain did not fall at Brunanburh, he was evidently dead or otherwise absent from the political scene a few years later, if the traditions surrounding Saint Catroe reveal an accurate chronology. Catroe was a Scot or Gaelic-speaking Pict, a native of Perthshire, who passed through Strathclyde while on pilgrimage. There he received hospitality from King Dyfnwal, ruler of *terram Cumbrorum*, 'the land of the Cumbrians', and stayed with him for a time. He subsequently travelled to the Continent, to the Frankish kingdoms, ending a successful ecclesiastical career as abbot of Metz where he is venerated as a patron saint. According to a contemporary Life, written at Metz approximately 12 years after Catroe's death in c.971, the saint was a relative of King Dyfnwal.[26] Although the nature of their kinship is not described, it raises three interesting possibilities: either Catroe's ancestry was part-British, or Dyfnwal's part-Scottish, or their families were connected by marriage. The saint's name appears to be Brittonic rather than Gaelic, containing a first element derived from *cad*, 'battle', which could be Pictish or British. His father Fochereach bore a Gaelic name and was presumably a Scot or a Gaelic-speaking Pict, but the name of his mother Bania could be Gaelic or Brittonic. Both parents were said to be of royal blood so a political marriage between either of their families and the Strathclyde dynasty is not implausible. Dyfnwal ab Owain certainly showed his kinsman an appropriate level of hospitality befitting a high-status guest. The author of the Life believed that Catroe was brought to Strathclyde by Constantine mac Áeda, although this should mean no more than a guarantee of the pilgrim's safety to the frontier of Alba and the provision of an armed escort. There may be a veiled hint of mac Ailpín superiority in the foisting of a Gaelic monk on the goodwill of the Britons, but, on the other hand, Dyfnwal's hospitality may have been given willingly to his guest, quite regardless of kinship or of subservience to Constantine. The generosity of the Strathclyde court included safe passage to the border between the Britons and the *Normannorum*, 'Northmen', the Scandinavian rulers of Northumbria. At a frontier settlement called *Loida*, perhaps near the River Lowther in Westmorland, the pilgrim was met by a local lord of Viking stock who escorted him to York. There a certain King Erichius gave further assistance before Catroe continued his journey southward to London. 'Erichius' is usually identified as Eric or Erik, a mysterious figure whose sporadic rule of York in the late 940s and early 950s occurred some years after Catroe's pilgrimage. This might or might not be the famous Norwegian warlord Erik Bloodaxe.[27]

Edmund and Malcolm

At the time of Catroe's journey the dominant English king was Athelstan's brother Edmund who had shared in the great victory of 937. Athelstan's hegemony over the North did not dissolve after his death in 939 and was maintained by Edmund's own achievements. The *Fragmentary Annals of Ireland* report Edmund's victory in 940 over Constantine mac Áeda, the Strathclyde Britons and a Dublin Viking called Olaf Cuarán.[28] This battle may have reaffirmed West Saxon authority over the old northern alliance. Four years later Edmund fought in Northumbria against the same Olaf and again emerged victorious. By then, the elderly Constantine had entered monastic retirement after almost half a century in the kingship of Alba. For reasons unknown, but perhaps because of dynastic strife, his surviving son Ildulb did not immediately succeed him. Instead, the next king was Malcolm mac Domnaill, a son of Constantine's cousin and a great-grandson of Cináed mac Ailpín. Historians sometimes refer to this king as Malcolm I and the same convention will be followed here, partly to avoid confusion with his grandson Malcolm mac Cináeda and also with a namesake from Strathclyde whom we shall meet soon. Relations between Malcolm I and Edmund went beyond the grudging obligations of vassal and overlord to become something more akin to a working relationship, with Edmund recognising the new king of Scots as a trusted custodian of West Saxon interests in the North and as a bulwark against the Britons and Scandinavians. The growing friendship between Malcolm and his powerful English patron brought to an end the tripartite Norse–Celtic alliance of the 930s and left the Britons dangerously exposed to Edmund's ambitions. With no fear of an armed response from Alba, the West Saxon king launched a devastating raid on Strathclyde in 945, perhaps as a stark reminder to Dyfnwal ab Owain of the obligations of clientship – or maybe Dyfnwal simply had too many Viking friends.[29]

Details of the campaign are vague, but the late Welsh text *Brut y Tywysogyon* claims that the English 'slew cruelly those whom they found in their way, of the Britons and those who belonged to them', a statement which seems to encompass districts under Strathclyde rule but not inhabited by Britons.[30] If this tradition has any historical validity, it might point to victims not only on the Clyde but also in former Bernician lands around the Solway Firth, in which case Edmund may have been seeking to wrest control of this region.[31] That the raid had a punitive or vengeful aspect is shown by the brutal treatment meted out to two of Dyfnwal's sons who were blinded by Edmund's troops. The circumstances suggest that both princes were already held by the English king as captives or hostages. Dyfnwal himself survived the onslaught and retained, or was permitted to retain, the kingship of his realm, but overall authority on the Clyde was temporarily granted to Malcolm of Alba. The *Anglo-Saxon Chronicle* reported the sequence of events in a brief summary:

> King Edmund harried all Cumberland and let it all to Malcolm, king of Scots, on the condition that he be his together-worker on sea and on land.[32]

The term 'together-worker' is a literal translation of Old English *midwyrhta* and perhaps conveys the nature of Edmund's association with Malcolm more accurately than 'ally', the latter being more commonly used of equal partners. As the favoured *midwyrhta* of an English overking, Malcolm may have been perceived by the Britons and others not as Edmund's trusted henchman but as his lackey in the North. The term 'Cumberland' here refers to Strathclyde, the land of the Cumbrians, rather than to the later English county. Its 'letting' to Malcolm implies a temporary grant of suzerainty over Dyfnwal and a short-term diversion of tribute to the mac Ailpín treasury. These benefits were conditional on Malcolm's continued support of West Saxon policy.[33] Permanent absorption of Strathclyde into the kingdom of the Scots is not implied by the *Anglo-Saxon Chronicle*, while the Welsh Annals merely state that 'Strathclyde was wasted by the Saxons' and make no mention of Malcolm.

After Edmund's assassination in 946, his younger brother Eadred succeeded him. The new king at once made a show of force in Northumbria, apparently against rebels, before receiving from the loyal *midwyrhta* Malcolm a renewal of oaths.[34] Malcolm's usefulness to the West Saxon dynasty was proved again in 949 by a raid on Northumbria in which he harassed the troublesome Anglo-Scandinavian elite of York. The Irish annals report what may be a second raid in 952 in which the Scots acted in alliance with the English and Britons, the latter presumably Strathclyders rather than Welshmen.[35] The annalists give neither the location of the attack nor the names of the rulers involved, but, if the context has been interpreted correctly, the fighting took place on the northern margins of Northumbria. Irish tradition assigned victory to the Scandinavians, presumably those of York. The Britons, we may assume, were led to war by Dyfnwal ab Owain.

An outbreak of dynastic infighting among the Scots claimed the life of Malcolm I in 954, the year in which the aforementioned 'Eric' was expelled from Northumbria by his subjects. In Alba the kingship passed to Ildulb, son of Constantine mac Áeda, but at York the line of kings came to an end. The Anglo-Scandinavian elites of Northumbria gave up their independence by accepting the authority of Eadred of Wessex. On the Clyde the indomitable Dyfnwal was still king. His realm had endured invasion and defeat, two of his sons had been savagely mutilated, but he remained in power as sovereign lord of an ancient kingdom. Many of his contemporaries in other lands had fallen to the perils of the age yet he was destined to play an active role in northern politics for a further 20 years. He was perhaps still reigning when Ildulb of Alba, who ruled the Scots from 954 to 962, made war on Strathclyde and Northumbria. In the words of *Berchan's Prophecy*, Ildulb's campaigns brought 'woe to the Britons and Saxons' and gained new territory 'from a foreign land, by might'.[36] In this instance the 'foreign land' was Northumbria and the annexed territory lay in Lothian in what had once been the kingdom of Gododdin. The chief prize was Edinburgh, ancient Din Eidyn, a place continuously held by English rulers based at Bamburgh since the Bernician expansion of the seventh century.[37] Capturing the citadel was an act of great symbolism and a major triumph for mac Ailpín ambitions south of the Forth. By wresting the heartland of Lothian out of English hands for the first time in more than 300 years Ildulb was helping to shape the Anglo-Scottish border we see today. But the long years of Northumbrian rule had left an indelible mark on the region and its inhabitants: the Votadini of old were a distant memory and there was to be no belated revival of Brittonic language and culture.

After Ildulb's death in 962 two rival mac Ailpín kings reigned in swift succession, or perhaps jointly in an uneasy power-sharing arrangement. One of these was Dub, son of Malcolm I, for whom the sources preserve no record of dealings with Strathclyde. In 965 Dub defeated in battle his rival or co-ruler Cuilén, Ildulb's son, but died in the following year while campaigning near the Moray Firth. Cuilén then became sole king of Alba and reigned for a further five years. An entry under 971 in the Irish annals notes his downfall:

Cuilén, Ildulb's son, king of Alba, was killed by the Britons in a battle rout.[38]

Irish tradition claimed that the Britons slew Cuilén *at tigh tenedh*, 'in a burning house' and that his brother Eochaid was slain alongside him. The *Scottish Chronicle* identifies the killer as Amdarch or Radharc, Dyfnwal's son, who slew Cuilén and

Eochaid 'for the sake of his daughter, in *Ybandonia*'.[39] Amdarch or Radharc has been seen as an otherwise unknown Strathclyde prince bearing the more familiar name Rhydderch. The form *Radharc* and other forms such as *Radhard* seem to support this emendation, but *Amdarch* and its own variants appear in more than one manuscript of the *Scottish Chronicle* and might correspond to a genuine Brittonic name. The place *Ybandonia* where Cuilén died has been equated with Abington in Lanarkshire, presumably because of a superficial phonetic similarity, but this has rightly been questioned.[40] Ybandonia is more likely to be a Brittonic or Gaelic name, albeit one corrupted and clumsily Latinised, whose original form has been lost through scribal error in the process of transmission and recopying. An alternative place-name, together with more detail about the nature of the grievance against Cuilén, appears in the twelfth-century *Chronicle of Melrose*:

> He was a foolish man. It is said that Radhard slaughtered him in *Loinas* because of the rape of his daughter, whom the king had carried off for himself.[41]

Loinas corresponds closely to old forms of the name 'Lothian', but could also mean Lennox, the vale of the River Leven running south from Loch Lomond. Lennox was a domain of the kings of Strathclyde and later became a Scottish earldom. Both Lennox and Lothian provide plausible settings for tenth-century hostilities between Britons and Scots, with neither region seeming more likely than the other. Dyfnwal, the father of Amdarch or Rhydderch, was almost certainly Dyfnwal ab Owain, the veteran king of Strathclyde and survivor of many northern wars. His granddaughter was perhaps in her teens or twenties in 971 so he may have been approaching old age at the time of her violation by Cuilén. The circumstances suggest a visit by the king of Alba to Dyfnwal's court, followed by a severe abuse of hospitality.[42] Nothing more is heard of Amdarch/Rhydderch after this incident, but his brothers and their father continued to play significant roles in northern politics until the end of the century and into the new millennium.

Vassals and Overlords

With Northumbria now firmly attached to the authority of the West Saxon kings, the boundaries of England were taking shape. Since 959 the English had been ruled by Edgar, a son of Edmund and nephew of Athelstan. He may have owed his position to the support of powerful Anglo-Scandinavian elites in the northern and eastern parts of his realm. His contact with the northern Celtic kingdoms was minimal throughout most of his reign, at least until the accession in Alba of Cináed II in 971. Cináed was a son of Malcolm I, the king whose amicable relations with Edgar's father make him the most Anglophile of all tenth-century Scottish monarchs. Cináed's reign began with a raid on Strathclyde, but this ended in defeat for his *pedestres*, 'land forces', at *Moin Vacoruar* or *Vacornari*, a *moin* or 'moss' presumably within the territory of the Britons.[43] A suggestion that the battle was fought on the Cornie Burn near the former Bernician monastery of Abercorn on the Firth of Forth seems faintly plausible, but any area of boggy ground within a day's march of Clydesdale could be proposed. This rout of the Scots says much for the military capability of tenth-century Strathclyde and suggests that the kingdom was still a power to be reckoned with. The battle may have been the last of Dyfnwal's reign for, sometime before 973, he abdicated the kingship in favour of his son Malcolm. Amdarch or Rhydderch, the prince credited with slaying Cuilén two years earlier, was either dead or infirm or otherwise ineligible to rule. Perhaps Malcolm was the eldest able-bodied son and therefore the heir-designate? The two sons of Dyfnwal cruelly blinded by English soldiers in 945 might still have been alive, but neither of these maimed men would have been deemed fit to rule the kingdom. Malcolm duly became king, with Dyfnwal apparently retaining an advisory role.

In 973, Malcolm was one of a group of kings who met Edgar of Wessex at a formal ceremony on the River Dee. John of Worcester, our principal source for this event, reports it in the context of a formal submission by various Welsh and northern rulers to a West Saxon overlord. According to the twelfth-century Worcester chronicle, the meeting occurred immediately after a circumnavigation by Edgar of the coasts of *Britannia*, a voyage in which he was escorted by a huge English fleet. Here the chronicler probably used the term *Britannia* to simply mean 'Wales' rather than the island of Britain as a whole.[44] Mooring at Chester, Edgar allegedly summoned the other rulers to attend upon him, commanding them to swear oaths of allegiance as his vassals. He then boarded a boat on the nearby river and took the helm while his fellow kings hauled the oars. The Worcester chronicle named the northerners as Maccus Haraldsson of the Hebrides, Cináed II of Alba and Malcolm 'king of the Cumbrians'. Mention is also made of a King Dyfnwal whom we can identify as Malcolm's father. The other attendees came from Wales or, in one case, from the Norse earldom of Orkney. A great deal of controversy surrounds this event and scepticism has been raised about its historicity. It may be little more than a twelfth-century fiction promoted by English propagandists to glorify the old West Saxon dynasty or, if its origins are indeed early, it might be based on folklore about Edgar. Contemporary or near-contemporary sources are mostly silent on the matter, the exception being a Life of Saint Swithun, written c.1000, in which eight kings are said to have submitted to Edgar on a single day. If the Chester gathering did occur, it need not have been the display of subservience envisaged by John of Worcester but a meeting of independent rulers who regarded each other as peers and equals.[45] The image of one king being rowed along the Dee by others can be explained in terms requiring no connotations of homage or subservience. By grasping the helm Edgar may simply have taken a role expected of the host, in which case the Worcester version reflects a later exaggeration of his status. On the other hand, the position of helmsman surely conveyed the symbolism of command and authority to contemporary observers. Assuming that the royal conclave actually happened, and that it was not a ceremony of submission, we should picture the two Strathclyde envoys as potential allies with whom Edgar wished to discuss specific issues. The relationship between Edgar and Cináed, for instance, was evidently based on stabilising the volatile Bernician frontier between their realms. The two men were already acquainted, for Cináed had visited the English court on at least one occasion and, according to the *Scottish Chronicle*, had held Edgar's son as a hostage. Their discussions at Chester, or at a later meeting, may have resulted in the formal cession of Lothian to Alba, thereby bringing a temporary suspension to the grim cycle of raid and counter-raid. Edgar's dealings with Strathclyde are unreported, but the old warlord Dyfnwal ab Owain would have driven a hard bargain in any negotiations. The ruling king Malcolm ap Dyfnwal, a man whose brothers had been blinded by West Saxon soldiers, was no more likely than his father to offer unconditional friendship to Edgar. During the latter's reign there is no hint in the sources of English attacks on Strathclyde, nor of new campaigns to regain lost Bernician lands north of the Solway, so perhaps a mutual non-aggression pact was indeed crafted at Chester in 973.

The sources hint at hostile relations between Britons and Scots in the last quarter of the tenth century. Raids mounted by Cináed II against Strathclyde had been strongly resisted and his army had suffered a heavy defeat at *Moin Vacoruar*. The *Scottish Chronicle* informs us that Cináed 'walled the banks of the fords of Forthin', a statement usually associated with the crossings of the River Forth at the ancient fords of Frew.[46] If this is indeed a reference to fortifications or defences being erected at Frew, the anticipated threat lay across the river in what had formerly been western Manau. The most likely aggressors in this region were warbands from Strathclyde striking north to plunder erstwhile Pictish estates in Menteith. On geographical grounds it is less likely that the Forth defences were thrown up against the English, whose nearest military forces lay far to the south beyond the recent Scottish gains in Lothian. Another theatre of tenth-century conflict between Scots and Britons may have lain in the Firth of Clyde, where an ancient boundary between Cenél Comgaill and the kings of Alt Clut seemingly divided the Cowal peninsula. Our attention is drawn to the nearby Isle of Bute where the monastery at Kingarth, a major religious centre within Cenél Comgaill territory, has yielded stone sculpture bearing stylistic features reminiscent of the Govan School. If the Kingarth monuments were indeed produced in the Govan style, it is possible that they were commissioned by a British elite. From this we might infer that the monastery of St Blane's, and perhaps the whole of Bute, fell under the sway of Strathclyde during the tenth century.[47] Such a scenario might even provide a context for Kingarth's saint being known in later Irish tradition as 'triumphant Blane of the Britons'.

The Govan stonecarving tradition: interlace patterns on the shaft of the Arthurlie Cross. Drawing reproduced from J.R. Allen & J. Anderson, *The Early Christian Monuments of Scotland* (Edinburgh, 1903).

In 975, the year of Edgar's death, the veteran Strathclyde king Dyfnwal ab Owain left his homeland to embark on a spiritual journey to Rome. There he became a monk, renouncing the cares of the secular world and adopting the clerical tonsure. That he was able to undertake such a pilgrimage says much for the respect in which he was held by his neighbours and fellow monarchs, for his journey would have taken him through many lands. If, like his kinsman Catroe, he travelled overland to the south coast of England, he would have passed through Anglo-Scandinavian settlements in Northumbria, English territory in Mercia and thence into the core domain of the West Saxon kings. Guarantees of safe passage for himself and his entourage would have been necessary, and the fact that these were given by friends and former enemies alike suggests that his kingdom was not at that time engaged in hostilities along its southern border. Dyfnwal was already a man of advanced years and, whether through age or infirmity, he died before the year was out.[48] His son Malcolm continued in the kingship for a further 22 years, a period for which the history of Strathclyde passes unnoticed in the surviving sources. Cináed II, Malcolm's contemporary on the throne of Alba, was slain in 995 by the treachery of fellow Scots. Malcolm himself died two years later. He was succeeded either immediately or soon after by his brother Owain, a fifth son of Dyfnwal and perhaps the last-born.

Another gap in the recorded history of the North Britons follows Malcolm's death, with little definite information becoming available for a further 20 years. In the *Anglo-Saxon Chronicle* an entry under the year 1000 refers to a raid by Aethelred, son of Edgar, on *Cumberland*. Here, as in 945, the setting is territory ruled by the Clyde Britons.[49] The target of Aethelred's aggression was presumably Owain ap Dyfnwal although the motive for the raid is unknown. Aethelred had no great military reputation and is better known for paying Viking warlords large sums of money to leave his kingdom in peace. Because of these *Danegeld* payments he was perceived by contemporaries as weak and ill-advised, hence his nickname *Unraed*, 'Poor counsel'. His assault on *Cumberland* suggests some specific grievance, possibly arising from Owain's relationship with the Scandinavians. Did the king of Strathclyde allow his harbours on the Ayrshire coast or on the Solway to be used by Vikings, receiving in return a share of pirate loot or a slice of Danegeld?[50] Whatever the reasons behind Aethelred's attack he ravaged *Cumberland* comprehensively, plundering 'nearly all of it' according to the *Anglo-Saxon Chronicle*. Things might have turned out even worse for the Britons if the English fleet, sailing north to rendezvous with the army, had not encountered bad weather in the Irish Sea. The ships were presumably heading for the Firth of Clyde but were forced to change course, their captains steering instead towards the Isle of Man. From Aethelred's viewpoint the failed rendezvous was somewhat offset when his naval force looted Scandinavian colonies along the Manx coastline. Strathclyde, however, may have had a rather lucky escape. Had the weather not intervened, the kingdom might have endured a repeat of the devastating siege of Alt Clut, this time directed at the new royal centres of Govan and Partick. Alternatively, and despite the rhetoric in the *Anglo-Saxon Chronicle*, Aethelred's targets may have been more limited: Scandinavian coastal settlements in Ayrshire and Galloway, or districts where local British elites routinely gave aid and refuge to Vikings. Such co-operation between Britons and Norsemen was no doubt a frequent occurrence. In a period when English power was weak and ineffectual the 'Cumbrians' of Strathclyde might even have participated in the latest wave of Scandinavian raids.

Viking warlords were still active in the western seaways during these years, among them Ragnall 'Lord of the Isles' whose domain lay in the Hebrides, and a Norse dynasty based at Waterford in south-east Ireland. The most serious threat to Aethelred's England came, however, from the East, from across the North Sea. In the last years of the tenth century the Danish king Sveinn Forkbeard launched a series of raids, some of them directed at other Scandinavian groups such as those on the Isle of Man. When Sveinn turned his attention to Aethelred's kingdom he was paid off with Danegeld, but remained an ever-present threat. The eleventh century had barely begun when he embarked on a major campaign against the English, his objective being to bring them under his direct rule. Ten years of warfare eventually took a heavy toll on Aethelred and, in 1013, he fled to Normandy with his family, seeking exile with his brother-in-law Duke Richard who was himself a descendant of Vikings. England was seized by Sveinn who installed his teenage son Cnut as king, a move welcomed not only by the Scandinavian settlements in the Danelaw but also by many Englishmen. Aethelred's eventual return received a lukewarm reception and, when he died in 1016, part of the English aristocracy rejected his son Edmund in favour of Cnut. War broke out between the two sides, but it proved inconclusive and a truce was agreed, followed by a partition which separated Edmund's Wessex from lands loyal to Cnut. Edmund's death a few months later gave Cnut an opportunity to claim the entire kingdom.

These important events unfolding in England were watched closely by the northern kings, whose own interests were likely to be affected by any major shift in the balance of power further south. Strathclyde entered the eleventh century under the rule of Owain ap Dyfnwal who by then was probably in his fifties or sixties. His contemporary in the kingship of Alba was Malcolm II whose 30-year reign spanned the first third of the new century. Among modern historians Malcolm is often referred to as Malcolm mac Cináeda, his father having been Cináed II whose own father had also been called Malcolm. The various occurrences of the name *Máel Coluim*, 'Follower of Saint Columba', in this period can be somewhat confusing, hence the usefulness of patronyms or numerals to differentiate between namesakes who were contemporaries or near-contemporaries. We have already encountered one of these namesakes in the person of the Clyde king Malcolm ap Dyfnwal who met Edgar at Chester in 973. Since *Máel Coluim* is a Gaelic name with no meaning in Brittonic speech, it might seem odd to encounter it in the Strathclyde royal house. The explanation can be found in political marriage which occasionally led to 'foreign' names being bestowed on the children of inter-dynastic unions. This process may account for the bestowing of *Ildulb*, 'Hildulf', a name of Frankish or Scandinavian origin, on a tenth-century mac Ailpín prince who became a king of Alba. The appearance of the name *Malcolm* among the Britons likewise implies one or more marriages between their dynasty and the mac Ailpíns.

Berchan's Prophecy calls Malcolm II of Alba *biodhba Bretan*, 'enemy of the Britons', but no mention of Scottish campaigns against Strathclyde appears in other sources so the label might be rhetorical rather than historical. Malcolm's chief adversaries lay on his north-eastern frontier, in Moray, where a family claiming descent from the Cenél Loairn kings of Argyll challenged his authority, and further south in the Northumbrian borderlands. At that time the northern part of Northumbria, formerly Bernicia, was still ruled by an English earl at Bamburgh, while the erstwhile Anglo-Scandinavian realm of York was now also an earldom. The two earls were answerable to the king of England and had an important role in protecting his northern interests. Having previously served monarchs of West Saxon stock, they found themselves, in 1016, acknowledging the half-Danish, half-Polish Cnut as their sovereign. Earl Uhtred of Bamburgh affirmed his allegiance to the new king by placing hostages, presumably members of his own family, under royal protection. According to the *Anglo-Saxon Chronicle*, Cnut ordered Uhtred's assassination in 1016, but this appears to be a misdating and the murder should be more correctly assigned to a period later than 1018. In that year Uhtred and his people faced a major invasion by the combined armies of Alba and Strathclyde.

The Battle of Carham

An eleventh-century Irish text, *The Wars of the Gaels against the Vikings*, describes the high-king Brian Boru raiding across the sea to take tribute from 'Saxons and Britons' in Argyll, Alba and Lennox. This garbled report is usually seen as rhetoric designed to enhance Brian's fame, but its early date makes it worthy of consideration.[51] If it has any historical basis, and if raids were indeed directed at Lennox, then the plundered Britons were those of the Clyde. There is no other hint of Strathclyde involvement in Brian's campaigns. In 1014, at Clontarf near Dublin, he defeated the Scandinavians in a great battle. The sources list Scots of Alba among the participants, together with Britons from Wales and Cornwall, but the men of Clyde are not mentioned.

In an entry under the year 1015 the Welsh Annals report the death of Owain ap Dyfnwal. His successor was a namesake, perhaps a nephew, who forged or maintained a military alliance with the Scots. In English sources the younger Owain has the epithet *Calvus*, 'The Bald', this presumably being the Latin equivalent of a Brittonic word similar to modern Welsh *Moel*. At the time of his accession the prospect of war between Alba and England lay simmering uneasily, nor were tensions eased when the fall of the West Saxon dynasty merely brought Cnut to power. The Scottish king Malcolm II had already attacked northern English territory in 1006, the first year of his reign, by laying siege to Durham. This venture had left him nursing a wounded pride after the siege was lifted by Northumbrian forces under Uhtred, the future earl of Bamburgh. Malcolm's subsequent troubles in Moray put his southern ambitions on hold, but he revived them in 1018 in partnership with Owain the Bald. The two kings led their armies into Tweeddale, perhaps approaching separately before joining together at a pre-arranged rendezvous.[52] Turning east along the valley, they eventually met Earl Uhtred's Northumbrians at Carham on the south bank of the Tweed.[53] Although the ensuing battle was a victory for the allies, its political significance has been doubted by some modern commentators. Later English and Scottish chroniclers called it a 'great' battle and, while not being contemporary with the event, these traditions do suggest that both sides regarded it as important. A more contemporary text is an eleventh-century history of the Franks, written by Ralph ('Rodolfus') Glaber, which refers to Malcolm and Cnut waging a protracted war. If Ralph's testimony can be trusted on this point, we should view Carham as a key moment in an ongoing conflict, perhaps a turning-point. Within a few years of the battle, possibly as early as 1019, Cnut and Malcolm reached a negotiated settlement by which the Tweed became the new Anglo-Scottish frontier.[54] All lands north of the river were ceded to the king of Alba who in return swore an oath of allegiance to Cnut. It is possible that the package of incentives offered to Malcolm included the slaying of Earl Uhtred who, as a net loser of estates under the terms of the treaty, may have been among its most vociferous opponents. Uhtred's brother Eadwulf, known as 'Cuttlefish', became the new earl of Bamburgh and passively observed the formal transfer of territory to the Scots.

Owain the Bald may have died at Carham or, like Malcolm of Alba, he perhaps returned home laden with the spoils of victory. Nothing more is heard of him, nor is there any mention of Strathclyde for the next 12 years. In this period the kingdom seems to have grown smaller, shrinking back to the old heartlands in Clydesdale. This is one inference to be drawn from an entry in the Irish annals noting the death in 1034 of Suibhne, 'Sweeney', king of the Gall Gáidhil. Suibhne may have been a ruler of Galloway where Norse–Irish colonies had long been answerable to the Viking lords of Dublin.[55] In the eleventh century his domain seemingly constituted an independent kingdom stretching north from the Solway to encompass Gall Gáidhil settlements in Ayrshire. If Suibhne was not king of some other region, such as the Hebrides, then he could have been a precursor of the later lords of Galloway who first appear in the twelfth century.[56] Any Gall Gáidhil expansion beyond the northern parts of Ayrshire is likely to have been at Strathclyde's expense and would no doubt have been resisted. A plausible timescale for such expansion is the period after the passing of Owain the Bald, the victor of Carham, who probably remained militarily strong throughout his reign. That he was dead before 1030, leaving behind a weaker heir, is suggested by a raid in that year by Norse-Irish from Dublin assisted by English forces. The victims were unspecified 'Britons', but those of Strathclyde are probably meant, in which case the 'English' may be identified as Northumbrians.[57] In 1038, another raid, this time by Northumbrians acting alone, plundered Strathclyde 'with sufficient ferocity'.[58] The raiders were led by Eadwulf, son of Uhtred and earl of Bamburgh, who thus avenged his father's defeat on the Tweed 20 years earlier.

The Conquest of Strathclyde

In 1042, the kingship of England passed to Edward, known as the Confessor, last sovereign of the old West Saxon royal house. Edward's father was Aethelred, the rival of Cnut, but his mother was Emma of Normandy whom Cnut had married after Aethelred's death. Emma and Cnut had a son, Harthacnut, who ruled after Cnut while Edward lived in exile with his mother's Norman kin. Harthacnut died and Edward became king, bringing henchmen from Normandy as members of his entourage. These were the first Normans to gain real influence in England, for Edward placed them in positions of trust and authority, a move regarded as provocative by some among the English elite. Edward's reign roughly coincided with that of his Scottish contemporary Macbethad, Shakespeare's Macbeth, a *mormaer* or 'great steward' of Moray, who seized the kingship of Alba in 1040. Tensions began to rise between the two kingdoms and, in 1054, Edward sent an army across the Tweed under the command of Siward, earl of Northumbria. A battle was fought and the Scots suffered a heavy defeat. Siward deposed Macbethad from the kingship and replaced him with Malcolm, 'son of the king of the Cumbrians'. This Malcolm was not, as commonly believed, Macbethad's successor Malcolm III, whose father Donnchad (Shakespeare's 'Duncan') had been slain by Macbethad in 1040. With a clear mac Ailpín ancestry stretching back 200 years, it is inconceivable that Malcolm III would have been described as anything other than

'Donnchad's son'.[59] The man foisted on the Scots by Siward in 1054 was clearly a different Malcolm, a 'Cumbrian' prince and thus a member of the Strathclyde royal family. To have a legitimate claim on the throne of Alba, regardless of how many Northumbrian swords backed his candidacy, he must have been eligible by blood. His claim probably derived from a political marriage between the king of Strathclyde and a mac Ailpín princess. The names of his parents are not recorded, but the chronological context points to his father being the son or successor of Owain the Bald, while his own name might identify his mother as a daughter of Owain's ally Malcolm II of Alba. It is feasible that the military co-operation forged between the victorious allies of 1018 may have been sealed by a marital union between their offspring.

Macbethad was slain in 1058 in a battle against Malcolm, Donnchad's son, who duly became Malcolm III, king of Scots. This implies that Macbethad had regained the kingship after being deposed by Siward and that he continued to rule for a few more years.[60] We may envisage the Cumbrian Malcolm being ousted by Macbethad either in battle or through assassination, the latter scenario fitting the Shakespearean image of 'Macbeth' rather neatly. In wider political terms we might wish to know why a Briton or half-Briton was deemed suitable by Earl Siward as a replacement for Macbethad. The Strathclyde prince was clearly Edward's choice too, and we might wonder why England's king chose him over his name-sake. Contrary to widespread belief, there is no evidence of English support for Malcolm III during his bid to topple Macbethad in 1058. Taken as a whole, the various sources seem to hint at hostility rather than friendship between Malcolm III and Edward, while at the same time suggesting friendship between Edward and Strathclyde. An English army evidently gave 'the king of the Cumbrians' a brief but valuable period of influence at the royal court of Alba by placing his son on the Scottish throne. At the same time, and according to a near-contemporary Northumbrian source, the priests John and 'Magsuen' were consecrated as bishops of Glasgow by the archbishop of York.[61] As the later Scottish diocese of Glasgow was not yet in existence these two men were almost certainly bishops of Strathclyde. It is likely that they were Britons, or non-Britons serving British communities. The name *Magsuen* is unintelligible and might be a scribal error for a Brittonic name like *Masguen* or *Maswen*. The hints of ecclesiastical and military co-operation between Edward's England and the Clyde kingdom, with Northumbria as the link, point to a political accord forged in opposition to the mac Ailpín dynasty. The relationship was surely unequal, given the huge resources at Edward's disposal. Strathclyde's king, the 'king of the Cumbrians', is not named in any source, but he was perhaps the last British ruler on the Clyde. It seems likely that he acknowledged Edward as overlord in exchange for protection from Macbethad and, after 1058, from Malcolm III. British territory may have been ceded to Edward as part of the deal, or British territorial claims on lost provinces rescinded, with the area we know today as 'Cumberland' perhaps being restored to English rule.[62]

Malcolm III submitted to Edward in 1059, but became a troublesome vassal, ravaging Northumbria in 1061 and giving hospitality to the rebel earl Tostig four years later. Edward's death in 1066 led to the Norman invasion and conquest of England, an upheaval exploited by Malcolm who saw an opportunity to raid Northumbria again. Bereft of any guarantee of English protection, the Clyde Britons now felt the full force of Malcolm's aggression. He may have nurtured a special grievance against them, seeing them as English stooges and never forgiving their attempt to intrude one of their own princes into the kingship of Alba 12 years earlier. His plundering of their territories can be dated to the period 1066 to 1070. In the latter year the northern English earl Gospatric, holding office under Norman authority, retaliated against Scottish raids by attacking *Cumberland*. This territorial name, as we have seen, is usually synonymous with Strathclyde but the distinction between the 'Land of the Cumbrians' and the English county of Cumberland becomes less clear as we reach the end of the eleventh century. Here, in reference to Gospatric's campaign, we are probably seeing a Northumbrian invasion of Strathclyde.[63] Our source for this event is a twelfth-century chronicle from which we learn that Gospatric led his army to *Cumberland* because it lay under the 'dominion' of Malcolm, king of Scots, who had seized it by 'violent subjugation'.[64] What this 'dominion' entailed in political terms is difficult to assess but it was plainly not achieved by peaceful means. The key issue is whether or not the Clyde Britons regained their independence at some later date. In other words, did their ancient royal dynasty follow its West Saxon counterpart into oblivion between 1066 and 1070? While acknowledging the lack of firm evidence this question can be answered with a cautious *Yes*. The downfall of Anglo-Saxon England seems to have been accompanied by the Scottish conquest of Strathclyde and the final defeat of the Men of the North.

10

IDENTITIES

The Bishops of Glasgow

In 1093 Malcolm III, king of Scots, died in battle near the River Aln in Northumbria. The next few years witnessed a struggle for the succession from which Edgar, one of Malcolm's sons, eventually emerged as king. Edgar was in turn succeeded by his brother Alexander in 1107. A younger brother, David, was granted a portion of the Scottish kingdom to rule in his own right. The grant was a bequest of Edgar and represented a division of authority between David and Alexander on the latter's accession to the throne. David's territory encompassed Lennox, Glasgow and Clydesdale together with districts further south in Dumfriesshire and parts of the Tweed and Teviot valleys. As ruler of these lands he held the title *Cumbrensis regionis princeps*, 'prince of the Cumbrian region'.[1] The political implications behind Edgar's bequest are clear and unambiguous: the old kingdom of Strathclyde had ceased to exist and its people were now ruled by a Scottish prince.

As ruler of the Cumbrian *regio*, David held sway over a substantial area between Clyde and Solway. He did not, however, receive the whole of the erstwhile British kingdom. Renfrewshire initially lay outside the territory bequeathed by Edgar, as did some parts of northern Ayrshire formerly under British rule. It is likely that these lands were not Edgar's to give, and that they did not belong to his kingdom at that time. The simplest explanation is that these districts were ruled by independent lords of the Gall Gáidhil owing no allegiance to the kings of Alba. At some point during his principate David brought Renfrewshire under his authority, thereby expanding his *regio* across the former southern heartland of the Clyde kings. Sometime between 1114 and 1118 he created a bishopric at Glasgow on the site of an ancient church allegedly founded by Saint Kentigern in the sixth century. The extent of the new bishop's ecclesiastical jurisdiction was established by an inquest of landholdings in the Cumbrian region, a process instituted by David himself.[2] This was essentially a survey of the old kingdom of Strathclyde, specifically of its major estates and other assets. When David succeeded to the kingship of Scots in 1124, he delegated the administrative functions of his princedom to the bishop of Glasgow who became, in all but name, the new ruler on the Clyde. During David's reign the bishops exploited this role to their advantage, promoting their diocese as the successor of the North British kingdom with themselves as the heirs of its native dynasty. This gave their diocese a legitimacy and ancestry it otherwise lacked, for it was essentially a recent Gaelic foundation closely associated with the Scottish kings and ultimately dependent on their continuing patronage. Any connection between Glasgow's new bishops and the old royal dynasty of the Britons was based on illusion and propaganda. The authority of the bishops over their extensive territory relied on a complete dismantling of the former kingdom's identity and its swift replacement with a version of 'Scottishness' appropriate to the Cumbrian region's ethnic, linguistic and cultural affiliations. At the heart of this transformation lay the location of Glasgow itself. The place was conveniently close to the post-870 centre of royal power and ecclesiastical ritual at Govan, but far enough away to allow the latter to be set aside and downgraded. It was vital for David and his bishops that the premier church of the North British kings should be deprived of status and rendered obsolete. As long as Govan survived as a major religious centre, its non-Scottish royal associations would not be forgotten and it might remain a potential focus for dissent. It was duly stripped of its importance and relegated to a lesser role as a subordinate church of Glasgow. The former royal estate of Partick across the river became a residence of the bishops in a move consistent with their dual role as powerful lords and landowners.

It is likely that David dispossessed a portion of the old British aristocracy during his principate of their homeland. Some noble families had undoubtedly disappeared after the subjugation of Strathclyde by Malcolm III in the 1060s, but others may have survived in sufficient numbers to cause concern 40 years later. David's entourage included knights from many lands – Normans, Bretons, Flemings and Englishmen – many of whom received generous gifts of land within his princedom. These estates were available for redistribution because they had recently become vacant: their previous incumbents had been ousted on the points of Scottish swords, either during Malcolm's reign or Edgar's. David himself may have been responsible for another phase of dispossessions as part of an ongoing policy of Gaelicisation. One casualty of the demise of a Brittonic-speaking elite was the native language itself. By c.1100 all social advancement in the region depended on an ability to speak Gaelic, the language of the new masters. Access to powerful patrons and wealthy sponsors was no longer available to any ambitious Briton who chose to remain monolingual. Those Britons who wished to retain their position in the social hierarchy had to adopt the speech of the Scots. In such circumstances monolingual families were doomed to loss of status and would have become targets for dispossession. Others may have survived by adapting quickly to Gaeldom, especially in districts where contact with Gall Gáidhil neighbours had already produced a bilingual class. How long Brittonic survived as a living language is uncertain, but it was in terminal decline before the middle of the twelfth century. It is feasible that the ancient tongue continued to be used among older generations of the peasantry, perhaps in peripheral communities far from the centres of power, before dying out altogether by c.1200.[3]

The bishops of Glasgow played a key role in Gaelicisation by promoting themselves as the heirs of Strathclyde's former dynasty. Central to this carefully crafted vision of continuity was the elevation of Kentigern as patron saint of the old British kingdom and as a figure of authority from whom his twelfth-century 'successors' derived their right to rule. In Chapter 3 we discussed the *vitae* of Kentigern written at this time and noted the relationship between the saint and his royal patron Rhydderch Hael. In one passage of the *Vita* written by Jocelin of Furness at the behest of his namesake in the episcopate of Glasgow the secular authority of the bishops was asserted in unambiguous terms. Kentigern, having been appointed as the first bishop, is shown receiving from Rhydderch complete overlordship of the Clyde kingdom. This transfer of power occurred at a ceremony in which the king, kneeling in homage at Kentigern's feet, 'handed over to him the dominion and princedom over all his kingdom'.[4] Behind this fictional scenario lies a sequence of twelfth-century events that was thereby legitimised by historical precedent: the end of David's principate over the Cumbrian *regio* on his succession to the Scottish throne and his subsequent transfer of certain administrative powers to the bishops of Glasgow. As king of Scotland David nevertheless retained overlordship of the *regio* and continued to grant landholdings there to his friends and subordinates.

Other aspects of the Scottish takeover of Strathclyde become relevant at this point, for the creation of the new bishopric precipitated an ecclesiastical power-struggle. In England the archbishops of both York and Canterbury claimed Glasgow as a subordinate.[5] These claims formed part of a wider disagreement between the two archbishoprics over Canterbury's demand of allegiance from York. The latter sought to boost its status by claiming authority over the Glasgow diocese, while Canterbury saw itself as having an ancient right to primacy over the whole of Britain deriving from Saint Augustine's mission to Kent in the sixth century. Between these two conflicting views the bishops of Glasgow strove to maintain their ecclesiastical autonomy. In this they were assisted by kings such as David who, while paying homage to the Norman monarchs of England, hoped to keep the Scottish Church free from the jurisdiction of Anglo-Norman archbishops. However, an additional concern for Glasgow lay in moves by David and his immediate successors to seek papal approval for the designation of St Andrews as the first Scottish archbishopric.[6] Had this plan succeeded, the bishop of Glasgow, together with all others in the Scottish kingdom, would have been subject to the authority of St Andrews. Under the pressure of a three-pronged ecclesiastical assault – from Canterbury, York and St Andrews – the Glasgow bishops fought hard to preserve their autonomy. Their strategy included an attempt to convince the papal authorities at Rome that their diocese had once been an independent kingdom, ruled by kings who were neither Scottish nor English, a distinct realm served by royal bishops of whom they themselves were the legitimate heirs.[7] This required them to adopt a pseudo-British identity and to construct an appropriate history for their diocese. The first cathedral at Glasgow was not consecrated until 1136, but gained an aura of antiquity when the Kentigern hagiographers portrayed it as the lineal successor of a sixth-century church. Similar historical links between the Gaelic bishopric and the conquered British kingdom were devised in the cathedral precincts to be presented as genuine traditions handed down through the centuries. These were disseminated to a wider audience through the *vitae* of the patron saint who, in his twelfth-century guise as chief bishop of Strathclyde, owed allegiance to no ecclesiastical superior except the Pope. Charters associated with grants of royal land at this time deliberately mention a 'Welsh' component in the population of the Glasgow diocese, thereby allowing the bishops to portray themselves as ministering to the indigenous *Straecledwealas* just as Kentigern had allegedly done six centuries earlier. In the time of Bishop Jocelin (1175–99) the ecclesiastical independence of Glasgow was finally acknowledged by the papacy and the prospect of subordination receded. There was to be no archiepiscopal status for St Andrews after all. It is surely ironic that the Scottish bishops of Glasgow, who played such a key part in the downgrading of Govan and the dismantling of British identity, should borrow that same identity in pursuit of their own short-term purposes. The imagined 'Welshness' of twelfth-century Strathclyde apparently fooled the papal authorities. We should not allow ourselves to be duped by such a carefully crafted charade. By c.1150 British identity among the local populace was dying rather than flourishing and the Britons themselves were starting to think of themselves as Scots. Furthermore, Glasgow Cathedral was primarily a Scottish Gaelic foundation whose brethren had no real affection for British culture, not least because they resented its close affiliation with Govan. Bishop Jocelin, the prime mover in many of the events and processes of the time, recognised the urgent need to detach Glasgow's present from Govan's past. His efforts in this regard were successful. When he died in 1199, the kings who had once patronised the older church already belonged to a bygone age, which is precisely where Jocelin and his contemporaries wanted them to be.

Brets and Brettos

References to Britons among the inhabitants of Scotland in the twelfth, thirteenth and fourteenth centuries seem at first glance to provide evidence for late survival of Brittonic speech. Closer examination reveals much of this data to be ambiguous, at least in so far as linguistic affiliations are concerned. A document of 1305 issued by Edward I, king of England, relating to the administration of Scotland mentions 'the custom of the Scots and the Brets' in reference to unspecified laws.[8] It is possible that these laws include those described in a thirteenth-century legal code giving a scale of fines for crimes committed against people of different social class. In this text murder was penalised by the payment of a 'blood-fine' to the victim's family, this compensation being defined by the Gaelic term *cro* and its Brittonic equivalent *galnes*. Two other types of payment, *mercheta* (a marriage tax) and *kelchyn* (an additional blood-fine), were also borrowed from British legal terminology.[9] Although the title by which the text is commonly known today, *Leges inter Brettos et Scotos*, 'Laws among Britons and Scots', appears to be a seventeenth-century addition, the antiquity of its clauses need not be doubted. It clearly derives from an earlier document whose compiler desired to find equivalence between Scottish and British compensation systems. The most likely context for such a text is the immediate aftermath of the fall of Strathclyde, in which case a date between 1070 and 1100 seems plausible.[10] Whether any of its clauses were still relevant in 1305 when Edward I prohibited the 'customs' of the Scots and Britons is doubtful.

In lands that had once been the southern provinces of tenth-century Strathclyde, people were still identifying themselves as Britons in the 1100s. Some were clearly of high status and may have been descended from the old native aristocracy. A charter granting land in Ayrshire was witnessed c.1190 by Gille Críst *Bretnach*, 'Gilchrist the Briton', while further south near Dumfries a man called Gilcudbricht *Bretnach* witnessed an earlier charter in the 1130s.[11] In a recent study of Strathclyde's final phases Dauvit Broun suggested that *Bretnach* might denote contact with Wales rather than a claim to North British ancestry. As Professor Broun rightly observes, personal names prefixed with Gaelic *gille-*, 'servant (of a saint)', were unlikely to be bestowed in Brittonic-speaking families.[12] On the other hand, a Gaelic-speaker might identify himself as a *Bretnach* in contexts where a claim to British ancestry conferred some specific advantage, such as in property disputes over land formerly held by Britons. It is therefore possible that Gille Críst and Gilcudbricht were not only of British stock but were also proud of their heritage and incurred no disadvantage by displaying it. In Brittonic the equivalent of *gille-* was *gos-*, a prefix rendered obsolete by the widespread adoption of Gaelic speech but still being used in the late twelfth century.[13] Near

Peebles on the eastern periphery of Strathclyde in c.1200 men with names such as Gospatric, Gosmungo and Goso[s]uold appear in a list of inhabitants, along with Queschutbrit, 'Servant of Saint Cuthbert', whose name carries a form of *gos* reminiscent of Welsh *gwas*.[14] It is not known if any of these individuals thought of himself as *Bretnach* so their names might be due to contemporary trends among speakers of Gaelic or English in the Peebles area rather than to residual memories of British ancestry. One of the last references to a British element in the population of medieval Scotland comes from an inscription said to have been carved on the old bridge at Stirling: 'I am free march as passengers maie ken, to Scots to Britains and to Englishmen'.[15] By the time these words were carved it is extremely unlikely that anyone in Scotland could be considered a Briton in any meaningful sense.

Places and People

So thorough was the disappearance of Britishness in twelfth-century southern Scotland, particularly within the bounds of the Glasgow diocese, that the entire history of the Clyde Britons was almost forgotten in their former heartlands. Of their kings only Rhydderch Hael was remembered, chiefly because of his role in the story of Kentigern. All other kings were deemed irrelevant to the propagandist purposes of Glasgow Cathedral and had no place in the new pseudo-history of the diocese. Further south, in the English county of Cumberland, a memory of the last kings of Strathclyde seems to be preserved in local folklore. At Penrith a curious amalgam of tenth-century monuments in the churchyard is said to be the grave of a giant called Ewan Caesarius, a figure also associated with the nearby earthwork of Castle Hewen.[16] As both sites lie within a region that fell under the sway of the Clyde kings after c.900, the folklore might commemorate one of the Owains who ruled in the tenth and eleventh centuries. It has been suggested that the sixth-century hero Owain ab Urien may be the figure in question, but, despite his prominence in later Arthurian saga, his deeds in folklore take place further north. As we saw in Chapter 3, he appears in the Kentigern hagiography in a context suggestive of southern Lothian. In the Lake District hills a feature known as Dunmail Raise, 'Dyfnwal's Cairn', stands on the old boundary between the ecclesiastical dioceses of Carlisle and York. It probably commemorates a king of Strathclyde.[17] As with the Owain place-names a firm identification is impossible, but a plausible candidate is Dyfnwal ab Owain who died in 975 while on pilgrimage to Rome. If Dunmail Raise and Castle Hewen really do commemorate two kings of Strathclyde in what was once their tenth-century borderland, the point is worthy of comment. Both sites currently have names of medieval origin bestowed by English-speakers long after the demise of Brittonic. Perhaps the original names incorporated British equivalents of 'castle' and 'raise' which were subsequently translated into recognisable English forms? The original names probably arose among local Britons familiar with folk-tales recounting the deeds of the kings, but how long such lore survived after those same communities adopted an English identity is unknown.

Place-names provide one of the few legacies of the North Britons in lands formerly ruled by the Clyde dynasty. Aside from the two English examples mentioned above, there are many more of wholly Brittonic origin and some that look distinctly 'Welsh' to modern eyes. Penpont in Dumfriesshire is a compound of *pen*, 'head', and *pont*, 'bridge', both of which are very common in the place-names of Wales. The meaning of Penpont is 'Bridge-head' or 'Bridge-end'. On the outskirts of Dumfries the place-name Terregles, recorded in the fourteenth century as *Travereglys*, has the same meaning as Trefeglwys in mid-Wales, namely *tref yr eglwys*, 'church hamlet'.[18] The town of Tranent, 10 miles east of Edinburgh in the ancient heartland of Gododdin, was recorded in the twelfth century as *Treuernent*, a name corresponding to Welsh *tref yr nant*, 'valley hamlet', found in the place-names of modern Wales as Trefnant.[19] These names represent a small sample of numerous 'Welsh' elements preserved in the toponymy of areas once inhabited by the North Britons. Most are isolated relics of the indigenous language among later names of Gaelic or English origin. In some instances a non-Brittonic name provides evidence of the former inhabitants, the most famous example being Dumbarton, from Gaelic *Dun Breatainn*, 'Fort of the Britons'. A similar but less well-known example is *Clach nam Breatainn*, 'Stone of the Britons', on the higher slopes of Glen Falloch above the road between Dumbarton and Crianlarich. In place-names of English origin the element *cumber* usually denotes a settlement of Britons, as at Cummersdale in the county of Cumberland and of course the latter name itself. In the seaways off the Ayrshire coast the same element was adopted by Scandinavians as a prefix to Old Norse *ey*, 'island', in the name *Cumbrae*, 'Island of the Britons'. The Lanarkshire town of *Cumber*nauld, however, seems to derive its name from Gaelic *comar na allt*, 'confluence of streams'.

Few visible traces of the North Britons are instantly recognisable today. Unlike the Picts, whose symbol stones make them enigmatic and interesting, the Britons have traditionally had a low profile in public perceptions of Scotland's heritage. This situation might now be changing. A programme of study and excavation at Govan and at other sites around the Clyde has brought a uniquely North British sculptural tradition into the public eye. The collection of carved stones displayed at the old parish church of Govan provides visitors with a tangible link to the kingdom of Strathclyde and shows the North Britons as key players in early Scottish history. In the modern era Strathclyde underwent a form of rebirth 900 years after its last king was overthrown, re-emerging as a territorial unit during a restructuring of UK local government in 1973. Although its administrative role has since suffered a second disappearance, the old name continues to be used in various high-profile contexts in the Glasgow region. The local constabulary, for instance, still uses the old name of the kingdom for its area of jurisdiction. For much of the last quarter of the twentieth century it was almost easy to believe that the *Straecledwealas* had survived into modern times like their compatriots in Wales. Even now, when the post-1973 'region' of Strathclyde no longer exists, the name of the ancient kingdom still plays a role in the life of Greater Glasgow. But what became of the kingdom's inhabitants, the North Britons, a people who left behind a scatter of Welsh place-names and some richly carved stones? The simple answer, in a genetic or biological sense, is that they survived the death of their language and culture. They remained on the lands of their ancestors, living as they had ever lived, to become an integral part of the Scottish nation.

NOTES

Introduction

1 Chadwick 1976, 70.
2 Miller 1976, 269.

Chapter 1

1 Hartley and Fitts 1988. The notion of a 'confederacy' should not be pressed too far: the Brigantes may simply have been an East Pennine people who held several western groups under their sway. On this topic see most recently Breeze 2008.
2 On this and subsequent Roman campaigns in Scotland see Breeze 1996.
3 Ammianus Marcellinus, xxvii, 8.
4 Esmonde-Cleary 1989, 142.
5 On Gildas see the papers collected in Lapidge and Dumville 1984.
6 Gildas, 21.
7 Gildas, 23.
8 Wilmott 1997.
9 Dark 1992.
10 Chadwick 1949, 143; Blair 1947, 59.
11 Morris 1973, 213.
12 Morris 1973, 214.
13 Miller 1975.
14 Williams 1980, 75.
15 Chadwick 1976, 88.
16 *HE*, i, 15; ASC 455.
17 Blair 1947, 55.
18 Dumville 1989, 218.
19 Watson 1926, 421.
20 Binchy 1970; Sawyer and Wood 1977.
21 Higham 2007.

Chapter 2

1 Examples include Shaw 1964 and Morris 1973.
2 On these points Dumville 1977 is an essential introduction.
3 Koch 1997, but see also Isaac 1999 for caveats.

4 Bromwich 1961.

5 Bartrum 1966.

6 Miller 1976, 258.

7 Dumville 1986, 14.

8 For a summary of the traditional view of Votadinian geography see Jackson 1969, 69–75. For a suggestion that the Votadini dwelt further south around Corbridge see the recent paper by David Breeze (2008).

9 Driscoll and Yeoman 1997, 228.

10 Jackson 1953, 705.

11 Hope-Taylor 1977, 287–9.

12 Skene 1868, i, 173.

13 Jackson 1955, 83, n.13.

14 Smith 1990, 281.

15 Smith 1990, 284.

16 Morris-Jones 1918, 47.

17 Bromwich 1961, 477.

18 Smith 1990, 289.

19 Smith 1990, 288.

20 Watson 1926, 343.

21 Driscoll 2005, 148.

22 Scott 1997, 33.

23 Driscoll and Forsyth 2004, 4. Andrew Breeze (2007) regards *Damnonii* as a scribal error for *Dumnonii*. He may be right.

24 On Patrick see the papers collected in Dumville et al. 1993.

25 Patrick, *Epistola*, 2.

26 Patrick, *Epistola*, 11.

27 Macquarrie 1997, 9.

28 e.g. Miller 1976, 266.

29 See Chapter 4.

30 Alcock and Alcock 1990.

31 The name comes from an old story about Robert the Bruce.

32 Watson 1926, 103.

33 Fraser 2009, 16.

34 *HB*, 62.

35 Chadwick 1949, 148.

36 Williams 1980, 75 n.16.

37 *HE*, i, 12.

38 For recent views on this topic see Fraser 2008.

39 *HE*, i, 1.

40 Fraser 2009, 148.

41 Campbell 2001.

Chapter 3

1 Thomas 1968, 97.
2 Forsyth 2005, 117.
3 Forsyth 2005, 124, 129.
4 Watson 1926, 163.
5 Smith 1990, 292.
6 Smith 1990, 294.
7 *HE*, iii, 4.
8 Hill 1997, 28.
9 Duncan 1978, 78.
10 Broun 1991,146; Clancy 2001, 7.
11 Clancy 2001, 21–3.
12 Lowe 1999.
13 *AC*.
14 Shead 1969, 223.
15 Outside the Kentigern hagiography she appears only in the Welsh genealogical tract *Bonedd y Seint*, 'Descent of the Saints'.
16 Forsyth 2005, 127.
17 Cameron 1968.
18 Driscoll 2005, 153.
19 Watson 1926, 193.
20 Macquarrie 1997, 192.
21 Fraser 2005.

Chapter 4

1 Woolf 2003, 356.
2 Higham 2007, 78.
3 *HE*, v, 24.
4 *HB*, 57.
5 *HB*, 61.
6 *HB*, 62.
7 Fraser 2009, 149.
8 *HB*, 63.
9 e.g. Smyth 1984, 21.
10 Fraser 2009, 126.
11 O'Sullivan and Young 1995, 35.
12 Rowland 1990, 95; Isaac 1998.
13 MacQueen 1990, 61.
14 MacQueen 1990, 64.
15 MacQueen 1990, 62.
16 MacQueen 1990, 63.
17 Koch 2006, 1499.
18 McCarthy 2002, 372–3.
19 Reid 1951, 155.

20 Alcock 1983, 4.
21 Laing and Longley 2006, 164.
22 For an English translation of Sir Ifor's comments on Taliesin see Williams 1975.
23 Williams 1975, xli.
24 Jackson 1969, 103–4, 107.
25 Chadwick 1949, 144.
26 Fraser 2009, 130.
27 Ekwall 1947, 371.
28 Mills 1976, 127.
29 Williams 1975, xlix.
30 Isaac 1998, 65.
31 Hogg 1946.
32 Collingwood 1908.
33 Morris-Jones 1918, 77.
34 McCarthy 2002, 366.
35 Broun 1991, 150.
36 Williams 1975, 75.
37 Jackson 1949b.
38 Sims-Williams 1996.
39 *VC*, i, 15.
40 Macquarrie 1997, 82.
41 Macquarrie 1997, 60.
42 On Nudd and Senyllt see Bromwich 1961, 5, 507–8.
43 Morris-Jones 1918, 47.
44 Bromwich 1961, 147.
45 Macquarrie 1997, 82.
46 Bromwich 1961, 107, 241.
47 Jarman 1960, 16.
48 Pennar 1989, 87.
49 Macquarrie 1986, 18.
50 *VSK*, 33.
51 Bromwich 1961, 199.
52 Rowland 1990, 100.
53 Williams 1980, 82 n.49.
54 Jackson 1963, 31 n.3.
55 Jones 1975; Gruffydd 1994.
56 *HB*, 63.
57 *HE*, ii, 14; iv, 23.
58 Rowland 1990, 101.
59 Bromwich 1961, 308.
60 On this poem see Breeze 2001.
61 Koch 1997, xxxii.
62 Koch 1997, 175.
63 On the origins of the name *Elmet* see Hind 1980.
64 Miller 1976, 265–6.
65 *VSK*, 22.

Chapter 5

1　Bromwich 1961, 209.
2　Pennar 1989, 73.
3　Jarman 1978.
4　Chalmers 1807, i, 246.
5　Skene 1876.
6　Bower, iii, 31.
7　Armstrong 1950, 52–3.
8　Phythian-Adams 1996, 35.
9　Graham 1913, 33.
10　Taylor 1931, 116.
11　Birley 1954.
12　Gardner 1925.
13　Clarkson 1995.
14　Laing and Longley 2006.
15　Taylor 1931, 113.
16　Taylor 1931, 114
17　Chadwick 1976, 100.
18　Watson 1926, 368.
19　Tolstoy 1985, 161–88.
20　Bromwich 1961, 209.
21　Winchester 1987, 19.
22　Phythian-Adams 1996, 35–6.
23　Miller 1975, 106–9.
24　Phythian-Adams 1996, 86.
25　Smith 1967, xxxci n.4; xxxviii n.1.
26　Lovecy 1976, 37.
27　Dumville 1988, 3; Higham 1993, 83.
28　Lovecy 1976, 37.
29　Higham 1986, 254.
30　Stephens 1888.
31　See Jackson 1969 for a synopsis, Jarman 1988 for the English translation used here, Koch 1997 and Isaac 1999 for references to recent scholarship.
32　Rowland 1995, 33.
33　Jarman 1988, 24.
34　Jarman 1988, 18.
35　See Koch 1997 and, for a more sceptical view, Isaac 1999.
36　Rowland 1995, 35.
37　e.g. Cessford 1995.
38　Jarman 1988, 24, 58 and 70.
39　Koch 1997, xxiii.
40　Ross 1991.
41　Jackson 1969, 13.
42　Jarman 1988, xxiii.
43　Fraser 2009, 131.
44　On this point see Clarkson 1993 and Cessford 1996.

45 Rivet and Smith 1979, 302–4.
46 Morris-Jones 1918, 69 n.1.
47 Jackson 1969, 83.
48 Jackson 1969, 83.
49 Hope-Taylor 1977, 287–91.
50 Jackson 1969, 84.
51 Jackson 1969, 13.
52 Williams 1980, 47.
53 Dumville 1988, 3.
54 On the early English settlements at Catterick see Wilson et al. 1996.
55 Williams 1980, 67.
56 Hope-Taylor 1977, 296.
57 Hope-Taylor 1977, 295.
58 McDiarmid, 1983, 16 n.15.
59 Jackson 1949a, 28.

Chapter 6

1 Bromwich 1961, 481.
2 Rowland 1990.
3 Bromwich 1961, 8.
4 *HE*, i, 34.
5 Alcock 1981, 184.
6 *HE*, i, 22.
7 For a useful summary of Áedán's wars see Macquarrie 1997, 103–16.
8 Smith 1990, 311.
9 Chadwick 1949, 125.
10 *HE*, i, 34.
11 Charles-Edwards 1983, 49 but see Wallace-Hadrill 1988, 226–8 for a different perspective.
12 Bromwich 1961, 54.
13 *HE*, ii, 2.
14 See Anderson 1922, 141 for the theory and Chadwick 1963b, 180 for its flaws.
15 *HE*, ii, 12.
16 *HE*, ii, 9.
17 Anderson 1922, 201.
18 Smyth 1984, 65.
19 *HE*, ii, 14; Hope-Taylor 1977.
20 *AC* 626; *HB*, 63.
21 Chadwick 1959, 24.
22 *HE*, ii, 14.
23 Corning 2000, 8.
24 Chadwick 1963a, 164.
25 Corning 2000, 7.
26 *VC*, i, 1.
27 *HE*, ii, 20.

28 Woolf 2004.

29 *HE*, iii, 1.

30 *HE*, iii, 1–2; Corfe 1997.

31 *HB*, 57.

32 Rollason 2004.

33 Stancliffe 1995a, 57.

34 Wade-Evans 1950, 82.

35 Smyth 1984, 23.

36 *HE*, iii, 6.

37 *AU/AT* 638 = 640.

38 Stancliffe 1995a, 58; Fraser 2009, 171.

39 Jackson 1959.

40 Clarkson 2001, 111–14.

41 On the disputed location of Maserfelth see Stancliffe (1995b) and Thacker (1995).

Chapter 7

1 *HE*, iii, 15.

2 *AU/AT* 642 = 643.

3 Fraser 2009, 179.

4 Koch 1997, lxiv.

5 *AT* 622 = 624.

6 Fraser 2009, 164–5.

7 *AU/AT* 637 = 639.

8 On the Cowal–Alt Clut boundary see Rennie (2006). I am grateful to Hugh Andrew for useful discussions on this point and for providing me with unpublished notes by Betty Rennie.

9 Fraser 2005.

10 Clarkson 2001, 152.

11 Margary 1973, 488.

12 Margary 1973, 490.

13 *AU/AT* 642 = 643.

14 Nicolaisen 1960.

15 Halsall 1989, 166.

16 Margary 1973, 491.

17 Clarkson 2001, 132–5.

18 Koch 1997, 27.

19 Koch 1997, lxxx.

20 Jackson 1969, 66.

21 Dumville 1988, 7.

22 Sharpe 1995, 358.

23 *VC*, iii, 5.

24 Fraser 2005, 107; Anderson 1973, 152–5.

25 Smyth 1984, 63.

26 *HE*, iii, 21.

27 Smyth 1984, 23.

28 *HE*, iii, 24.

29 *HB,* 65.

30 *ASC* 952. Andrew Breeze (2007) suggests an identification with Stirling.

31 Jackson 1969, 72n.; Fraser 2008, 22–5.

32 *HB,* 65.

33 *AU* 658 = 657.

34 *HE*, iii, 24.

35 Smyth 1984, 24–5.

36 *HE*, iii, 4.

37 Higham 1997, 234.

38 *HE*, iii, 24.

39 *HE*, iii, 25.

40 James 1984.

41 *VW,* 17.

42 *VCP,* 27.

43 McCarthy 1999.

44 *AU/AT* 684.

45 *HE*, iv, 26.

46 See Woolf 1998 and Sellar 1985 for two contributions to the debate.

47 Evans 2008.

48 Fraser 2002. For an alternative view, suggesting that the battle occurred further north, see Woolf 2006.

49 *HE*, iv, 26.

50 *AU/AT* 678 = 677.

51 Miller 1980, 310.

52 *HE*, iv, 26.

Chapter 8

1 *AU/AT* 694 = 693.

2 *AU* 681/2.

3 Fraser 2005, 108; Watson 1926, 193.

4 Miller 1980, 310.

5 Smyth 1984, 25–6.

6 *HE*, v, 24.

7 *AU/AT* 711. James Fraser suggests the River Leven in Lochaber as an alternative setting for the battle (Fraser 2005, 104, n.5).

8 Fraser 2009, 273.

9 *AU/AT* 717.

10 Watson 1926, 387.

11 *AU/AT* 711; *ASC* 710.

12 HE, v, 21.

13 *HE*, v, 24.

14 *AC* 768.

15 Brooke 1991a; Hill 1991, 38

16 Bede, *Continuatio*, 297.

17   Driscoll and Forsyth 2004.

18   Fraser 2009, 312.

19   Anderson 1922, 239.

20   *HRA*.

21   Driscoll 2004, 8.

22   Fraser 2009, 318.

23   Forsyth 2000; Breeze 1999.

24   Woolf 2005, 39.

25   Wagner 2002, 48.

26   On the symbol see Cummins 1999, 103.

27   *AU* 780.

28   Macquarrie 1993, 12.

29   Broun 1998, 82.

30   Woolf 2007, 52–4.

31   On Cináed's origins see Woolf 2007, 93–8.

32   *Scot Chron*; Woolf 2007, 101–2.

33   *AU* 870; *AC* 870.

34   Woolf 2007, 110.

35   Clancy 2006, 1819.

36   Fragmentary Annals.

37   *AU* 871.

38   *AU* 872.

39   Smyth 1984, 215–29; Kirby 1962.

40   Broun 2004, 129–34.

41   Anderson 1922, 355.

42   Driscoll 2003; Driscoll 2004.

43   Clancy 1996.

44   Driscoll 1998, 102–3.

45   Ritchie 1994; Driscoll, O'Grady and Forsyth 2005.

46   Driscoll, O'Grady and Forsyth 2005, 156.

47   Spearman 1994. The horseman appears on the cover of this book.

48   Driscoll, O'Grady and Forsyth 2005, 145.

49   Clancy 2008.

50   *AU* 878; *Scot Chron*.

51   MacQuarrie 1993, 13; Smyth 1984, 216.

52   Woolf 2007, 120.

53   Hudson 1994, 57.

54   Duncan 2002, 12.

55   Watson 1926, 132.

56   Anderson 1922, 366–7.

57   Woolf 2007, 125.

58   Anderson 1922, 368.

59   e.g. Smyth 1984, 218.

60   Woolf 2007, 156.

Chapter 9

1 Macquarrie 1993, 15.
2 Hudson 1994, 58.
3 Hudson 1988, 148; Hudson 1994, 72.
4 Jackson 1955, 86–7; Jackson 1963.
5 Jackson 1963, 82.
6 Higham 1986, 321.
7 Woolf 2007, 154.
8 On Aethelflaed see Wainwright 1959.
9 Radner 1978.
10 Anderson 1922, 402–3.
11 Woolf 2007, 144.
12 Davidson 2001.
13 Woolf 2007, 147.
14 *ASC* 927.
15 Woolf 2007, 151.
16 Smyth 1984, 228.
17 Lapidge 1981, 91 n.140.
18 Anderson 1922, 445.
19 Hudson 1988.
20 Woolf 2007, 167.
21 *AU* 937.
22 Woolf 2007, 171.
23 Cavill, Harding and Jesch 2004.
24 Halloran 2005. The Burnswark hypothesis was challenged on philological grounds (Cavill 2008) but has recently been re-stated (Halloran 2010). I am grateful to Kevin Halloran for allowing me to see the latter paper in advance of publication.
25 Clarkson 2001, 188.
26 On the Life of Catroe see Dumville 2001.
27 Woolf 1998; Woolf 2007, 187–8.
28 Anderson 1922, 431.
29 Woolf 2007, 183.
30 Anderson 1922, 449.
31 Hudson 1994, 84.
32 *ASC* 945; translation in Duncan 2002, 23.
33 Hudson 1994, 85; Woolf 2007, 184.
34 Anderson 1922, 450.
35 *AU* 952; Hudson 1994, 87.
36 Hudson 1994, 89.
37 *Scot Chron*; Woolf 2007, 194–5.
38 *AU* 971.
39 Anderson 1922, 475–6.
40 Macquarrie 1993, 16.
41 Anderson 1922, 476.
42 Woolf 2007, 205.
43 *Scot Chron*; Woolf 2009, 209–10.

44 Alex Woolf, pers. comm.
45 For recent discussions see Thornton 2001 and Williams 2004.
46 Watson 1926, 53.
47 Laing 1998; Laing, Laing and Longley (1998), 553.
48 *AU/AT* 975.
49 Hudson 1994, 106.
50 Woolf 2007, 222.
51 Anderson 1922, 525; Hudson 1994, 114.
52 Woolf 2007, 238.
53 On this battle see Duncan 1976.
54 Woolf 2007, 240.
55 Brooke 1991b.
56 Woolf 2007, 253.
57 *AT* 1030; Woolf 2007, 254.
58 *HRA*; Anderson 1922, 583.
59 Duncan 2002, 40.
60 Woolf 2007, 263. A king called Lulach evidently reigned for a few months before Macbethad's death.
61 Durkan 1999, 89.
62 Woolf 2007, 263.
63 Woolf 2007, 270 and, for a different view, see Broun 2004, 138.
64 *HRA*.

Chapter 10

1 Broun 2004, 141.
2 Scott 1997, 30.
3 Jackson 1955, 88.
4 *VSK*, 33.
5 Durkan 1999.
6 Broun 2004, 155–7.
7 Broun 2004, 167.
8 Broun 2004, 125.
9 Jackson 1955, 88.
10 Duncan 1975, 108.
11 Watson 1926,191; Clancy 2001, 12 n.39, where *Gilcudbricht* replaces Watson's erroneous *Gilendonrut*.
12 Broun 2004, 121–2.
13 Brooke 1991b, 106.
14 Watson 1926, 134.
15 Grant 1892, 331.
16 Collingwood 1923; Clare 1979.
17 Phythian-Adams 1996, 74.
18 Watson 1926, 359.
19 Watson 1926, 360.

BIBLIOGRAPHY

Part 1: Primary Sources: Editions and Translations

AC Annales Cambriae (Welsh Annals). J. Morris (ed.) *Nennius: British History and the Welsh Annals* (Chichester, 1980)

ASC Anglo-Saxon Chronicle. A. Savage (ed.) *The Anglo-Saxon Chronicles* (Godalming, 1997)

AT Annals of Tigernach. Selected English translations in A.O. Anderson (ed.) *Early Sources of Scottish History, AD 500 to 1286*. Vol. 1 (Edinburgh, 1922)

AU Annals of Ulster. Selected English translations in A.O. Anderson (ed.) *Early Sources of Scottish History, AD 500 to 1286*. Vol. 1 (Edinburgh, 1922). See also S. Mac Airt and G. Mac Niocaill (eds) *The Annals of Ulster to AD 1131* (Dublin, 1983)

Ailred, *Vita Niniani* (Life of Ninian). A.P. Forbes (ed.) *The Historians of Scotland: V - Lives of St Ninian and St Kentigern* (Edinburgh, 1874)

Aneirin, *Y Gododdin*. A.O.H. Jarman (ed.) *Aneirin: Y Gododdin* (Llandysul, 1988)

Bede, *Continuatio*. J. McClure and R. Collins (eds) *Bede: The Ecclesiastical History of the English People* (Oxford, 1994)

Berchan's Prophecy. Selected English translations in A.O. Anderson (ed.) *Early Sources of Scottish History, AD 500 to 1286*. Vol. 1 (Edinburgh, 1922). See also B.T. Hudson (ed.) *The Prophecy of Berchan* (Westport, 1996)

Bower, Walter, *Scotichronicon*. Books 3 and 4. J. and W. MacQueen (eds), *Scotichronicon* (Aberdeen, 1989)

Fragmentary Annals of Ireland. Selected English translations in A.O. Anderson (ed.) *Early Sources of Scottish History, AD 500 to 1286*. Vol. 1 (Edinburgh, 1922). See also J.Radner (ed.) *The Fragmentary Annals of Ireland* (Dublin, 1978)

Gildas, *De Excidio Britanniae*. M. Winterbottom (ed.) *Gildas: the Ruin of Britain and Other Works* (Chichester, 1978)

HB Historia Brittonum. J. Morris (ed.) *Nennius: British History and the Welsh Annals* (Chichester, 1980)

HE Bede, *Historia Ecclesiastica Gentis Anglorum*. J. McClure and R. Collins (eds) *Bede: The Ecclesiastical History of the English People* (Oxford, 1994)

HRA Historia Regum Anglorum (History of the Kings of England) attributed to Symeon of Durham. J. Stevenson (ed.) *Simeon of Durham: a History of the Kings of England* (London, 1858)

Patrick, *Epistola* and *Confessio*. A.B.E. Hood (ed.) *St Patrick: His Writings and Muirchu's Life* (Chichester, 1978)

Scot Chron The Scottish Chronicle. Selected English translations in A.O. Anderson (ed.) *Early Sources of Scottish History, AD 500 to 1286*. Vol. 1 (Edinburgh, 1922)

Taliesin. M. Pennar (ed.) *Taliesin Poems* (Felinfach, 1988)

VC Adomnán, *Vita Sancti Columbae*. R. Sharpe (ed.) *Adomnán of Iona: Life of Saint Columba* (London, 1995)

VCP Bede, *Vita Sancti Cuthberti Prosaica* (Prose Life of St Cuthbert). B. Colgrave (ed.) *Two Lives of Saint Cuthbert* (Cambridge, 1940)

VSK Jocelin of Furness, *Vita Sancti Kentigerni* (Life of St Kentigern). A.P. Forbes (ed.) *The Historians of Scotland: V - Lives of St Ninian and St Kentigern* (Edinburgh, 1874)

VW Stephen of Ripon, *Vita Sancti Wilfrithi* (Life of St Wilfrid). B. Colgrave (ed.) *The Life of Bishop Wilfrid by Eddius Stephanus* (Cambridge, 1927)

Part 2: Modern Scholarship

Alcock, L. (1981) 'Quantity or Quality: the Anglian Graves of Bernicia', pp.168–85 in V.I. Evison (ed.) *Angles, Saxons and Jutes* (Oxford)

Alcock, L. (1983) '*Gwŷr y Gogledd*: an Archaeological Appraisal' *Archaeologia Cambrensis* 132: 1–18

Alcock, L. and Alcock, E. 'Reconnaissance Excavations . . . . 4: Excavations at Alt Clut, Clyde Rock, Strathclyde, 1974–5' *Proceedings of the Society of Antiquaries of Scotland* 120: 95–149

Anderson, A.O. (1922) *Early Sources of Scottish History, AD 500 to 1286*. Vol. 1 (Edinburgh)

Anderson, M.O. (1973) *Kings and Kingship in Early Scotland* (Edinburgh)

Armstrong, A.M., Mawer, A., Stenton, F.M. and Dickins, B. (1950) *The Place-Names of Cumberland*, Parts 1 and 2 (Cambridge)

Bartrum, P.C. (ed.) (1966) *Early Welsh Genealogical Tracts* (Cardiff)

Bassett, S. (ed.) (1989) *The Origins of Anglo-Saxon Kingdoms* (Leicester)

Binchy, D.A. (1970) *Celtic and Anglo-Saxon Kingship* (Oxford)

Birley, E. (1954) 'The Roman Fort at Netherby' *Transactions of the Cumberland and Westmorland Antiquarian and Archaeological Society*, Second Series 53: 6–39

Blair, P.H. (1947) 'The Origin of Northumbria' *Archaeologia Aeliana* 25: 1–51

Breeze, A. (1999) 'Simeon of Durham's Annal for 756 and Govan, Scotland' *Nomina* 22: 133–7

Breeze, A. (2001) 'Seventh-Century Northumbria and a Poem to Cadwallon' *Northern History* 38: 145–52

Breeze, A. (2007) 'Some Scottish Names, Including Vacomagi, Boresti, Iudanbyrig, Aberlessic and Dubuice' *Scottish Language* 26: 79–95

Breeze, D. (1996) *Roman Scotland* (London)

Breeze, D. (2008) 'Civil Government in the North: the Carvetii, the Brigantes and Rome' *Transactions of the Cumberland and Westmorland Antiquarian & Archaeological Society*, Third Series 8: 63–72

Bromwich, R. (ed.) (1961) *Trioedd Ynys Prydein: the Welsh Triads* (Cardiff)

Brooke, D. (1991a) 'The Northumbrian Settlements in Galloway and Carrick: an Historical Assessment' *Proceedings of the Society of Antiquaries of Scotland* 121: 295–327

Brooke, D. (1991b) 'Gall-Gaidhil and Galloway', pp.97–116 in R.D. Oram and G.P. Stell (eds) *Galloway: Land and Lordship* (Edinburgh)

Broun, D. (1991) 'The Literary Record of St Nynia: Fact and Fiction' *Innes Review* 42: 143–50

Broun, D. (1998) 'Pictish Kings, 761–839: Integration with Dal Riata or Separate Development?', pp.71–83 in S. Foster (ed.) *The St Andrews Sarcophagus: a Pictish Masterpiece and its International Connections* (Dublin)

Broun, D. (2004) 'The Welsh Identity of the Kingdom of Strathclyde, c.900–1200' *Innes Review* 55: 111–80

Cameron, K. (1968) 'Eccles in English Place-Names', pp.87–92 in M.W. Barley and R.P.C. Hanson (eds) *Christianity in Britain, 300–700* (Leicester)

Campbell, E. (2001) 'Were the Scots Irish?' *Antiquity* 75: 285–92

Cavill, P., Harding, S. and Jesch, J. (2004) 'Revisiting *Dingesmere*' *Journal of the English Place-Name Society* 36: 25–38

Cavill, P. (2008) 'The Site of the Battle of Brunanburh: Manuscripts and Maps, Grammar and Geography', pp.303–19 in O. Padel and D. Parsons (eds) *A Commodity of Good Names: Essays in Honour of Margaret Gelling* (Donnington)

Cessford, C. (1995) 'Where are the Anglo-Saxons in the *Gododdin* Poem?' *Anglo-Saxon Studies in Archaeology and History* 8: 95–8

Cessford, C. (1996) 'Yorkshire and the *Gododdin* Poem' *Yorkshire Archaeological Journal* 68: 241–3

Chadwick, H.M. (1949) *Early Scotland* (Cambridge)

Chadwick, H.M. (1959) 'Vortigern', pp.21–33 in H.M. Chadwick, N.K. Chadwick, K. Jackson, R. Bromwich, P.H. Blair and O. Chadwick, *Studies in Early British History* (Cambridge)

Chadwick, N.K. (1963a) 'The Conversion of Northumbria: a Comparison of Sources', pp.138–66 in N.K. Chadwick (ed.) *Celt and Saxon: Studies in the Early British Border* (Cambridge)

Chadwick, N.K. (1963b) 'The Battle of Chester: A Study of Sources', pp.167–85 in N.K. Chadwick (ed.) *Celt and Saxon: Studies in the Early British Border* (Cambridge)

Chadwick, N.K. (1976) *The British Heroic Age* (Cardiff)

Chalmers, G. (1807–24) *Caledonia* (London)

Charles-Edwards, T.M. (1983) 'Bede, the Irish and the Britons' *Celtica* 15: 42–52

Clancy, T.O. (1998) 'Govan, the Name, Again' *Report of the Society of Friends of Govan Old* 8: 8–13

Clancy, T.O. (2001) 'The Real St Ninian' *Innes Review* 52: 1–28

Clancy, T.O. (2006) 'Ystrad Clud', pp.1818–20 in J.T. Koch (ed.) *Celtic Culture: an Historical Encyclopedia.* Vol. 5 (Santa Barbara)

Clancy, T.O. (2008) 'The Gall-Ghaidheil and Galloway' *Journal of Scottish Name Studies* 2: 19–50

Clare, T. (1979) *Interim Report on Excavations at Castle Hewen 1978–79 and the Question of Arthur* (Kendal)

Clarkson, T. (1993) 'Richmond and Catraeth' *Cambrian Medieval Celtic Studies* 26: 15–20

Clarkson, T. (1995) 'Local Folklore and the Battle of Arthuret' *Transactions of the Cumberland & Westmorland Antiquarian & Archaeological Society*, Second Series 95: 282–4

Clarkson, T. (2001) *Warfare in Early Historic Northern Britain.* Unpublished PhD thesis, University of Manchester.

Collingwood, W.G. (1908) 'Report on an Exploration of the Romano-British Settlement at Ewe Close, Crosby Ravensworth' *Transactions of the Cumberland & Westmorland Antiquarian & Archaeological Society*, Second Series 8: 355–68

Collingwood, W.G. (1923) 'The Giant's Grave, Penrith' *Transactions of the Cumberland & Westmorland Antiquarian & Archaeological Society*, Second Series 23: 115–28

Corfe, T. (1997) 'The Battle of Heavenfield', pp.65–86 in T. Corfe (ed.) *Before Wilfrid: Britons, Romans and Anglo-Saxons in Tynedale* (Hexham)

Corning, C. (2000) 'The Baptism of Edwin, King of Northumbria: a New Analysis of the British Tradition' *Northern History* 36: 5–16

Cummins, W.A. (1999) *The Picts and their Symbols* (Stroud)

Dark, K. (1992) 'A Sub-Roman Re-Defence of Hadrians Wall?' *Britannia* 23: 111–20

Davidson, M.R. (2001) 'The (Non-)Submission of the Northern Kings in 920', pp.200–11 in N.J. Higham and D.H. Hill (eds) *Edward the Elder, 899–924* (London)

Driscoll, S.T. (1998) 'Church Archaeology in Glasgow and the Kingdom of Strathclyde' *Innes Review* 49: 94–114

Driscoll, S.T. (2003) 'Govan: an Early Medieval Royal Centre on the Clyde', pp.77–85 in R. Welander, D. Breeze and T.O. Clancy (eds) *The Stone of Destiny: Artefact and Icon* (Edinburgh)

Driscoll, S.T. (2004) *Govan from Cradle to Grave*. Friends of Govan Old Lecture Series. (Glasgow)

Driscoll, S.T. and Forsyth, K. (2004) 'The Late Iron Age and Early Historic Period' *Scottish Archaeological Journal* 26: 4–11

Driscoll, S.T., O'Grady, O. and Forsyth, K. (2005) 'The Govan School Revisited: Searching for Meaning in the Early Medieval Sculpture of Strathclyde', pp. 135–58 in S.M. Foster and M. Cross (eds) *Able Minds and Practised Hands: Scotland's Early Medieval Sculpture in the Twenty-First Century* (Leeds)

Driscoll, S.T. and Yeoman, P. (1997) *Excavations Within Edinburgh Castle, 1988–91* (Edinburgh)

Dumville, D.N. (1977) 'Sub-Roman Britain: History and Legend' *History* 62: 173–92

Dumville, D.N. (1986) 'The Historical Value of the Historia Brittonum' *Arthurian Literature* 6: 1–26

Dumville, D.N. (1988) 'Early Welsh Poetry: Problems of Historicity', pp.1–16 in B.F. Roberts (ed.) *Early Welsh Poetry: Studies in the Book of Aneirin* (Aberystwyth)

Dumville, D.N. (1989) 'The origins of Northumbria: some aspects of the British background', pp.213–22 in S. Bassett, (ed.) *The Origins of Anglo-Saxon Kingdoms* (Leicester)

Dumville, D.N. et al. (1993) *St Patrick, AD 493–1993* (Woodbridge)

Dumville, D.N. (2001) 'St Cathroe of Metz and the Hagiography of Exoticism', pp.172–88 in J. Carey, M. Herbert and P. O'Riain (eds) *Studies in Irish Hagiography: Saints and Scholars* (Dublin)

Duncan, A.A.M. (1975) *Scotland: the Making of the Kingdom* (Edinburgh)

Duncan, A.A.M. (1976) 'The Battle of Carham, 1018' *Scottish Historical Review* 55: 20–8

Duncan, A.A.M. (2002) *The Kingship of the Scots, 842–1292: Succession and Independence* (Edinburgh)

Durkan, J. (1999) 'The Glasgow Diocese and the Claims of York' *Innes Review* 50: 89–101

Ekwall, E. (1947) *The Oxford Dictionary of English Place-Names*. Third edition. (Oxford)

Esmonde-Cleary, S. (1989) *The Ending of Roman Britain* (London)

Evans, N. (2008) 'Royal Succession and Kingship Among the Picts' *Innes Review* 59: 1–48

Forsyth, K. (2000) 'Evidence of a Lost Pictish Source in the *Historia Regum Anglorum* of Symeon of Durham', pp.19–32 in S. Taylor (ed.) *Kings, Clerics and Chronicles in Scotland, 500–1297: Essays in Honour of Marjorie Ogilvie Anderson on the Occasion of her Ninetieth Birthday* (Dublin)

Forsyth, K. (2005) '*Hic Memoria Perpetua*: the Early Inscribed Stones of Southern Scotland in Context', pp. 113–34 in S.M. Foster and M. Cross (eds) *Able Minds and Practised Hands: Scotland's Early Medieval Sculpture in the Twenty-First Century* (Leeds)

Fraser, J.E. (2002) *The Battle of Dunnichen, 685* (Stroud)

Fraser, J.E. (2005) 'Strangers on the Clyde: Cenél Comgaill, Clyde Rock and the Bishops of Kingarth' *Innes Review* 56: 102–20

Fraser, J.E. (2008) 'Bede, the Firth of Forth and the Location of *Urbs Iudeu*' *Scottish Historical Review* 87: 1–25

Fraser, J.E. (2009) *From Caledonia to Pictland: Scotland to 795* (Edinburgh)

Gardner, W. (1925) 'The Roman Fort at Caerhun, Co. Caernarvon' *Archaeologia Cambrensis* 5: 307–41

Graham, T.B.H. (1913) 'Annals of Liddel' *Transactions of the Cumberland & Westmorland Antiquarian & Archaeological Society*, Second Series 13: 32–38

Gruffydd, R.G. (1994) 'In Search of Elmet' *Studia Celtica* 28: 63–79

Halloran, K. (2005) 'The Brunanburh Campaign: a Reappraisal' *Scottish Historical Review* 84: 133–48

Halloran, K. (2010) 'Etbrunnanwerc' *Scottish Historical Review* (forthcoming)

Halsall, G. (1989) 'Anthropology and the Study of Pre-Conquest Warfare and Society: the Ritual War in Anglo-Saxon England', pp.155–77 in S.C. Hawkes (ed.) *Weapons and Warfare in Anglo-Saxon England* (Oxford)

Hartley, B. and Fitts, L. (1988) *The Brigantes* (Gloucester)

Higham, N.J. (1986) *The Northern Counties to AD 1000* (London)

Higham, N.J. (1993) *The Kingdom of Northumbria, AD 350–1100* (Stroud)

Higham, N.J. (1997) *The Convert Kings: Power and Religious Affiliation in Early Anglo-Saxon England* (Manchester)

Higham, N.J. (2007) 'Historical Narrative as Cultural Politics', pp.68–79 in N.J. Higham (ed.) *Britons in Anglo-Saxon England* (Woodbridge)

Hill, P. (1987) Traprain Law, the Votadini and the Romans' *Scottish Archaeological Review* 4: 85–91

Hill, P. (1991) 'Whithorn: the Missing Years', pp.27–44 in R.D. Oram and G.P. Stell (eds) *Galloway: Land and Lordship* (Edinburgh)

Hill, P. (1997) *Whithorn and St Ninian: the Excavation of a Monastic Town* (Stroud)

Hind, J.G.F. (1980) 'Elmet and Deira – Forest Names in Yorkshire?' *Bulletin of the Board of Celtic Studies* 28: 541–52

Hogg, A.H.A. (1946) 'Llwyfenydd' *Antiquity* 20: 210–11

Hope-Taylor, B. (1977) *Yeavering: an Anglo-British Centre of Early Northumbria* (London)

Hudson, B.T. (1988) '*Elech* and the Scots in Strathclyde' *Scottish Gaelic Studies* 15: 145–9

Hudson, B.T. (1994) *Kings of Celtic Scotland* (Westport)

Isaac, G.R. (1998) '*Gweith Gwen Ystrat* and the Northern Heroic Age of the Sixth Century' *Cambrian Medieval Celtic Studies* 36: 61–70

Isaac, G.R. (1999) 'Readings in the History and Transmission of the *Gododdin*' *Cambrian Medieval Celtic Studies* 37: 55–78

Jackson, K.H. (1949a) 'The *Gododdin* of Aneirin' *Antiquity* 23: 25–34

Jackson, K.H. (1949b) 'Arthur's Battle of Breguoin' *Antiquity* 23: 48–9

Jackson, K.H. (1955) 'The Britons in Southern Scotland' *Antiquity* 29: 77–88

Jackson, K.H. (1959) 'Edinburgh and the Anglo-Saxon Occupation of Lothian', pp.35–47 in P. Clemoes (ed.) *The Anglo-Saxons: Studies in some Aspects of Their History* (London)

Jackson, K.H. (1963) 'Angles and Britons in Northumbria and Cumbria', pp.60–84 in H. Lewis (ed.) *Angles and Britons* (Cardiff)

Jackson, K.H. (ed.) (1969) *The Gododdin: the Oldest Scottish Poem* (Edinburgh)

James, E. (1984) 'Bede and the Tonsure Question' *Peritia* 3: 85–98

Jarman, A.O.H. (1960) *The Legend of Merlin* (Cardiff)

Jarman, A.O.H. (1978) 'Early Stages in the Development of the Merlin Legend', pp.335–48 in R. Bromwich and R.B. Jones (eds) *Astudiaethau ar yr Hengerdd* (Cardiff)

Jarman, A.O.H. (ed.) (1988) *Aneirin: Y Gododdin* (Llandysul)

Jones, G.R.J. (1975) 'Early Territorial Organisation in Gwynedd and Elmet' *Northern History* 10: 2–27

Kirby, D.P. (1962) 'Strathclyde and Cumbria: a Survey of Historical Development to 1092' *Transactions of the Cumberland & Westmorland Antiquarian & Archaeological Society*, Second Series 62: 71–94

Koch, J.T. (ed.) (1997) *The Gododdin of Aneirin: Text and Context from Dark-Age North Britain* (Cardiff)

Koch, J.T. (2006) 'Rheged', pp.1498–9 in J.T. Koch (ed.) *Celtic Culture: an Historical Encyclopedia*. Vol. 4 (Santa Barbara)

Laing, L. (1998) 'The Early Medieval Sculptures from St Blane's, Kingarth, Bute' *Pictish Arts Society Journal* 12: 19–23

Laing, L., Laing, J. and Longley, D. (1998) 'The Early Christian and Later Medieval Site at St Blane's, Kingarth, Bute' *Proceedings of the Society of Antiquaries of Scotland* 128: 551–65

Laing, L. and Longley, D. (2006) *The Mote of Mark: a Dark Age Hillfort in South-West Scotland* (Oxford)

Lapidge, M. (1981) 'Some Latin Poems as Evidence for the Reign of Athelstan' *Anglo-Saxon England* 9: 61–98

Lapidge, M. and Dumville, D.N. (eds) (1984) *Gildas: New Approaches* (Woodbridge)

Lovecy, I. (1976) 'The End of Celtic Britain: a Sixth-Century Battle Near Lindisfarne' *Archaeologia Aeliana* Fifth Series 4: 31–45

Lowe, C. (1999) *Angels, Fools and Tyrants: Britons and Anglo-Saxons in Southern Scotland* (Edinburgh)

McCarthy, M.R. (1999) 'Carlisle and Saint Cuthbert' *Durham Archaeological Journal* 14–15: 59–67

McCarthy, M.R. (2002) 'Rheged: an Early Historic Kingdom near the Solway' *Proceedings of the Society of Antiquaries of Scotland* 132: 357–82

McDiarmid, M.P. (1983) 'The *Gododdin* and Other Heroic Poems of Scotland', pp.1–17 in J.D. McClure (ed.) *Scotland and the Lowland Tongue* (Aberdeen)

Macquarrie, A. (1986) 'The Career of St Kentigern of Glasgow: *Vitae, Lectiones* and Glimpses of Fact' *Innes Review* 37: 3–24

Macquarrie, A. (1993) 'The Kings of Strathclyde, c.400–1018', pp.1–19 in A. Grant and K.J. Stringer (eds) *Medieval Scotland: Crown, Lordship and Community* (Edinburgh)

Macquarrie, A. (1997) *The Saints of Scotland: Essays in Scottish Church History, AD 450–1093* (Edinburgh)

MacQueen, J. (1990) *St Nynia* (Edinburgh)

Margary, I.D. (1973) *Roman Roads in Britain*. Third edition. (London)

Miller, M. (1975) 'The Commanders at Arthuret' *Transactions of the Cumberland & Westmorland Antiquarian & Archaeological Society*, Second Series 75: 114–9

Miller, M. (1976) 'Historicity and the Pedigrees of the Northcountrymen' *Bulletin of the Board of Celtic Studies* 26: 255–80

Miller, M. (1980) 'Hiberni Reversuri' *Proceedings of the Society of Antiquaries of Scotland* 110: 305–27

Mills, D. (1976) *The Place-Names of Lancashire* (London)

Morris, J. (1973) *The Age of Arthur* (London)

Morris-Jones, J. (1918) 'Taliesin' *Y Cymmrodor* 28: 1–290

Nicolaisen, W. (1960) 'Some Early Name-Forms of the Stirlingshire Carron' *Scottish Studies* 4: 96–104

O'Sullivan, D. and Young, R. (1995) *The English Heritage Book of Lindisfarne* (London)

Pennar, M. (ed.) (1988) *Taliesin Poems* (Felinfach)

Pennar, M. (ed.) (1989) *The Black Book of Carmarthen* (Felinfach)

Phythian-Adams, C. (1996) *Land of the Cumbrians: a Study in British Provincial Origins, AD 400–1120* (Aldershot)

Reid, R.C. (1951) 'Dunragit' *Transactions of the Dumfriesshire & Galloway Natural History & Antiquarian Society* 29: 155–64

Rennie, E.B. (2006) *The 'Cowal' Shore and Gazetteer of Archaeological Sites* (Glendaruel)

Ritchie, A. (ed.) (1994) *Govan and its Early Medieval Sculpture* (Stroud)

Rivet, A.L.F. and Smith, C. (1979) *The Place-Names of Roman Britain* (London)

Rollason, D. (2004) (ed.) *Durham Liber Vitae and its Context* (Woodbridge)

Ross, S. (1991) *Ancient Scotland* (Moffat)

Rowland, J. (1990) *Early Welsh Saga Poetry: a Study and Edition of the Englynion* (Cambridge)

Rowland, J. (1995) 'Warfare and Horses in the Gododdin and the Problem of Catraeth' *Cambrian Medieval Celtic Studies* 30: 13–40

Sawyer, P.H. and Wood, I.N. (eds) (1977) *Early Medieval Kingship* (Leeds)

Scott, J.G. (1997) 'The Partition of a Kingdom: Strathclyde, 1092–1153' *Transactions of the Dumfriesshire & Galloway Natural History & Antiquarian Society* 72: 11–40

Sellar, W.D.H. (1985) 'Warlords, Holy Men and Matrilinear Succession' *Innes Review* 36: 29–43

Sharpe, R. (ed.) (1995) *Adomnán of Iona: Life of St Columba* (London)

Shaw, R.C. (1964) *Post-Roman Carlisle and the Kingdoms of the North West* (Preston)

Shead, N.F. (1969) 'The Origins of the Medieval Diocese of Glasgow' *Scottish Historical Review* 48: 220–5

Sims-Williams, P. (1996) 'The Death of Urien' *Cambrian Medieval Celtic Studies* 32: 25–56

Skene, W.F. (1868) *The Four Ancient Books of Wales* (London)

Skene, W.F. (1876) 'Notice of the Site of the Battle of Ardderyd or Arderyth' *Proceedings of the Society of Antiquaries of Scotland* 6: 91–8

Skene, W.F. (1886) *Celtic Scotland: a History of Ancient Alban. Vol. 1: History and Ethnology* (Edinburgh)

Smith, I.M. (1990) *The Archaeological Background to the Emergent Kingdoms of the Tweed Basin in the Early Historic Period.* Unpublished PhD thesis, University of Durham.

Smyth, A.P. (1984) *Warlords and Holy Men: Scotland, AD 80–1000* (London)

Snyder, C. (2003) *The Britons* (Oxford)

Spearman, R.M. (1994) 'The Govan Sarcophagus: an Enigmatic Monument', pp.33–45 in A. Ritchie (ed.) *Govan and its Early Medieval Sculpture* (Stroud)

Stancliffe, C. (1995a) 'Oswald, Most Holy and Most Victorious King of the Northumbrians', pp.33–83 in C. Stancliffe and E. Cambridge (eds) *Oswald: Northumbrian King to European Saint* (Stamford)

Stancliffe, C. (1995b) 'Where Was Oswald Killed?', pp.84–96 in C. Stancliffe and E. Cambridge (eds) *Oswald: Northumbrian King to European Saint* (Stamford)

Stephens, T. (1888) *The Gododin of Aneurin Gwardrydd* (London)

Taylor, T.T. (1931) 'Liddel Strength' *Transactions of the Dumfriesshire & Galloway Natural History & Antiquarian Society* 16: 112–19

Thacker, A. '*Membra Disjecta*: The Division of the Body and the Diffusion of the Cult', pp.97–127 in C. Stancliffe and E. Cambridge (eds) *Oswald: Northumbrian King to European Saint* (Stamford)

Thomas, A.C. (1968) 'The Evidence from North Britain', pp.93–122 in M.W. Barley and R.P.C. Hanson (eds) *Christianity in Britain, 300–700* (Leicester)

Thornton, D.E. (2001) 'Edgar and the Eight Kings, AD 973' *Early Medieval Europe* 10: 49–80

Tolstoy, N. (1985) *The Quest for Merlin* (Sevenoaks)

Wade-Evans, A.W. 'Prolegomena to a Study of the Lowlands' *Transactions of the Dumfriesshire & Galloway Natural History & Antiquarian Society* 27: 54–84

Wagner, P. (2002) *Pictish Warrior, AD 297–841* (Oxford)

Wainwright, F.T. (1959) 'Aethelflaed, Lady of the Mercians', pp.53–69 in P. Clemoes (ed.) *The Anglo-Saxons: Studies in some Aspects of their History* (London)

Wallace-Hadrill, J.M. (1988) *Bede's Ecclesiastical History of the English People: a Historical Commentary* (Oxford)

Watson, W.J. (1926) *A History of the Celtic Place-Names of Scotland* (Edinburgh)

Williams, A. (2004) 'An Outing on the Dee: King Edgar at Chester, AD 973' *Medieval Scandinavia* 14: 229–44

Williams, I. (ed.) (1975) *The Poems of Taliesin* (Dublin)

Williams, I. (1980) *The Beginnings of Welsh Poetry: Studies by Sir Ifor Williams.* Edited by R. Bromwich. (Cardiff)

Wilmott, T. (1997) *Birdoswald: Excavations of a Roman Fort on Hadrian's Wall and its Successor Settlements, 1987–92* (London)

Wilson, P.R., Cardwell, P., Cramp, R.J., Evans, J., Taylor-Wilson, R.H., Thompson, A. and Wacher, J.S. (1996) 'Early Anglian Catterick and Catraeth' *Medieval Archaeology* 40: 1–61

Winchester, A.L. (1987) *Landscape and Society in Medieval Cumbria* (Edinburgh)

Woolf, A. (1998) 'Pictish Matriliny Reconsidered' *Innes Review* 49: 147–67

Woolf, A. (2003) 'The Britons: from Romans to Barbarians', pp.345–80 in H.-W. Goetz, J. Jarnut and W. Pohl (eds) *Regna and Gentes: the Relationship between Late Antique and Early Medieval Peoples and Kingdoms in the Transformation of the Roman World* (Leiden)

Woolf, A. (2004) 'Caedualla *Rex Brettonum* and the Passing of the Old North' *Northern History* 41: 5–24

Woolf, A. (2005) 'Onuist Son of Uurguist: Tyrannus Carnifex or a David for the Picts?', pp.35–42 in D. Hill and M. Worthington (eds) *Aethelbald and Offa: Two Eighth-Century Kings of Mercia.* BAR British Series 383. (Oxford)

Woolf, A. (2006) 'Dun Nechtain, Fortriu and the Geography of the Picts' *Scottish Historical Review* 85: 182–201

Woolf, A. (2007) *From Pictland to Alba, 789–1070* (Edinburgh)

INDEX